TEXAS COAST

this book has been
Donated
in
Loving
Memory
of

Candace Lyn Johnson

TEXAS COAST

DISCOVER DELIGHTS ALONG THE GULF COAST OF TEXAS.

BY ROBERT RAFFERTY

★

TexasMonthlyPress

Texas Monthly Press, Inc.
P.O. Box 1569
Austin, Texas 78767

A B C D E F G H

Library of Congress Cataloging-in-Publication Data

Rafferty, Robert.
   Texas coast.

   Includes index.
   1. Texas—Description and travel—1981–   —Guide-books. 2. Coasts—Texas—Guide-books. I. Title.
F384.3.R33   1986   917.64′0463   85-28811
ISBN 0-87719-005-4 (pbk.)

Cover design by Hixo, Inc.

To my wife, Lyn,
who provides me with the warmth
of a summery day on the coast
even in mid-winter.

CONTENTS

★★
ACKNOWLEDGMENTS

Details, details, details! A guidebook is only as good as the truth of its details, so I'm indebted to a number of people for help in gathering and verifying the thousands and thousands of them in this book.

In general, I'd like to thank the various chambers of commerce and convention and visitors bureaus along the coast for their invaluable assistance in providing the tons of material about their areas necessary for laying the groundwork for my visits.

In particular, I'd like to offer an extra-special thank you to the following individuals who went far and beyond the call of duty to ensure the research visits that my wife and I made to their cities were especially fruitful and enjoyable:

Teresa Reinhardt, Port Arthur Convention and Visitors Bureau.

Kate Cambridge, Hamilton Associates, Galveston.

Timothy M. Kingsbury, Galveston Historical Foundation.

Kathy Berry, Brazosport Chamber of Commerce.

Lanette Nolte, Port Aransas Tourist and Convention Bureau.

Ede Day and Lisa Rose, Corpus Christi Convention and Tourist Bureau.

Jim Hough, Port Mansfield Chamber of Commerce.

Mike Rodrigues, Confederate Air Force, Harlingen.

I'd also like to give credit to my wife, Carolyn Banks Rafferty, who took time out from her own writing career to help with the research, give her strong opinions on my selections for the listings, and do all the proofreading of the various drafts and the final copy of the original manuscript.

Robert Rafferty

★★★

INTRODUCTION: PLEASE READ THIS FIRST!

American beachcombers rhapsodize about the East Coast beaches, but only a few have discovered the captivating charms of the Third Coast—the sandy stretches along the Gulf of Mexico. The Texas reaches of the sun-blessed Gulf Coast are the subject of this guidebook.

What's it like?

There's no one answer to that question. Portions of the Texas coast are remote, others glitzy. Descriptions range from one news article's assessment of "funky" to the glamorous tag line dreamed up by a Corpus Christi adman: "The Texas Riviera."

As you delve into this book you'll see that both descriptions are correct.

So why the shouting title above?

Studies show that many readers skip the introductions to guidebooks and jump right into the listings, thereby missing some of the guidelines that are essential to making the most of those listings—including qualifying statements explaining how and why some listing just may not pan out. Reading the Introduction is especially important in this book, because the Texas coast contains such a wide variety of attractions. In addition, there are a number of things you should be aware of before you go, so you can pick the place that's best for you.

Organization

A quick look at the Table of Contents will show that the listings are organized so they run down the coast from north to south: from Port Arthur on the Louisiana border to South Padre Island and Brownsville on the Mexican border.

The Coast Highway

Unfortunately, there is no coast highway that goes from border to border. The one in the north, starting at Sabine Pass and going through Galveston to Brazosport, pretty much ends there and doesn't reappear until Port Aransas. The next leg only goes from Port Aransas down Mustang Island and then along a few miles of the northern shore of Padre Island just past Corpus Christi. A few miles of paved road are also on the southern end of Padre Island. And that's it for driving along the Gulf.

True, you can drive along the shore of some of the Gulf bays, and there are some long stretches of beach here and there that you can navigate if you have a four-wheel-drive vehicle or don't mind getting stuck. For the most part, however, ordinary vehicles have to take inland routes to the connecting roads that jut out like fingers to the Gulf for the majority of the trip down the coast.

It should be noted, too, that Texas invests a lot of money in its roads, so they are generally in good shape. The other side of this, however, is that a number of construction companies work continuously to maintain and upgrade the roads, so expect detours and occasional traffic jams. For the most up-to-date information on construction projects on your route, check with the highway department or, if you're a member, the AAA before leaving home.

Our Fragile Beaches

There are more than 360 miles of Texas coast on the Gulf of Mexico, and most of it is beach. But if you are expecting wide, white sandy beaches, you may be in for a disappointment. First of all, most of those on the northern half of the coast are dirt colored and coarse textured, and with few exceptions, they are narrow. Not until you hit Mustang and Padre islands do the beaches start to get the pristine and expansive look of the ones on travel posters.

And our beaches are fragile.

The combination of natural erosion and thoughtless overdevelopment and overuse is eating away at the state's shoreline at an alarming rate, and some beaches are already starting to disappear. An Army Corps of Engineers' study, for example, projects that there will be little or no usable beach in Brazoria County by the year 2010. The Brazoria County Park Commission has recognized this threat and initiated a long-range program to save these beaches. Unfortunately, at this time, Texas lacks a comprehensive state program dedicated to saving our coastal beaches.

Most experts agree that seawalls and other man-made construction projects are virtually ineffective against erosion. In fact, they often speed up that natural process—evidenced by the continued narrowing of Galveston's once fine beach since the building of that seawall. Experts also agree that the best method of protecting the beach is by assisting nature in strengthening the front line of sand dunes. This means giving the beach space instead of building right on top of it. It also means that those of us who visit the beaches should realize what recreational treasures they are and, in addition to supporting efforts to save them, use them with tender loving care.

Industry vs. Tourism

Let's face it, on much of the coast industry ranks ahead of tourism as the prime provider of jobs, and this is not in any way belittling the attractions of the beaches and Gulf itself. Ports, refineries, and other heavy industries that depend on cheap ocean transport play a major role here. The exceptions—Galveston Island, smaller towns like Port Aransas and Port Mansfield, and the developed areas on both ends of Padre Island—are found where there is little or no heavy industry. And sometimes the plants are located well away from the tourist areas, as in Corpus Christi. But, in any case, the industries are there, and you should expect them. In some cases, they are part of the sights to see and are mentioned in the listings.

The good news is that the growing importance of tourism to the economy is being recognized by the various chambers of commerce and convention and visitors bureaus along the coast, and they are striving, with the cooperation of industry, to make these areas more attractive to visitors.

★★
THE LISTINGS

Each city listing begins with the name of the county in which it is located, the city's population according to the 1980 census or a more recent statistic if official, and (in parentheses) the telephone area code. Mileages given are generally calculated from the Texas Department of Highways and Public Transportation's Official Highway Travel Map and may differ slightly from your actual driving mileage.

A GET-ACQUAINTED DRIVING TOUR

The purpose of these tours is to give you a chance to get acquainted with the main streets, traffic, distances, and the general location of the major sights and tourist attractions before you have to venture out to a specific one. They work best when you take the tour early in your visit. With only a few exceptions, all the streets listed in each tour in this guide are included in the map at the beginning of each section on a city. You can use these maps, or get a more detailed one from the local chamber of commerce, to mark out your route before you start. Or, to avoid confusion and map shuffling, read the directions into a portable tape recorder, and let it be your guide as you play it back in your car as you go.

TOUR & GUIDE SERVICES

Chambers of commerce, visitors bureaus, and other places where you can get free information about the area—and maybe help in getting accommodations—are listed, along with tour guides and tour services for hire.

GUIDEBOOKS

Only those guidebooks targeted on that particular area are included. A listing of guidebooks covering larger sections of the coast is included at the end of this Introduction.

POINTS OF INTEREST

These are places of interest to visitors in the area that don't fall into one of the specific categories that follow, such as museums or historic places.

BIRD'S-EYE VIEW

These are the best sites to get a panoramic view of the area. There aren't many high places, natural or man-made, along the coast so there aren't many of these listings.

HISTORIC PLACES

Whether you are a history buff or just curious about our heritage, the coastal cities tell a story that's worth your time.

MUSEUMS

One of the nice things about the museums on the coast is they are all small enough to see everything there is to see—and many have a lot worth seeing—in an hour or two or, at the most, a leisurely afternoon. This makes them pleasant diversions from sand and sun or good rainy-day excursions, rather than the tiring undertakings that larger museums tend to become.

GALLERIES

Art lives on the coast! And fortunately, it also comes in small doses that fit into a vacation schedule with ease.

MUSIC & THEATER

This section contains details on music halls, symphony orchestras, little theaters, and other performing arts.

COLLEGES & UNIVERSITIES

In addition to describing educational programs, these listings include the institutions' offerings for both the short- and long-term visitor.

SHOPPING

For the essentials, the major shopping malls are listed. For the nice-to-have things as well as the unique and different, a selection of specialty shops is listed.

OUTDOORS & SIDE TRIPS

This category includes beaches, state and county parks, picnic areas, nature and hiking trails, and other places to go outdoors. The recommended side trips are rarely more than an hour's drive away and are well worth the effort.

KIDS' STUFF

Special places for kids of all ages.

SPORTS & ACTIVITIES

Birdwatching, boating, fishing, golf, hunting, tennis, and a variety of other sports activities available to visitors are covered. Of these, only fishing and hunting require licenses, since both these sports are closely regulated by the Texas Parks and Wildlife Department. The fees for hunting and fishing licenses range from as low as $5 for a 14-day sport-fishing license for Texas residents up to $200 for a nonresident general hunting license valid for all game and birds that can be legally taken. Most fees for both residents and nonresidents are grouped around the lower end of the scale. Licenses may be purchased at approximately 5,000 locations around the state, including many bait shops and convenience, hardware, and sporting goods stores. Free annual guides on both freshwater and saltwater fishing and on hunting may be obtained by writing Texas Parks and Wildlife Department, 4200 Smith School Road, Austin 78744.

ANNUAL EVENTS

People like to celebrate the events that make them unique. On the coast this takes the shape of festivals and other activities that run from Port Arthur's Cav-Oil-Cade Celebration to Brownsville's Charro Days. All such celebrations bring people together in the spirit of fun as well as civic pride.

ACCOMMODATIONS

Depending on what's available, these listings may be divided into sections covering hotels, motels, and such other accommodations as beach houses, condominium rentals, and bed-and-breakfast homes. Each of these has distinct advantages when matched against the size of your party, the length of your stay, and your other living-at-the-beach preferences, as well as the price you can afford.

Beach houses and condo rentals, for example, offer a lot more space and privacy than the average hotel or motel room. They also cost more. But if you have a large family or share with friends or rent by the week, a beach house or condo can work out cheaper in the long run. These also include kitchens that offer you the opportunity to save by eating some meals there instead of having to eat out all the time. Some of these boast expensive interior decorating and all the refinements of a luxury home with a rental price to match. Others are decorated in stark simplicity and cost much less. Most have daily rates but usually require a minimum stay of two or three days. Many people reserve the same place for the same time from year to year, so make reservations early.

Price ranges for accommodations are given at the beginning of each section using the symbols $ to $$$$. Since supply and demand determine prices, these vary from city to city. Prices also ride the curve of the seasons, especially in the more popular tourist areas. The highest prices are charged during "high season," which usually starts right before the schools let out for the summer and ends right after they open again in the fall. Dead low season is usually in January and February. Naturally, the cheapest lodging bargains are available during low season, but the *best* bargains can usually be found weekdays just before and after high season. During this time, the weather is still good, the restaurants and other attractions haven't closed or changed to winter hours, and the crowds have dwindled and space is available.

The price symbols do not take into account local room taxes, which range from about 7 to 11 percent. To reduce the shock of seeing it added to the bill, ask about the local room tax before you make a reservation.

Many chain hotels or motels have free 800 numbers listed. In most cases, this number contacts a central reservation bureau, but occasionally it will connect you directly with the hotel or motel.

RESTAURANTS

Finding restaurants worthy of listing in this guide was a difficult and often disappointing task. The key to listing a restaurant was simple: cleanliness, ambience, and price were factors, but the main test was whether the kitchen lived up to its promises on the menu. Even if it didn't promise much, as long as that was delivered in full, it was in. If it promised a great deal and couldn't deliver, it didn't make it.

There are a lot of restaurants of every type imaginable on the coast. In checking them out, I found that a lot of people who are in the restaurant business shouldn't be. Too often the food was overcooked, overpriced, sloppily prepared, and served lukewarm by a waitperson whose knowledge of the amenities of waiting tables was limited to interrupting a conversation to ask, "Is everything all right?"

It's also logical to expect that many restaurants on the coast serve well-prepared, fresh seafood. But logic doesn't seem to apply to restaurants. If you're looking for the culinary delights of fresh seafood, all I can say is "Good luck!" There are plenty of seafood restaurants, but—surprisingly—the majority of them serve the more convenient frozen seafood rather than taking the trouble to use the bounty of the deep that's available on the nearby dock. And then, only a few seafood chefs along the coast seem to know that there are other ways to prepare a catch, whether frozen or fresh, besides frying. Not that there's anything wrong with frying, but it doesn't always bring out the best in seafood.

Fortunately, a scattering of restaurants have learned that seafood can also be broiled, boiled, baked, poached, stewed, or steamed. And you can be sure that every one of these restaurants with culinary versatility is listed.

Out-of-state visitors should be aware that Texas has local option liquor laws that permit the voters in a designated area to decide if liquor will be available and, if so, under what conditions. This has resulted in boundary-line situations where a restaurant or bar on one side of a street can sell liquor by the drink, while on the other side of the street, you can get only beer and wine—or nothing alcoholic. I've tried to make it clear in each instance where this situation exists so you won't be surprised if you run into it.

CLUBS & BARS

This category has been treated rather lightly because clubs change frequently to keep up with the fads. To rate a listing here a club had to have at least an air of permanence about it, and even then, this category will probably have more "dead" listings than any other. If you are really interested in the latest in nightlife, check the *Texas Monthly* magazine listings, the local newspapers, the Yellow Pages, or the chamber of commerce or visitors bureau. Or just ask the beach crowd.

OFFBEAT

If you're looking for something different, this listing may fill the bill.

THINGS CHANGE

Time takes its toll. It took a long time to research, write, edit, print, and distribute this book. In the meantime, things have been changing. Restaurants, for example, are notorious for changing their names, management, and menus or moving to a new location. For various reasons, such as the owner's health, places close. Or disaster strikes—we had to delete the listings for one restaurant and an interesting specialty shop because they burned down between the time we visited and the final editing date.

This is why telephone numbers are included. You can call and check that all is still as listed here before you go. Just remember, phone numbers change too, so if you have trouble reaching a listing, call Information.

WHAT'S INCLUDED & WHAT'S NOT

Everyone who has ever traveled on the coast has their own favorite place—a certain restaurant, motel, fishing hole, or charter captain. It would be nice if I could include them all, but this is a guidebook, not the Yellow Pages; so it has limits.

Also, everything is relative. A hotel or motel, restaurant, or what-have-you in an area where it doesn't have much competition might be listed even though it wouldn't have had it been where more choices were available. Not that being the only game in town was justification for listing a truly wretched place; it still had to be worthy to earn its place in this book.

I've also skipped a few small coastal towns, either because they really don't have enough accommodations to take care of the visitors who come there now or they offer nothing so outstanding that I'd want to recommend making them a specific destination.

If you think I erred in leaving out your favorite and you're willing to share it with the rest of the world, I'd be happy to hear from you. Perhaps we can include it when this book is revised. Write me: Robert Rafferty, % Texas Monthly Press, P.O. Box 1569, Austin 78767.

OTHER GUIDEBOOKS & BOOKS OF INTEREST

East Texas Chamber of Commerce. *East Texas Vacation Guide.* Longview, Texas.

Fehrenbach, T. R. *Lone Star: A History of Texas and Texans.* New York: American Legacy Press, 1983.

Fodor's Travel Guides. *Texas.* New York, 1985.

McIlvain, Myra Hargrave. *Texas Auto Trails: The Southeast.* Austin: University of Texas Press, 1982.

Miller, George Oxford, and Tull, Delena. *Texas Parks and Campgrounds: North, East, and Coastal Texas.* Austin: Texas Monthly Press, 1984.

Miller, Ray. *Eyes of Texas Travel Guide: Gulf Coast Edition.* Houston: Cordovan Corporation, 1977.

Mobil Oil Corporation. *Mobil Travel Guide: Southwest and South Central Area.* Chicago: Rand McNally, 1984.

Morton, Robert A., *et al. Living With the Texas Shore.* Durham, North Carolina: Duke University Press, 1983.

Sharpe, Patricia, and Weddle, Robert S. *Texas.* Austin: Texas Monthly Press, 1982.

Sherley, Connie. *Fisher Annotated Travel Guides: Texas and the Southwest 84/85.* New York, 1984.

Texas Department of Highways and Public Transportation. *Texas Travel Handbook.* Austin.

Tyler, Paula Eyrich and Ron. *Texas Museums: A Guidebook.* Austin: University of Texas Press, 1983.

★★★

SYMBOLS USED IN THIS BOOK

RESTAURANT GUIDE
The restaurants are listed according to type. The following symbols indicate the cost of a typical meal for one person, exclusive of drinks, tax, and tip:

$: under $7
$$: $7–$17
$$$: $17–$25
$$$$: over $25

The word "bar" at the end of a restaurant listing indicates that liquor and mixed drinks are available.

WHEELCHAIR ACCESSIBILITY SYMBOLS
W   This place is accessible to persons in wheelchairs; the entrance is at least 32 inches wide, and no more than two steps are at the entrance. However, not all facilities (restrooms, elevators, etc.) are accessible.
W variable   This place is accessible only in part.
W +   This place and all its major facilities are accessible.
W but not all areas   This place has special facilities for the handicapped but is not accessible in its entirety; for example, state parks.
No symbol   This place is accessible only with great difficulty or not at all.

CREDIT CARDS
The following symbols note what credit cards are accepted at clubs, bars, and restaurants:

AE	American Express
DC	Diners Club
MC	MasterCard
V	Visa
Cr.	All major credit cards
No cr.	No credit cards

★ PORT ARTHUR ★

JEFFERSON COUNTY   ★   63,053   ★   (409)

Port Arthur, Beaumont, and Orange are linked as the Golden Triangle. That's a catchy title and sounds like public relations hype, especially for Port Arthur, a city whose lifeblood is oil. It pours through a monstrous refinery complex that is listed as one of the world's largest, at times processing up to 10 percent of the nation's crude. Add the huge petrochemical plants, and it's easy to see why the city lays claim to the title "Energy City" and boasts "We Oil the World."

In truth, however, even though Port Arthur is an industrial city that doesn't look much like gold on the outside, those willing to explore will find veins of the precious ore in all parts of the city.

Recently this area has felt the sharp sting of the decline in the oil industry. From a tourist standpoint, however, this situation brings to mind the old saw that every dark cloud has a silver lining. With the industrial tax base eroding, the city leaders had to look again at their neglected natural and other attractions for visitors. The result is a recognition of the tourist potential and renewed emphasis on making the city more attractive to visitors. This can only lead to good things for all.

1

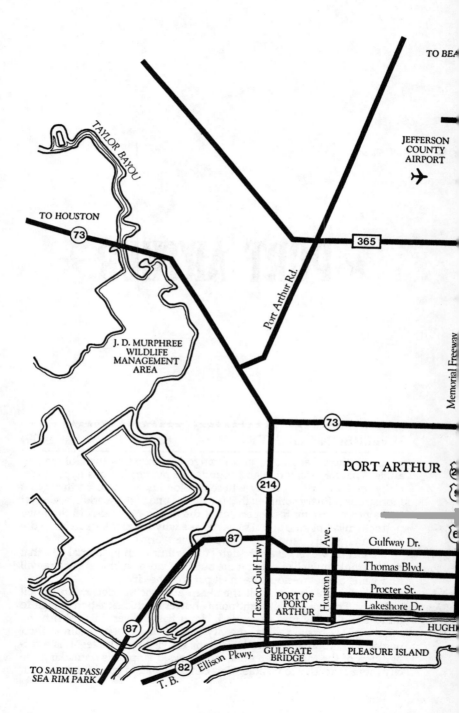

TO BEA·

JEFFERSON
COUNTY
AIRPORT
✈

TAYLOR BAYOU

TO HOUSTON

73

Port Arthur Rd.

365

J. D. MURPHREE
WILDLIFE
MANAGEMENT
AREA

Memorial Freeway

73

PORT ARTHUR

214

87

Texaco-Gulf Hwy.

Ave.

Houston

Gulfway Dr.

Thomas Blvd.

PORT OF
PORT
ARTHUR

Procter St.

Lakeshore Dr.

87

HUGH·

PLEASURE ISLAND

82 Ellison Pkwy.

GULFGATE
BRIDGE

TO SABINE PASS/
SEA RIM PARK

T. B.

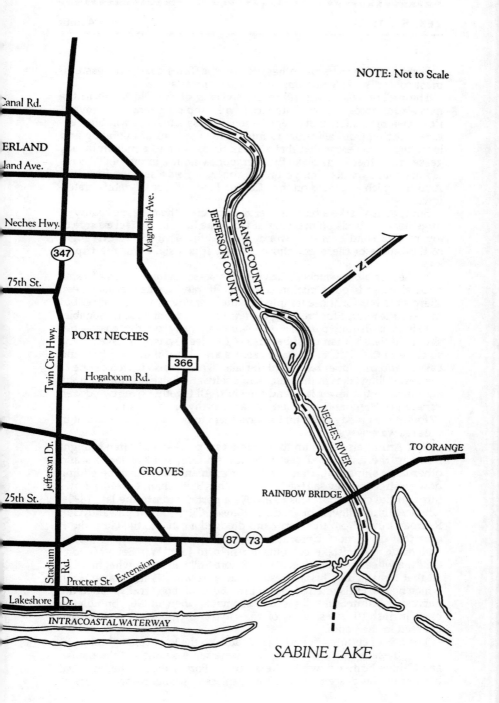

NOTE: Not to Scale

Canal Rd.

ERLAND

land Ave.

Magnolia Ave.

Neches Hwy.

JEFFERSON COUNTY

ORANGE COUNTY

347

N

75th St.

Twin City Hwy.

PORT NECHES

366

Hogaboom Rd.

NECHES RIVER

Jefferson Dr.

GROVES

TO ORANGE

25th St.

RAINBOW BRIDGE

87 73

Stadium Rd.

Procter St. Extension

Lakeshore Dr.

INTRACOASTAL WATERWAY

SABINE LAKE

3

Perhaps more than any other area on the Texas coast, this eastern-most corner is a kaleidoscope of colorful contrasts.

The nature lover can thrill to the spillover of the Old South in the moss-laden trees that are interlaced with tropical palms. The mysterious swamps, salt marshes, and bayous give sanctuary to wildlife creatures ranging from alligators to hundreds of species of migrating and local birds. It is estimated that at peak times close to a million ducks, geese, and other birds make their temporary homes in the 74,000 acres of marshland parks, refuge areas, and rice fields surrounding Port Arthur, which is located on the "Central Fly-way" for migrating waterfowl.

But it doesn't take a birdwatcher to appreciate the majestic beauty of huge flocks of birds on the wing. It would be hard not to feel a surge of joy in nature and a sense of wonderment at the sight of a sunrise flight of thousands of these graceful creatures. It is a sight worth a trip in itself.

While it is a birdwatcher's delight, this seasonal inundation of game birds also sends out a clarion call to the hunter. Game wardens keep sharp eyes out for those tempted by the seeming overabundance, but there's little excuse for breaking the law since bag limits are reasonable.

This is a fishing paradise, too—one of many on the coast—but slightly different than most because of the deep waters of Lake Sabine so close to the Gulf. Freshwater catches are plentiful in the rivers and bayous and the upper reaches of the lake, which is also touted as one of the best sailing lakes in the state, while saltwater fish eager for the hook are found in the lower lake and the Gulf. All together over two dozen varieties of fresh- and saltwater fish are worthy of an angler's time. Not to forget the greedy crabs that always seem to be waiting for the bait in the area waterways.

Port Arthur also lives up to its name as a port—a fact often brought home to the uninitiated visitor by the startling sight of tankers and other large ships that, from a block or so inland, appear to be gliding down a street as they sail the Sabine-Neches Ship Channel, which flows through the city. But it wasn't always a port. Not until the late 1890s, when Arthur Stillwell pushed his Kansas City, Pittsburgh, and Gulf Railroad down from the North and dredged a canal to the Gulf, did it earn that distinction. Unfortunately for Stillwell, he ran out of money and made the mistake of going for help to John W. "Bet-a-Million" Gates, a wheeler-dealer speculator. Before Stillwell knew what hit him, all that remained of his interests in the area was his first name, with which he had christened his new port. "Bet-a-Million" really reaped the harvest of Arthur Stillwell's accomplishments when, in 1901, Spindletop blew in just 10 miles north of the city, and the "black gold" rush ushered in the boom.

The mix of cultures in Port Arthur adds to the local color. Prominent among these is Cajun. Although there are some outposts of the Louisiana Cajuns farther down the Texas coast, Port Arthur is the only real bastion of the descendants of the displaced Acadians—whose tragic tale is told in Longfellow's *Evangeline*—south of the Louisiana line. One of the many fine things the Cajuns brought with them is a distinctive style of cooking. While too many so-called cooks on the coast seem to dislike fish cookery (evidenced by the way they mistreat it in the kitchen), the Cajuns add a little back-bayou culinary sorcery and seasoning and thus distinguish their seafood dishes from the ordinary. Cajun cooking is not to everyone's taste. Then again, what style of cooking is? But it is definitely distinctive and worth a try.

Perhaps even more enjoyable than their cooking is the philosophy these hard-working people express when their work is done: "Laissez les bons temps rouler." Loosely translated that means "Let the good times roll," and they make sure the good times roll and roll and roll at their favorite night spots and the many local festivals.

Also in the cultural mix are the good ole boy Texans, the older-than-they-think Janis Joplin–era rock'n'rollers (this was her home town), the Lone Star version of southern gentlefolk, the epitome of the urban cowboy, Mexican Americans, blacks, and the newcomers—Vietnamese who have migrated to the area and now have their own enclaves. The polyglot population is also laced with descendants of the Dutch who are centered in Nederland, a city in its own right but lacking distinguishable boundaries with Port Arthur except to the quick-eyed observer of city-limit signs that flash by on the highway.

Sabine Pass is another place difficult to separate out when talking about Port Arthur. Although 14 miles away, the town was annexed by Port Arthur in 1978. But even before that, the people in both places thought of them as one. One reason, perhaps, is that only two roads lead to Sabine Pass: the coast road from Galveston and High Island, which is rarely open because of erosion, and the road from Port Arthur, which is rarely closed. This little town in the corner of Texas has the distinction of having been laid out by Sam Houston in 1836. A high point in the town's history was the Civil War battle fought there in which a handful of Confederates with a few cannon whipped a Federal invasion force more than a hundred times its strength. Its present-day claim to fame rests on great fishing and the fact that it boasts of one of the most famous seafood restaurants on the coast. Sabine Pass is also the resting place for towering, out-of-service, offshore oil rigs, as well as being the gateway to Sea Rim State Park.

Winter temperatures usually range from the mid 40s to the low 60s, in summer from the low 70s to the low 90s. Perhaps because of all the wetlands, humidity can run high, especially in the summer.

A GET-ACQUAINTED DRIVING TOUR

The first thing to note is that Port Arthur has both numbered streets and numbered avenues. The way to retain your sense of direction—and your sanity—is to remember that the numbered streets run east and west while the numbered avenues run north and south.

A good starting place is the Civic Center on Texas 73 near 9th Avenue.

Visit the Visitors Bureau (see Tour & Guide Services) first, and then, armed with a city map and brochures, you'll be able to get more out of the tour.

Go east, past the library to 9th Avenue and turn right under Texas 73. A little over a mile down, on your right, you'll see the Hughen School. What makes this school so special is not just the work being done here to train severely physically handicapped children, but the number of celebrities who are supporting that work and the school. If you look close you'll see the drive into the school is called Bob Hope Street. The high school also bears the name of that famous benefactor. Jimmy Durante donated the indoor swimming pool. And every year, football coach Bum Phillips sponsors a fund-raising golf tournament for the school.

Just past the Hughen School, turn left on 25th Street, which becomes Griffing Park Drive. Griffing Park is one of the nicer residential areas in the city with many large and carefully landscaped homes. Make your own route on one of the side streets, like Forest, Rosedale, or Evergreen. There are lots of curves and loops in this area, so don't get lost. When you're ready to continue the tour, work your way back to Griffing Park Drive and 9th Avenue and turn left.

St. Mary's Hospital is on your right just past 22nd Street. About half a mile farther, you'll see several flags flying from flagpoles on your left. These mark Howard's Supermarket at 950 9th Avenue. It looks like any other supermarket, but this is a little neighborhood store grown up into a super store—homegrown and one-of-a-kind, unique in these days of giant chains. Like the chains, it has prescription, bakery, florist, and gourmet food departments. But it also has quince, cactus leaves, fresh fish, fresh Mexican and oriental vegetables, a full-line hardware store, and a cafeteria decorated in old grocery store style that's a good place for a lunch stop. Howard's also recognizes who its customers are with signs in English, Spanish, and Vietnamese. The last because just past this store you'll be in a section heavily populated by Vietnamese. On your left is the Queen of Peace statue (see Points of Interest) they've erected, and Vietnamese stores and restaurants line the next few blocks.

Go on past 5th Street and turn right on Proctor. (The ill-fated rock star Janis Joplin was born on this street at 4048, but that's in the other direction, and her birthplace is no longer standing.) About a quarter mile down on the left in the 3300 block is the oldest large apartment complex in Port Arthur, Eddington Court, built in 1929. There are about 6,000 conch shells from the Grand Cayman Islands imbedded in the wall in front of this apartment building. A little farther on, also on the left, is Rose Hill Park, which includes public tennis courts. From here on through downtown almost all the intersecting avenues are named for cities. Another mile brings you to Lamar University in Port Arthur (see Colleges & Universities) with the Gates Memorial Library, which houses the city's historical museum (see Museums). Ahead is the old downtown area. It's deteriorating, but the city is making efforts to bring it back to life.

When you cross Austin Avenue, on your left at 436 Proctor is the marble front of the Keyhole Klub (see Offbeat), one of the relics of Port Arthur's gambling heyday. Turn left at the next corner, Fort Worth, then left again on 4th Street going east. On the right is the City Hall complex, several clean-lined buildings that contrast sharply with the seedy downtown buildings a block away. Stop at City Hall for an excellent view of the city and the lake from the fifth floor observation deck (see Bird's-Eye View).

Continuing on, next to City Hall is the courthouse, and on the left are the Port Arthur News Building and the police and fire stations. Farther along on your right, 4th Street sort of ambles into Lakeshore Drive. In the 1000 block is the Seamen's Memorial Sundial, a tribute to the men of the Texaco *Oklahoma* that was lost at sea in 1971. Just past this, take the right turn onto the Walking Wall (see Points of Interest). Drive along the wall. On your left is Woodrow Wilson Junior High. Note the school's dome which is covered with gold leaf ½₀₀₀ inch thick. On your right is the Intracoastal Waterway and Pleasure Island.

When you come off the Walking Wall, right in front of you will be Rose Hill Manor (see Historic Places), a palatial colonial-style residence built in 1906.

The tour bends back on itself again at this point on Lakeshore Drive, but U-turns aren't permitted here; so go up Woodworth Boulevard in front of Rose Hill and make a left on 4th. The classic Greek revival–style home at 2949 is the Fredrichsen Home built in 1915 and now restored to its former grandeur. Turn left at the first street after this, then right to put you (legally) back on Lakeshore. There are several historic homes along this street. Also built in 1915 was the Hogan Home at 2605. At 2549 Lakeshore is another classic Greek revival house, the Carl White Home built in 1915 for the British Consulate. The major historic attraction on this street, however, is the Pompeiian Villa, the pink house at 1953 Lakeshore (see Historic Places). This is the only house in Port Arthur listed in the National Register of Historic Places. Just past this, the three-story yellow brick building is the Masonic Temple, a relative newcomer built in 1928. Many of the other older homes along this street are now in the process of being restored.

As you pass City Hall, if you look to your right you may see some of the fading murals decorating the walls of the older buildings. They were painted as part of the Bicentennial Celebration to depict the heritage of the city and the United States. Ten of them are scattered around the downtown area.

The street ends at Houston. To your left is the Port of Port Arthur (see Points of Interest). See if a ship is at the dock. If so, you might want to call at the end of this driving tour to arrange for the Port tour. Turn right on Houston, continue until you've crossed 11th Street and turn left at the light on Thomas. This takes you into the refinery area. About all you'll see for the next mile is Texaco storage tanks and the refinery behind them. Turn left when Thomas ends. This is Martin Luther King Street, also called the Texaco-Gulf Highway, both long names for a narrow street. It is also Texas 82 and leads to Pleasure Island (see Points of

Interest) and Louisiana. On your right is the Gulf plant.

The Gulfgate Bridge over the Intracoastal Waterway is both narrow and steep (it rises 138 feet above the water surface to cross the 400-foot wide and 40-foot deep Sabine-Neches Ship Channel), so the driver shouldn't be sightseeing. But even the driver can get a grand view of Sabine Lake and across into Louisiana as the car comes down from the high point on the bridge. At the stop sign turn right and go back under the bridge. There are no trailer hookups or sanitary facilities, but camping is permitted all along this area, and in summer you'll see everything from pup tents to luxury motor homes lined up. There are also plans to build an amphitheater here, and a temporary set-up is presently being used for summer concerts covering a variety of popular musical interests ranging from rock to country and western. If you want a waterside view of the port, which is on your left, this is a good place to stop. In addition to seeing port operations, you can take a look at the shipping on the Intracoastal and some shrimp boats that home port here. At the marina, turn right onto Pleasure Island Boulevard. This time it's a long name for a short street. On the right, across from the marina, is the Marlinspike Marine (see Shopping). At the end are the Pleasure Island Hotel (see Hotels and Motels), Pier 600 Restaurant (see Restaurants), and the lake. This is also the base for several charter fishing boats.

Turn back to the main road. If you want to explore a little more of the island, take a right and wander around. There's not much more to see, but there are a number of good places to take a break, relax, and watch the passing ships. Otherwise, turn left and head back over the bridge. Be sure to make that left onto the bridge access road, or you'll wind up in Louisiana. Coming down off the bridge you can see all the refineries laid out in front of you.

The Get-Acquainted Tour ends here. If you want to get back to your starting point at the Civic Center, continue straight on Texas 82, across 87 onto 214, which will take you back to Texas 73. Turn right on 73 and follow it back to the start.

Want to expand the tour? Just take a left at Texas 87 and follow it out to Sabine Pass and Sea Rim State Park (see Outdoors & Side Trips). Don't worry—you can't get lost—Texas 87 is all there is.

TOUR & GUIDE SERVICES

CONVENTION AND VISITORS BUREAU
3401 Cultural Center
Texas 73 near 9th Ave. (inside the Civic Center)
985-7822 or 985-3581
Monday through Friday 8–5
W+

On the wall just outside the Visitors Bureau office, there's one of those maps that flashes a light at the spot you're seeking when you push a

button. It's a good way to get oriented, but if you really want information on just about anything in Port Arthur, the experts inside are the
ones to ask. "Where can I buy fresh shrimp?" "What's biting in the
lake?" These are the kind of questions you can get answered here.
They'll give you a good local map, brochures, an activities calendar,
directions, and suggestions for making the most of your time in the
area. With some advance notice they can arrange small group tours of
the oil refineries. They'll also find you a place to stay if you don't have a
reservation and may even be able to get it at a discount.

POINTS OF INTEREST

PORT OF PORT ARTHUR
East end of Houston Ave. near 4th St.
983-2029 or 983-2011
W

Small in size compared to Houston or other major ports on the coast,
this port still has a little bit of all normal port activities, and the size
makes it easier to become acquainted with each of them. Anyone may
tour by calling ahead for times and clearance to get through the guard at
the gate. Conducted group tours may be arranged through the Convention and Visitors Bureau. There's more to see when a large ship is in
port and the 75-ton gantry crane, appropriately named "Big Arthur," is
doing its thing. The best view is from the observation platform on the
roof of the main storage building. From there you can see most of the
port as well as the shrimp boats.

QUEEN OF PEACE PARK
9th Ave. near 9th St.
W

This pocket park was established by the parishioners of Queen of
Vietnamese Martyrs Church, which is across the street, as a remem-
brance of their escape from Vietnam and a thanks to the city that took
them in. The heart of the park is a pagoda-style pavilion covering a
statue of Mary, Queen of Peace, that is about three times life-size. It also
bears witness to the efforts of these refugees, most of whom found jobs
on the local shrimp boats, to show their spirit and their acceptance of
the responsibilities of becoming new Americans.

RAINBOW BRIDGE
Over the Neches River on Texas 87 north of city

This bridge is reportedly the tallest on the Gulf Coast, rising to the
height of a 20-story building. Built in 1938, it is one and a half miles
long, including approaches, and clears the river by 177 feet. The result
is a high arch that may make you feel like you're on a roller coaster. This
exceptional clearance for a bridge over a minor river is the result of over-
diligent designers who wanted to ensure that everything afloat at that

time could pass under it. The ship that proved the determinant was the *Patoka*, a U.S. Navy dirigible tender. On its aft deck, the *Patoka* had a huge mast, which was as tall as an oil derrick and was used to moor the Navy dirigibles. But as the best laid plans often go, by the time the bridge was actually built, the *Patoka* was out of service. The height does make for a spectacular view for everyone but the driver. If you look to the right as you approach the bridge from the Port Arthur end, you can see a ship storage area where a number of out-of-work tankers and other large ships are tied up waiting for work or disposal. At least some of the nightmares of driving this narrow, two-lane bridge will be relieved a little in a few years when the bridge being built next to it is completed, and then each bridge will carry one-way traffic.

THE REFINERIES
West and south of downtown along Texas 82, 87, and 73
Free group tours
W

From a distance at night, they look like cities of lights or Christmas trees lying on their sides. Unfortunately, the magic disappears in daylight. Still, this is what city boasters call "the world's largest oil refining–petrochemical complex," so it is worth seeing up close. Unless you're part of a pre-arranged tour, however, the only way you can see it is by roaming the highways around the plants. Both Texaco and Gulf do offer tours but usually require at least ten people in the group (no small children) and reservations two weeks in advance. For information write the plant managers or public relations departments. Gulf's address is P.O. Box 701, Port Arthur 77640, and Texaco's is P.O. Box 712, 77641. Or the Convention and Visitors Bureau will set it up for your group.

THE WALKING WALL
Between Lakeshore Drive and the Intracoastal Waterway from
Savannah to Woodworth
W

The Walking Wall is part of the city's $89 million flood protection system. The auto traffic is one way (south to north), and the speed limit a leisurely 15 mph on this mile-long levee, so even the driver can sightsee. Or you can park and walk, jog, just sit and wave at the passing ships on the Sabine-Neches Ship Channel (part of the 1,200-mile Gulf Intracoastal Waterway), or watch the activities over on Pleasure Island.

BIRD'S-EYE VIEW

PORT ARTHUR CITY HALL
444 4th St. near Fort Worth
983-3321
Monday through Friday 8–5
Free
W +

The first things you'll see when you get off the elevator on the fifth floor are the old photos and other memorabilia of Port Arthur that are on display in the Heritage Room. But the real sights are outside, visible from the balcony. City Hall sits close to the Intracoastal Waterway, so to the east, you can see most of Pleasure Island and Sabine Lake and, on a clear day, the Louisiana shore. From the far corner of the balcony, the port and the Gulfgate Bridge to Pleasure Island are also visible. Walking around the balcony gives you views of Lakeshore Drive and the Walking Wall, the downtown area including the old Goodhue Hotel (the tallest building in town and soon to be restored), and the acres and acres of refineries. If the weather isn't warm enough for balcony viewing, you can still see a lot through the windowed walls of the Heritage Room.

HISTORIC PLACES

POMPEIIAN VILLA
1953 Lakeshore near Richmond
983-7977
Monday through Friday 9–4
$2
W

Sometimes called the "Billion Dollar House," this building's history is almost as fascinating as the villa itself. At the turn of the century, three tycoons bought a strip of waterfront land on Lakeshore Drive where they planned to build adjoining "winter cottages." John W. "Bet-a-Million" Gates built a 20-room, Virginia-style colonial, and Isaac Ellwood, "the barbed wire king," built a modest, 10-room "cottage" that was an authentic copy of a Pompeiian home of 79 A.D. But shortly after it was completed, Ellwood sold it to the third member of the group, James Hopkins, president of the Diamond Match Company, who had never built on his lot. Hopkins brought his wife down from St. Louis, but when she arrived and faced the heat, mosquitoes, and muddy streets of early Port Arthur, she turned around and went back north. Later Hopkins traded the villa to banker and land developer James Craig for Craig's 10 percent of the stock in the newly formed Texas Company. When asked later why he gave up all this stock for the house, Craig replied, "Oil companies were a dime a dozen then. How did I know the Texas Company would survive?" But survive it did and became Texaco, and the stock traded for the house is now worth close to a billion dollars—hence the billion dollar name for the house. The Gates mansion was torn down in 1960, and in the early 1970s the Villa, one of the last houses remaining from the colorful early days of the city, was close to meeting the same fate. The Port Arthur Historical Society came to its rescue and restored it to its former opulence. The deep pink stucco exterior is supposedly as authentic of a Pompeiian home as the Doric columns supporting the portico and the peristyle, a three-sided courtyard that gives access to every room. The Villa has been refurnished with antiques that might be typical of the furnishings used by the Craig family: a Louis XVI parlor set, English Empire dining room table, Savannerie rug, an eighteenth-century diamond-dust mirror, Baccarat crystal, and Sheffield candelabras. The paintings include a portrait of "Bet-a-Million" Gates and his dog, Blondie. Always a colorful sight, the Villa is at its breathtaking best when decorated for the Christmas holidays.

ROSE HILL MANOR
100 Woodworth at Lakeshore
985-7292
Tuesday through Friday 8:30–5, Saturday 8:30–noon
Free
W ramp in rear
This palatial, colonial-style mansion was built in 1906 by Rome H. Woodworth, one of the city's early mayors, and remained in the Woodworth family until 1948 when it was deeded to the city. It is now maintained by the Rose Hill Committee, which is working on restoring the house to its original appearance both inside and out. This lovely home is often rented for weddings and other social and civic events, especially on weekends, so call to find out if it's open before making a trip there. You can also arrange a tour by calling ahead.

MUSEUMS

LA MAISON DES ACADIENS AND DUTCH WINDMILL MUSEUM
Nederland
Tex Ritter Park
1500 Boston near 17th St., five blocks west of Twin City Hwy.
722-0279 (Nederland Chamber of Commerce)
March through August, Tuesday through Sunday 1–5; September through February, Thursday through Sunday 1–5
Free
It's an unusual grouping, this: a park dedicated to the memory of a country singing star and containing two small museums commemorating two diverse groups, the Cajuns and the Dutch. The House of the Acadians is a replica of an early, rustic home of the French immigrants who settled in Louisiana after being forced out of Nova Scotia by the British in the eighteenth century. Their descendants are the Cajuns who came to Texas. If you're lucky, you may be entertained by some authentic Cajun guitar music and songs. Overshadowing this tiny house is the Windmill Museum next door. This 40-foot-high replica of a Dutch original has 25-foot blades that revolve; but since the fickle wind can't be depended on to move the blades when visitors are there, an electric motor propels them. Part of the museum features items owned by Tex Ritter, who was born in Nederland, and the rest is given over to

the Dutch and local artifacts and a gift shop where you can buy items imported from Holland, including wooden shoes. There's a pleasant gazebo under the shade trees between the two buildings if you want to rest awhile. And if you want any other information on Nederland, the Chamber of Commerce office is right across from the park at 1515 Boston.

PORT ARTHUR HISTORICAL MUSEUM
Gates Memorial Library
210 Stilwell at Proctor
982-7667
Monday through Friday 10–2
Free
W

Delora R. Gates donated this library building to the city in 1918 in memory of her husband, John W. "Bet-a-Million" Gates. And since money was no problem, she hired the same architects who designed New York's Grand Central Station. In addition to housing the library of Lamar University at Port Arthur and a rare book collection, the north wing contains the Port Arthur Historical Museum. Like most small museums, this one is crowded with an interesting hodgepodge of displays designed to tell the "complete" story of the city. If you take the time to browse, you'll find everything from a contract to pay a dowry executed by James Bowie in 1831 and a slave sale contract from 1838 to a photo of the first Queen of Port Arthur taken in 1923. Other items of interest to search out include an Edison Talking Machine and a $500 mortgage bond issued by Mexican General Santa Anna on his personal property to raise money for his army.

MUSIC & THEATER

PORT ARTHUR LITTLE THEATER
4701 75th St.
962-1340 or 722-7732
October through June
W

This local group usually presents five plays during its winter and spring season.

COLLEGES & UNIVERSITIES

LAMAR UNIVERSITY AT PORT ARTHUR
1500 Proctor near Stillwell
983-4921
W

This school's emphasis is on technical and vocational courses, and since 1975 when the Texas Legislature approved the merger of Port

Arthur College with Beaumont's Lamar University to establish a branch in Port Arthur, its enrollment has increased ten-fold, from about 150 to over 1,500. An interesting sidelight of the merger, however, is that the legislature did not authorize funds for building until eight years later in 1983. The people of Port Arthur solved that problem and ensured the continued growth of their school by donating buildings. The Renaissance-style Gates Memorial Library was one of those donated. Formerly the city library, it now is home to the student library and the university's rare book collection, as well as the city historical museum (see Museums). The building is recorded as a Texas Historic Landmark and entered in the National Register of Historic Places. Open Monday through Thursday 9–7:30 and Friday 9–5:30. The Ruby Ruth Fuller Building, with its stained-glass windows, was another donation. It was the home of the First Methodist Church from 1916 until the congregation donated it to LUPA in 1976. When it was a church it was often used as an auditorium for visiting speakers. It continues in that role, but in addition, it is used for visiting entertainers who put on shows open to both students and the general public. For information on show schedules call 724-0886. Tours of both these buildings can be arranged either through the school or the Convention and Visitors Bureau. Other activities open to the public include the school's continuing education programs. Some of these last only a few days and are open to visitors as well as residents. For information on these programs call the Student Services Division at ext 301.

SHOPPING

CENTRAL MALL
Texas 365 and Memorial Freeway (U.S. 69)
722-3299
W

Anchored by Beall's, Penney's, and Sears and containing the usual mix of chains and local stores, this one-floor mall should meet most routine shopping needs. The usual fast food places are here, too, plus a Luby's Cafeteria.

MARLINSPIKE MARINE
401 Pleasure Island Blvd. (across from the marina)
982-5603
W

If you want anything in canvas—for a yacht or not—this is the place to go. Awnings, sails, boat and truck covers, hunting and athletic gear, wind socks—if it can be made of canvas, Charles Pederson, his wife, and their talented crew will make it for you. Although they aren't made by the Pedersons, custom handbags are also carried. These are heavy-duty marine fabric bags with a hand-painted design. If you're willing to pay the price, the artist will paint a picture on one of your boat or just about anything else that you can provide a photo of.

PORTIA'S
Groves
5601 East Parkway in Cambridge Square (39th St. exit off Texas 73)
962-2245
W

   Portia and Kathy Livingston, mother and daughter, have decorated
their store with antiques (which they'll sell) as a fitting background to
their large stock of contemporary fashions and fine gifts. Blue jeans to
silk dresses in sizes 4 to 14.

SNOOPER'S PARADISE
Groves
5509 East Parkway in Cambridge Square (39th St. exit off Texas 73)
962-8427
W

   No tiny, cluttered antique shop this. Well, maybe a little cluttered, but
as for tiny, there are 26,000 square feet filled mostly with furniture and
other antiques from the 1800s. The owners, Jon and Terry Hampton,
make several trips a year to personally comb Europe for their stock.
They send out small catalogs several times a year announcing their
latest finds. You can ask to be put on their mailing list.

OUTDOORS & SIDE TRIPS

PLEASURE ISLAND
Take Texas 82 over Gulfgate Bridge
982-4675, ext 359
Free
   Slowly but surely, this 3,500-acre island located between the 400-foot-
wide Sabine-Neches Ship Channel and Sabine Lake is being developed
to live up to its name. Right now you can go fishing or crabbing from
four fishing piers or the 16.5 miles of breakwater, launch your boat from
one of three ramps, hire a charter boat for lake or Gulf fishing, picnic in
a park, camp almost anywhere (no hookups), watch or fly ultralight
aircraft just south of the bridge or (if you prefer something even smaller)
watch model airplanes being flown from a field just north of the bridge,
attend a concert in the temporary Music Park, stable or ride your horse
on the north end of the island, or just watch the world sail by. There is
also a hotel (see Hotels & Motels) and a restaurant (see Restaurants) on
the island. You can also drive to Louisiana by following Texas 82 south
over a toll causeway. Plans? Well, they are grandiose and may not all
come true, but in the future there may be a golf course, lighted tennis
courts, a small theme park, a skeet and trap shooting and indoor pistol
range, a trailer park, and (the inevitable final signs of development)
more condominiums.

TAYLOR BAYOU BOAT TOURS
Take Texas 73 west approximately 13 miles toward Winnie to Jap
Road, make a right and go about 1.2 miles, on left just before small
bridge
794-1749
Weather permitting, Wednesday through Sunday afternoons and
early evenings
Adults $5, children $2

Robert Denicourt, a French chef who speaks five languages, and his
artist wife, Lou, started these tours because they wanted to share the
joys of their bayou home with others. They wanted everyone to experience the marsh ecology and the alligators, birds, snakes, and other
marsh inhabitants up close. These off-the-cuff tours became so popular
that now they run their pontoon boat, "True to Lou," on one-hour, narrated excursions into Taylor Bayou regularly. Of course, there's just one
little boat (up to six passengers) and the rather relaxed schedule depends on when the customers show up. So if it's a time they say they're
running (see above) and the boat isn't tied up at the little landing near
the bridge at Jap Road, wait awhile, they're probably out on a tour. To be
sure, call in advance.

Beaumont

Take U.S. 69-96-287, approximately 17 miles northwest of Port Arthur.

Beaumont, along with Port Arthur and Orange, goes by the name the
"Golden Triangle." Major points of interest include the Babe Didrikson
Zaharias Memorial Museum, the Beaumont Art Museum, and the
Gladys City Boom Town.

BEAUMONT VISITORS INFORMATION CENTER
3875 IH-10 at Walden (just south of where U.S. 69-96-287 meets IH-10)
842-1596
Monday through Saturday 8:30–4:30
W

The center is easy to find because of the mock oil derrick on the roof.
The helpful people here will make your visit easy, too. In addition to the
usual brochures and information on accommodations, restaurants, and
current events, they will give you a detailed map of the city marked for
a self-guided tour.

BABE DIDRIKSON ZAHARIAS MEMORIAL MUSEUM
IH-10 at Gulf exit
833-4622
Open seven days 9–5
Free
W+

Although born in Port Arthur, where a golf course is named after her,
Mildred "Babe" Didrikson Zaharias grew up in Beaumont, and the city

has honored her as she honored it. The museum, which has a design that symbolizes the five Olympic circles, displays the memorabilia of "The Babe's" outstanding athletic career, which included earning the Associated Press title of Woman Athlete of the Year six times, winning Olympic golds, and being a champion pro golfer. There is also a very short film showing her in action and a 15-foot, 250-pound gold key given to Babe by the City of Denver.

BEAUMONT ART MUSEUM
111 9th between Ashley and Evalon
832-3432
Tuesday through Friday 10–5, Saturday and Sunday 2–5
Free
W

Plans are underway to move from this Southern Regency mansion set on a carefully landscaped city block to another building at Delaware and French, but the time of the move isn't determined yet, so call or check with the Visitors Center. The permanent collection of paintings, sculpture, and mixed media is mostly by Texas artists. There are also frequent traveling exhibits, and the lecture series is highly regarded. A fine arts library and sales gallery are on the second floor.

GLADYS CITY BOOM TOWN
On the Lamar University Campus at University Dr. and U.S.
69-96-287, which is known locally as Cardinal Dr.
838-8896
Tuesday through Friday and Sunday 1–5, Saturday 9–5, closed Monday
Adults 50¢, children 25¢
W

Operated by Lamar University as an outdoor living history museum, this is a reconstruction of the oil boomtown that appeared almost overnight after Spindletop blew its top on January 10, 1901. The fifteen wooden buildings grouped around a plank sidewalk square include a log cabin saloon, barber shop, livery stable, mortuary, and pharmacy and doctor's office. There are also pieces of heavy oilfield equipment on display. Also in the same area is the Lucas Gusher Monument, a national historic landmark that is a memorial to the Spindletop pioneers, and the Spindletop Museum, which contains exhibits relating to the history of oil exploration in the area before the Spindletop oil boom. This museum is open Monday through Friday 1–5 and is free. It's located at 950 E. Florida near Callaghan on the Lamar campus just to the east of Gladys City. Ask for directions at the Boom Town.

Orange

Take Texas 87 across Rainbow Bridge, approximately 18 miles northeast of Port Arthur.

Texas' easternmost city and third corner city of the Golden Triangle is one of the main beneficiaries of the philanthropy of the Nelda C. and H. J. Lutcher Stark Foundation. One result is Civic Plaza (sometimes called Cultural Plaza) where several sights worth seeing are concentrated within easy walking distance of each other.

CIVIC PLAZA
From Texas 87 in Orange take MacArthur Dr. (Bus. 90) and Green Ave. east to the plaza
Best parking at Green and 7th across from art museum, and Main and 5th across from library

FARMERS MERCANTILE
Division and 6th
W
This old-time, wooden-floored farm and general store was opened in 1928 and is still run by the same family who stocks many items that were in vogue on opening day. Everything from cream crocks and butter churns to the latest in farm supplies, plus groceries, is available.

FIRST PRESBYTERIAN CHURCH
Green and 8th
883-2097
W
The three stained-glass windows above the front door won prizes at the Chicago World's Fair in 1893, much of the marble was imported from Italy, the pews and woodwork are mahogany, and many of the decorations are overlaid in gold leaf. This is why it took four years (1908–1912) to build this stately memorial to the Lutcher family, and why the eye-pleasing fruits of this investment of time and money are still evident. It also has the distinction of being the first public building in the world to be air conditioned.

FRANCES ANN LUTCHER THEATRE FOR THE PERFORMING ARTS
Main between 6th and 7th
886-5535
W
A modern, 1,500-seat theater with offerings ranging from touring companies of Broadway shows to concerts and opera.

HERITAGE HOUSE MUSEUM
905 Division
886-5385
Tuesday through Friday 1–4, Sunday 1–5
Adults $1, children 50¢
W
A visit here will give you an idea of how the upper middle class lived in Orange in the early 1900s. This rambling, two-story home contains period furnishings plus changing historical exhibits.

STARK MUSEUM OF ART
Green at 7th
883-6661
Wednesday through Saturday 10–5, Sunday 1–5
Free
W

The building itself won an award for excellence of concept, design, and construction in the use of natural stone. And inside is an outstanding collection of art and artifacts relating to the American Indian and our western history. Significant among the exhibits are Indian pottery and artifacts, Audubon prints of birds of Louisiana and Texas, bronze sculpture by Remington and Russell, and paintings by the artists in the Taos School of New Mexico. Perhaps to offset the dignity of these impressive works, there is also a group of "Andy" Anderson's humorous "whittlings" in wood, such as "The Jury" and "The Shotgun Wedding." There is also a collection of Dorothy Doughty's porcelain models of American birds that rivals Audubon's prints and a series of Steuben glass bowls engraved with scenes representing the history of each of the fifty states.

W. H. STARK MANSION
Green at 6th
Entrance through the Carriage House, 610 W. Main
883-0871
Tuesday through Saturday 10–3:30
Reservations requested
$2

If the Heritage House reflects the life of the upper middle class, this one tells in many ways what it was like to be one of the richest families in the area at the turn of the century. The 15-room, three-story structure, with its many gables, galleries, and distinctive windowed turrets, shows the influence of several architectural styles. Today the house stands much as it did when the Stark family lived here, with its original furniture, rugs, family portraits, lace curtains, silver, ceramics, glass, woodwork, and lighting.

Sabine Pass

Take Texas 87 south, approximately 14 miles from Port Arthur.

This town is in the record books as having the lowest elevation in the state: eight feet above sea level. It was laid out in 1836 by Sam Houston and Philip A. Sublett with expectations that its location would undoubtedly make it a major city. But a series of hurricanes proved that it was too exposed for a port, so now, with the exception of the telltale signs of the oil industry, it remains much the same fishing town it has been for a century and a half.

SABINE PASS BATTLEGROUND STATE HISTORICAL PARK
One and a half miles south of Sabine Pass on FM Rd. 3322
971-2559 (Sea Rim State Park superintendent)
Open at all times
W

The story of the Civil War battle fought here sounds like a Texas Tall Tale, but it is true. Historians have proven that. On September 8, 1863, a Union fleet numbering some 20 vessels and 5,000 men tried to invade Texas through Sabine Pass. Facing them was Company F of the Texas Heavy Artillery, which consisted of a lieutenant, who was a young barkeep from Houston named Dick Dowling, and some 40-odd Irish dockworkers with six cannon in a small, unfinished fort called Fort Griffin, which consisted of some earthworks reinforced with railroad iron and ship's timbers. Company F had been ordered to spike its guns and withdraw by Confederate General John B. Magruder, but the unit had been together since early 1861 and was spoiling for a fight, so Dowling ignored the order. Four Union gunboats attacked the tiny Confederate force, bombarding Dowling's position. Dowling held fire until the ships were in close range, and the Irish gunners quickly disabled two of the ships. Directing their fire on the troop carriers, the Confederates forced them to turn tail. And with them went the rest of the fleet back to New Orleans. The final score: Dowling wound up with all six of his cannon and no casualties, while the Federal force lost two gunboats and 65 men were killed, wounded, or missing and 315 were captured. Needless to say, Dowling was a hero to Texans for the rest of his life. Time and erosion has wiped out all substantial evidence of the exact site of Fort Griffin, but the 56-acre park was placed on a probable site, and Dowling's exploit is commemorated with a statue. Also, "Dick Dowling Days" are still celebrated in Sabine Pass during Labor Day weekend. The tiny park offers covered picnic sites with water and restrooms, a boat ramp, and a fish-cleaning shelter. There are also some old concrete bunkers in the park, but these were used by the coast artillery in World War II, 80 years after Dowling. Even more impressive than the statue are the huge offshore drilling rigs, man-made islands many stories high, that are anchored in storage nearby. These dwarf the Dowling statue and illustrate how far technology has come since the days of Company F's heavy artillery.

SABINE PASS LIGHTHOUSE
Technically, it's in Louisiana, but you can see it across the Sabine-Neches Ship Channel from just below the battleground park. Built in 1856, this 85-foot tower sent the light through its Belgian-constructed lens as far as 18 miles into the Gulf. It was decommissioned in 1952 after almost a hundred years of service and now is owned by the Louisiana Game and Fish Department. The lens is on display at the Port Arthur Historical Museum.

SEA RIM STATE PARK

Texas 87, approximately 23 miles south of Port Arthur and 10 miles
west of Sabine Pass
971-2559
March through October, open seven days 8–10 for day use;
November through February, open 8–5 for day use; open at all times
for camping but gates closed at day use closing hours
Autos $2
W+ but not all areas

This park is unique because it is the only marshland park in the state.
But it is also the best beach park on the eastern end of the coast. The
highway divides the 15,109-acre park into its two distinct areas. South,
on the Gulf, is the Beach Unit with three miles of wide, sandy beach
and a little over two miles of a biologically important zone where salt
tidal marshlands meet the Gulf waters. Behind the beach is the park
headquarters, observation deck, and Interpretive Center, containing
a well-executed map and explanation of dune and marsh life, a small
aquarium, hunting and fishing information, brochures on area attractions, and a collection of seashells. This weathered wood complex also
has restrooms, showers, and concessions (summer only). If you want
follow-up on what you saw in the Interpretive Center, a 3,650-foot
boardwalk, called the Gambusia Nature Trail, wanders over the tidal
marshlands offering the opportunity for a close-up view. There are also
20 camping sites equipped with water and electrical hookups and a
dump station for $4 a night. Tent camping on the beach is $3. All camping in the park requires a permit. If you don't make it in before closing
time, a public beach is farther down the road but without facilities.
Across the highway, the Marshlands Unit has a boat ramp, a boat channel with canoe or pirogue trails that allow access to the marsh, and six
platforms and four observation blinds that provide an outstanding base
for nature lovers, birdwatchers, photographers, fishermen, and even
campers—but don't forget insect repellent. Hunting is permitted in
parts of the Marshland Unit on designated mornings during the regular
open migratory waterfowl season. Canoe rentals are available at the
Breeze Inn Again store on the highway to the east of the park. But
before you put your canoe in the water, get a trail map from the park
rangers and file a float plan with them. Airboat rides through this unit
are also sometimes available, the "sometimes" being determined by
whether Texas 87, the main route for tourists, is open to Galveston. Not
enough customers come through the Port Arthur way to make the rides
profitable. When running, the airboat takes about 30 minutes to cover
eight miles, and there's a good chance you'll see alligators (one stretch is
so thick with them it's called "Alligator Alley"), muskrats, raccoons,
ducks, and maybe even an otter. March through October 9–7, $7 for
adults, $4 for children. For further information on the park write the
Park Superintendent at P.O. Box 1066, Sabine Pass 77655.

SPORTS & ACTIVITIES

Baseball

The Beaumont "Gators," a San Diego Padres farm club, provide professional baseball for the Golden Triangle.

Birdwatching

Port Arthur is located in the Central Fly-way for waterfowl, so during the migratory season, birds are everywhere. Pleasure Island is one of the more accessible places to observe them. Not as accessible but also not as disturbed by civilization are McFaddin Marsh National Wildlife Refuge, along the coast west of Sea Rim State Park; Texas Point National Wildlife Refuge, south of Sabine Pass; the state's J. D. Murphree Wildlife Management Area, and the Audubon's Sidney Island.

J. D. MURPHREE WILDLIFE MANAGEMENT AREA
Texas 73, approximately five miles west of Port Arthur
736-2551
Call for days open
Birdwatching free, fees for hunting and fishing
You need a boat to get around this 8,407-acre preserve, but in season, it's worth the effort to see the migrating waterfowl in a natural habitat. For information write the director of the management area at Highway 73 and Parks and Wildlife Drive, Port Arthur 77640.

SIDNEY ISLAND
No one allowed on island without permission of Audubon warden
Accessible only by boat
735-4298
This island, east of the Rainbow Bridge near the Louisiana state line, is leased from the state by the National Audubon Society. Nesting season is from March until August, and the keep-off restrictions are rigidly enforced during that period. You can watch through binoculars from boats in the lake. Among the migratory birds and shorebirds to be seen here are the roseate spoonbills. For information write Sidney Island, Box 611, Bridge City 77611.

Fishing

No matter what else is going on along the coast, this sport is the biggest single draw. And Port Arthur is triply blessed because it offers lake, river and bayou, and Gulf fishing. And of course, there's excellent fishing in some of the wildlife areas (see Birdwatching). Saltwater catches include mackerel, red snapper, ling, speckled trout, drum, and redfish.

Saltwater fishing tournaments are normally held in May and October. From freshwater the anglers pull in bass, white perch, and catfish. Crabs are also in abundance. Bring your own boat (there are some rentals, but not many) and go it alone, or hire a guide. You can also charter a boat for both lake and offshore. Charters in the area run about $600 or $700 a day for up to six persons. Among the many guides in the area, Steve Dubois (962-3225) has a good reputation for knowing where the freshwater fish are biting, while Seaweed Kleiner (727-3886) and Joel Singleton (962-9604) are two of several who are both lake and offshore guides. There are no party boats operating from Port Arthur at present. For a complete list of guides and charter services, contact the Convention and Visitors Bureau (see Tour & Guide Services).

Golf

BABE DIDRIKSON ZAHARIAS MEMORIAL GOLF COURSE
75th St. and U.S. 69
722-8286
Open seven days, dawn to dusk
$4–$5
Eighteen-hole public course. Multi-use recreation center nearby. Lessons available.

PORT GROVES GOLF CLUB
Groves
5721 Monroe Blvd.
962-1261
Open seven days, 6:30 a.m. to dusk
$2.10 for nine holes
Nine-hole course open to public.

Hunting

Birds, birds, birds, and more birds! Plus deer, wild turkeys, and a number of other game animals can be hunted in the area. And now that the alligators have been protected into over-population, there's even an occasional season for them. Hunting is permitted in some of the wildlife preserves and Sea Rim State Park, and a number of hunting clubs and leases are available on private land. Once again, you can go it on your own, or hire a guide. Norris Guide Service (736-3023) is popular, and there are others. Guides cost about $70 a day per person for everything from lodging to dog, blind, and boat. A well-known hunting resort is located just five minutes away from the waterfowl hunting areas. For more information contact the Convention and Visitors Bureau (see Tour & Guide Services).

LABOVE SHOOTING RESORT
Sabine Pass
Texas 87 south
971-2258
$300–$500 a day per gun
   Waterfowl is the game. The air-conditioned lodge has carpeted bed-rooms and a bar. Fees cover lodging, meals, hunting, guides, decoys, and transportation to and from the blinds. For details write Box 1104, Sabine Pass 77655.

Jogging

   For interesting scenery as you jog, try the Walking Wall (see Points of Interest) and Pleasure Island (see Outdoors & Side Trips).

Tennis

   There are a number of courts scattered around town. Here are the locations of the lighted courts:

AURORA PARK
61st St. between 9th Ave. and U.S. 69

AUSTIN HIGH SCHOOL
2441 61st St.

BABE DIDRIKSON ZAHARIAS MEMORIAL GOLF COURSE
75th St. and U.S. 69
722-8286

DOORNBOS PARK
Nederland
Ave. H between S. 24th and S. 27th

EDISON JR. HIGH SCHOOL
3501 12th St.

JEFFERSON HIGH SCHOOL
2200 Jefferson Dr.

LINCOLN HIGH SCHOOL
1023 Lincoln

REYNOLDS PARK
4100 block of 36th St.

ROSE HILL PARK
2900 Proctor at Woodworth

WASHINGTON PARK
300 W. Thomas Blvd.

ANNUAL EVENTS

Details are available from the Port Arthur Convention and Visitors Bureau (985-7822 or 985-3581).

April

PLEASURE ISLAND MUSIC FESTIVAL
Pleasure Island, north of Gulfgate Bridge
Usually weekend late in April or early May
Admission
Variety is the spice of this festival. One year it's the big band sound, a pops orchestra, jazz, gospel, and western swing; and the next rock, country and western, rhythm and blues, and Cajun.

May

BUM PHILLIPS–BOB HOPE CELEBRITY GOLF TOURNAMENT
Port Arthur Country Club (796-1311) and Babe Didrikson Zaharias Memorial Golf Course (722-8286)
Weekend near end of month
Free
A charity tournament for the Hughen School. Bum Phillips, Bob Hope, and pro football stars are usually among the celebrities.

MEMORIAL WEEKEND S.A.L.T. FISHING RODEO
Headquarters: Pleasure Island Pier
Tickets $20 includes festival events.
Salt- and freshwater. Over $25,000 in prizes. Other Memorial Weekend events tied in.

June

CAJUN WEEKEND
Civic Center
Weekend early in month
Admission
Cajun music, dancing, Cajun food, and a carnival in the Cajun spirit of "Let the good times roll!"

September

CAYMAN ISLAND WEEKEND
Civic Center
Weekend early in month
Admission
   Over the years, Port Arthur and the Cayman Islands, one of the few remaining British crown colonies in the Caribbean, have built up a special relationship. This festival celebrates that with music—usually by a band from the islands—dancing, and food. The Convention and Visitors Bureau also has special travel packages to the Caymans available.

MEXICAN FIESTA
Civic Center
Weekend in middle of month
Admission
   Mexican music, food, arts and crafts, and entertainment.

October

CAV-OIL-CADE CELEBRATION
Most events in or around the Civic Center
963-1107 or 982-2561
Week near end of month
Most outdoor events free
Admission to some indoor events
   This is the big one for the city, celebrating its ties to the oil industry. The first Cav-Oil-Cade was held in 1952, and it has grown bigger and better every year. Downtown street parade, musical events that usually include a name group in concert, dances, crowning of the queen, golf and tennis tournaments, other competitions and contests of all kinds from fire-hose fights to bicycle races, banquets, regattas, and a fishing rodeo.

HOTELS & MOTELS

Rates for a double:
   $: under $35
  $$: $35–$50
$$$: over $50

BEST WESTERN AIRPORT TOWERS MOTOR INN
Nederland
200 Memorial (U.S. 69), near Jefferson County Airport
727-1631 or 1-800-528-1234
$
W

The Nederland address makes it sound like this bargain-priced motel is out of the way, but actually nothing is far away from anything in Port Arthur. This two-story motel has 116 rooms, a pool with wading area, a restaurant, and a lounge where you can dance on Friday and Saturday nights. Free airport transportation.

DRIFTWOOD MOTOR HOTEL
3700 Memorial (U.S. 69) at 36th St.
983-1633 or 1-800-251-1962
$$
W + two rooms
There's a little bit of everything here. Many of the 129 rooms in this two-story motel have a small, private balcony facing the free-form, grotto-style pool with Jacuzzi and hot tub set in a grassy central patio. For those who look at swimming more as exercise than a cooling break from sunbathing, there is also a larger pool near the restaurant. In fact, the large windows of The Landing Restaurant next door overlook that pool. Other amenities include a children's wading pool and playground, barber and beauty shops, and a lounge that is a popular dance spot with the locals. Although not part of the motel complex, a twin cinema is next door.

HOLIDAY INN PARK CENTRAL
Memorial (U.S. 69) at 75th St.
724-5000
$$$
W + two rooms
The 165 rooms offer in-room movies and accommodations that are a shade better than what's typical for this chain, and the amenities are in harmony with its status as a hotel rather than motel. The four-story building has a large and cheerful lobby and a restaurant that is brightened by both the decor and the large windows overlooking the pool and Jacuzzi. It also boasts Triangles, which the manager classes as a "high-energy" club. The local "energetics" seem to agree for this is one of the most popular spots in town for dancing to the music of a DJ while being showered by confetti and balloons and nibbling on the hearty free snacks. Right across the street is the municipal golf course. Free airport transportation.

HOLIDAY MOTOR HOTEL
3889 Gulfway (Texas 87) near 9th Ave.
985-2538
$$
W
It's small when compared to the newer hotels, only 62 rooms, and starting to show its age, but it is centrally located. More importantly, the congenial owner-manager has been here for ages, and the number of repeat guests indicates there must be some good reasons to stay here. In

addition to a pool and small restaurant, there is also a lounge. However, because of the peculiarities of Texas local option liquor laws, it's located in one of the few dry areas of the city. To get around this inconvenience, the lounge is set up as a private club to which motel guests are given automatic memberships. For a more elaborate meal, Leo & Willie's Restaurant is right down the street.

PLEASURE ISLAND HOTEL
580 Pleasure Island Blvd.
985-5573
$$$
W

If you want to be on the water, this is the place. It's located on Sabine Lake just past the Pleasure Island Marina. All the accommodations are one-bedroom apartments that can sleep up to six (provided privacy isn't a big deal). Each apartment has a private balcony overlooking the lake. Usually about 35 apartments are available either in the hotel building or the rental pool in the condominium next door. Some covered parking is provided under the buildings. There is a pool and Jacuzzi, and, even though each apartment has a kitchen, room service breakfast is available but only in the hotel building. Some sports equipment can be checked out. Weekly rates are available and reasonable. Thinking of a Memorial Day vacation here? Put in your reservations early. This is the headquarters for the Fishing Rodeo held that weekend.

RAMADA INN
3801 Texas 73 near 9th Ave., near the Civic Center
962-9858 or 1-800-2-RAMADA
$$$
W+ three rooms

From the marble and brass decor in the lobby to the jogging track around the tennis court, this chain motel adds luster to the city's accommodations. It has 130 rooms and suites and the customary swimming pool. In addition to the regular menu, Arthur's Restaurant offers a noon buffet and Sunday buffet brunch that are both attractive to the eye and bountiful. When you walk into Arthur's Pub you may feel as if you are entering a king-sized living room. There's a bar, of course, but there are also couches, comfortable chairs, and even bookcases. Entertainment is provided by a DJ and a piano bar. Courtesy transportation is available.

SABINE PASS MOTEL
Sabine Pass
5623 Greenwich, off Texas 87
971-2156
$$
W

A little hard to find, but take a right at the only four-way stop in town, and you'll be able to spot it on the left near the end of the football field. It's approximately eight miles from Sea Rim and has just about the closest rooms for rent near that state park. Unfortunately, its 32 plain-vanilla rooms are often filled by fishermen or oil rig crews, so reservations are essential.

RESTAURANTS

Putting on the Ritz

PIER 600
Pleasure Island
600 Pleasure Island Blvd. (sometimes called Pleasure Pier)
983-4542
5:30–10:30, Sunday brunch 11:30–2:30, closed Sunday and Monday evenings
$$$$
W+

A stunning view of the lake, upholstered wicker furniture, soothing green decor, stained glass, antiques, attractive artwork, and soft music make this a local favorite for a sumptuous evening. There are reports that the culinary skills of the kitchen are unpredictable and aren't always up to the impressive surroundings, but to be fair, the chef often makes culinary delights that surpass the vista. The emphasis is on seafood, but prime ribs, steaks, and Cornish hens are also on the menu. The impressive wine cellar includes such exquisite vintages as Château Lafite-Rothschild, Premier Grand Cru Pauillac for the well-heeled. A window seat at the Sunday champagne brunch provides a fine view of the weekend sailors in their fleet of small sailboats, reflecting hundreds of colors on the lake. Lounge and bar.

Barbecue

BRISKET ROOM
1101 Jefferson Dr. at Lewis, about two blocks south of Gulfway
982-6471
Monday through Saturday 11–9, Sunday 11–2
$–$$
W
A typical cafeteria-style barbecue place, except the locals say the barbecue is a little better and the portions a little bigger than at the other places in town. Beer.

Cajun

FARM ROYAL
2701 Memorial (U.S. 69-96-287) at 26th
982-6483
Serves breakfast, lunch, and dinner, closed Sunday
$$; No cr.
W

It looks like a typical roadside restaurant: crowded tables without tablecloths, and the aquarium by the door and a few paintings (for sale) by local artists are the only decorations. But what roadsider has a wine list or frog legs and quail on the menu? More important, it offers some flavorful, if mild, samples of Cajun cooking. To appreciate the menu you have to understand a little about Cajun food. For example, a *gumbo* is a cross between a soup and a stew and, though often heavy with seafood, is liable to have everything in it but the cook's apron. If crawfish, which the Cajuns call "mudbugs," is listed as *étouffée*, it'll probably be cooked in a mixture of flour and oil, smothered in peppers and onions, and served over rice. If you hesitate to experiment with the house Cajun specialties, the more familiarly named seafood dishes are usually good and plentiful. Ask about the *Farm Royal Cookbook*. Wine and beer.

Drive-In

MONCEAUX DRIVE IN
3349 Gulfway at 6th Ave.
982-3033
Monday through Saturday 10–10, closed Sunday
$; No cr.

This tiny take-out-only place offers hamburgers and the other routine fast food dishes, but two of the reasons it still is open at the same spot after more than 40 years are its crabfingers and steakfingers, which will have you licking your fingers. Smart to call ahead for faster service.

Seafood

THE BOONDOCKS
Take Texas 73 west toward Winnie to Jap Road, turn right and go 1.3 miles to small sign marking entrance road on left, approximately 13 miles from Port Arthur
796-1482
Tuesday through Friday 4–10, Saturday 12–10, Sunday 12–8, closed Monday
$$; AE, MC, V
W

This is one restaurant where the name tells it like it is—it is out in the boondocks of Taylor Bayou. But if you're a catfish lover, it's well worth the trip and the wait for a table (no reservations). Bill Northern started this restaurant in the mid seventies as a fish camp beer joint but found he had to stay open too many hours. So he decided to turn it into a small restaurant and serve only lunch and dinner. Since catfish were plentiful in the area, he worked out mild, medium, and spicy frying recipes and that became the house specialty. The duck hunters soon discovered it, and his little restaurant took off. The decorations come from his customers—thousands of business cards stapled to everything that doesn't move. For variety, the menu also includes huge chicken-fried steaks, shrimp, and other routine alternatives. When you've finished, ask for a gator bag, go outside, and hope the alligators show. The gators are temperamental and don't always come calling, plus they hibernate in cold weather, so that attraction is definitely seasonal and erratic. Beer, wine, and BYOB.

CARPEL'S
9999 Gulfway Dr. (Texas 87) alongside the Rainbow Bridge
962-5470
Tuesday through Thursday 5–10, Friday 5–11, Saturday 11–11,
Sunday 11–10, closed Monday
$$$
W

It's not as far out, but this restaurant's almost as hard to find as the Boondocks. The secret is to take the last road on the left just before you start to climb the Rainbow Bridge on the Port Arthur side. There's a sign, but you may miss it. And even when you make the turn, you may think you're headed wrong because the beginning of the dirt road is very bouncy. But persevere: go past the marina and through the riverside community—at 10 mph as requested, please—to the end of the road and the long, low building that is Carpel's. There are two medium-sized dining rooms, but if you want a water view (with the bridge looming over), try the long gallery filled with tables for two alongside the kitchen. The specialty is seafood, cooked with all the tender loving care it deserves. Not a great seafood house, but one of the better ones in the area. Half orders are available. Beer and wine.

LEO AND WILLIE'S
3825 Gulfway Dr. (Texas 87) and 10th Ave.
983-4451
Monday through Thursday 11–10, Friday and Saturday 11–11, closed Sunday
Reservations suggested
$$$
W inside steps

This centrally located seafood restaurant serves everything from lobster to hamburgers. Some menu highlights are *shrimp creole*, a crayfish platter, a cold platter of boiled shrimp, various seafood salads, and a stuffed crab that is unusual because it is made with all white-lump crab, no bread filling. Bar.

SARTIN'S
Sabine Pass
Texas 87 at Tremont, approximately 13 miles south of Port Arthur at beginning of Sabine Pass
971-2158
Open seven days 11–10
Reservations recommended, especially on weekend
$$; No cr.
W

If it isn't the best seafood restaurant on the coast (and if the kitchen was a little less erratic, it could be), it is certainly the best known. It seems that every travel and guidebook writer who gets within striking range makes a pilgrimage here to add to the piles of praise heaped upon this unpretentious restaurant. The Sartin family started this place as an outlet for the catch from their shrimp boats, which led to the slogan "Ours woke up in the Gulf this morning." Shrimp, oysters, crabs—all the simple seafood dishes you'd expect are on the menu, plus the daily catch special. But two things that make this restaurant a stand-out are the barbecued crabs and the "platter service." The crabs aren't really barbecued, they're deep fried, but the spices used in frying make them taste like no other crab dish around. And don't mistake the "platter service" for the usual seafood platter that is on the menu of almost every restaurant on the coast, including this one. No, that word "service" is the clue. The waitresses will bring an overflowing platter that changes with the season but usually includes cold crab claws, barbecued crabs, fried fish, fried shrimp, frog legs, french fries, cold slaw, and garlic toast. And she'll continue to serve you more and more of the same until you're ready to call it quits. Statistically, all the platter service you can eat usually takes about two hours. Sorry, you need at least three people to order platter service (at $12 each) and no doggy bags. You eat off paper plates, use rolls of paper towels instead of napkins, and deposit the shells and leavings in the trash can at the end of your table. Beer and wine. BYOB.

CLUBS & BARS

GET DOWN BROWN'S
5333 Twin City Highway near Hogaboom
962-8024
Tuesday through Friday 4 p.m.–2 a.m., Saturday 6–2, closed Sunday and Monday
W

The walls are painted to give the impression of a small town, and at times, especially on ladies' night and free barbecue or crawfish night, it seems as if the town is going to burst at the seams. The name comes from the nickname earned by the owner when he was a DJ. He has another club of the same name in Beaumont. Progressive country by a DJ keeps the dancers happy.

LEO'S
Sabine Pass
5035 S. Gulfway (Texas 87)
971-2789
Monday through Saturday 9 a.m.–2 a.m., Sunday noon–2 a.m.
W

On the left as you come into Sabine Pass, this old-style roadhouse is a popular haunt of the locals and the off-duty oil rig crews who flock to the bar, pool tables, and a large, DJ-hosted dance floor. A big added attraction is owner "Momma" Melba Hanner's Wednesday free lunch. For her free Thanksgiving dinner, Momma cooks for days and puts on a spread for all who want to come.

RODAIR CLUB
FM Rd. 365 about four miles west of intersection with U.S. 69-96-287, near the bridge
736-9001
Friday and Saturday 8:30–1 a.m., Sunday 3–8, closed rest of week
Cover $2.50; No cr.
W

If you think Cajun food is different, wait until you try the Cajun two-step (with a hip shake) to the fiddlin' of a live band. This white-frame building doesn't look like much—in fact, parts of it look like they are just one rusty nail away from falling down—but it's one of the great spots in Texas for hearing folk music that has bounded over from Louisiana and gotten an alligator lock on the local scene. Things can get rough, so stay calm, be polite, and leave any look-down-the-nose inhibitions at home. Then you'll be welcome to join in letting the good times roll. Beer and wine, but you can brown-bag it and BYOB.

OFFBEAT

KEYHOLE KLUB
436 Proctor near Austin
985-4117
W

Behind the marble front is a bar with pool tables in the rear, which seems in keeping with its neighbors in this seedy section of downtown. But if you look closely you can still see hints of what used to be, in the fading gold wallpaper and the huge key set in the middle of the ceiling. What used to be? Well, the Keyhole Klub was once one of the best-known gambling palaces on the coast. Upstairs, Jimmy and Harry Monsur, the two brothers who own the Klub, have kept the old gambling hall in top shape. No gaming tables or equipment, of course, but the lighting system that used to highlight the club's entertainers and exotic dancers is still working, the dance floor is waxed, and the gold leaf ceiling still glows in old-time, bordello-pink lighting. It's so well-preserved, in fact, that two movies with gambling sets have been shot here. It's unfortunate that the upstairs is not open to the public, but the Monsurs are keeping it up in hopes that someday they'll be able to turn back the clock and go back into business—not necessarily gambling, perhaps a nice supper club. When conditions are right, they'll be ready. Meanwhile, there are those who claim that the best hotdogs on the coast are grilled on the little stove behind the downstairs bar. Not a safe area for after dark visits.

★★★

BOLIVAR PENINSULA

PORT ARTHUR TO HIGH ISLAND VIA WINNIE

There are two ways to travel the Bolivar Peninsula along the coast from Port Arthur to Galveston, and both go through High Island. The Winnie route is longer because it zigzags inland at the beginning, but it is also the more dependable, since Texas 87 between Sea Rim State Park and High Island is (too) often closed because of storm damage and erosion. To travel the 50-mile Winnie route, take Texas 73 west to Winnie. Turn left (south) on Texas 124 to the coast just south of High Island where you can pick up the more dependable section of Texas 87 and go right (west) to Bolivar and Galveston.

PORT ARTHUR TO HIGH ISLAND VIA TEXAS 87

If this road is open, the Texas 87 route is shorter than the Winnie detour. Since it hugs the beach most of the way and also crosses or skirts several wildlife refuges, the drive usually is a little more interesting, especially during the bird migrations. Just follow Texas 87 west from Sabine Pass, passing Texas Point National Wildlife Refuge and going through Sea Rim State Park and McFaddin Marsh National Wildlife Refuge to the junction with Texas 124. Driving on the beach along here is not recommended because only a thin layer of sand covers the marsh mud.

ANAHUAC NATIONAL WILDLIFE REFUGE

Take Texas 124 to the junction with FM Rd. 1985 between High Island and Winnie, go west on 1985 approximately 10.5 miles to sign to refuge, then left on park road approximately three miles
267-3337
Open at all times
Free
W

This refuge is the winter home of large concentrations of waterfowl including roseate spoonbills, herons, egrets, pelicans, and snow and blue geese. Fishing and hunting are permitted in designated areas. For additional information, including birding lists of more than 250 species spotted here, write the refuge at Box 278, Anahuac 77514.

HIGH ISLAND TO PORT BOLIVAR

Unless your car sits high you probably won't be able to see the water or the narrow strip of beach (much of it is under water at high tide) along parts of this stretch because the road runs behind the line of protective dunes. What you will see are cattle and a scattering of oil wells. The first community of consequence is Gilcrist at Rollover Pass. Most of the houses here are single-family homes built up on stilts. The same is true for the rest of the communities you'll pass—all acknowledging the low elevation and the capriciousness of the Gulf. Usually a few beach houses are for rent in both Gilcrist and Crystal City, the next wide place in the road. From Crystal City to Port Bolivar, the beach widens, and in contrast to the condition in most of the area just passed through where the beach is eroding, the beach here is actually building seaward. Except for an occasional clump of houses or a fishing camp, this undeveloped stretch of beach is ideal for those seeking sun with solitude. It is also great for shell collecting, especially after a storm, and for birdwatching. A good place to picnic is Fort Travis Seashore Park (684-0333), just off Texas 87 about one and a half miles from the ferry slip. All that's there of the old fort are some ruins, but there are a few screened shelters, a playground, restrooms, and showers. A permit is required for camping (fee); reservations through the Galveston County Parks Department (766-2411).

BOLIVAR LIGHTHOUSE
Port Bolivar
Texas 87 near ferry slip

The first lighthouse was built here in 1852. It was made of cast iron, so the Confederates dismantled it for the metal during the Civil War. The present tower was completed in 1872 and kept in service until 1933. In addition to the lives it may have saved at sea, it also served as a storm shelter and saved many from floods during several hurricanes. It's now on private property, and no visitors are allowed.

BOLIVAR FERRY
Operated by Texas Department of Highways and Public Transportation
Leaves approximately every 20 minutes, 24-hour service
763-2386 for schedules
Free

Once aboard this ferry you can stay in your car or go up to the observation platform—just make sure you're back in your car when it's drive-off time. The trip takes about 15 minutes, long enough to enjoy the excellent view of Galveston, the five-mile dike jutting out from Texas City to the west, and the variety of ships and small boats using the Houston Ship Channel through Bolivar Roads. This is open water, which gets a little choppy at times, but the ferries run in just about anything short of a hurricane. As you approach the Galveston side, you can wave to the fishermen lined up along the shore at Seawolf Park on Pelican Island. Even though several ferries operate at peak times, the wait on summer weekends and holidays can get long on both sides. Take along a book and snacks. Or, on the Bolivar side, you can stop at ZUM's near the landing for a cool drink. The slogan at this bait shop is "Famous for Nothing," but it is famous locally for the graffiti on the walls. You don't need a car to ride. On nice days, a lot of people walk on board and make the round-trip just for the pleasant ride and the view. There are restrooms on board.

★ GALVESTON ★

★★★

GALVESTON COUNTY SEAT   ★   61,902   ★   (409)

In 1817 Jean Lafitte came to Galveston Island, ran off the Karankawa Indians, and set up a base. He stayed here until 1821 when the U.S. government forced him to leave after his men made the undiplomatic mistake of privateering against an American gunboat. Now if there is any consistency in the stories and legends about pirates, it is that they always buried their loot. That is why treasure hunters today would like to dig under the hospitals at the University of Texas Medical Branch, which covers the area where Lafitte was supposed to have lived.

Lafitte may or may not have buried treasure on the island, but there is little doubt that today Galveston Island is living up to its unofficial title as the Treasure Island of the Texas Coast.

If you last came here as a kid and remember it as a sleepy resort town, you may be surprised by its present vitality. Over the past 20 years, Galveston has had a real renaissance. Part of this is due to the unceasing labors of the volunteers and staff of the Galveston Historical Foundation, which saved whole areas of the city from the "progress" of the bulldozer and led the battle to restore and preserve the city's illustrious past. Part is due to the bounty of the Moody Foundation, which has

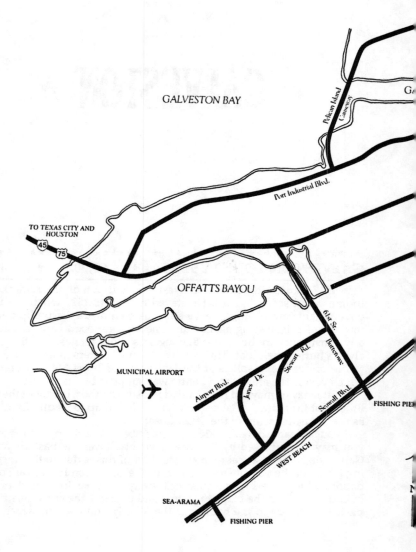

GALVESTON BAY

Pelican Island Causeway

Ga

Port Industrial Blvd.

TO TEXAS CITY AND
HOUSTON

45 75

OFFATTS BAYOU

61st St.

MUNICIPAL AIRPORT

Stewart Rd.

Buttercup

Airport Blvd.

Jones Dr.

Seawall Blvd.

FISHING PIER

WEST BEACH

N

SEA-ARAMA

FISHING PIER

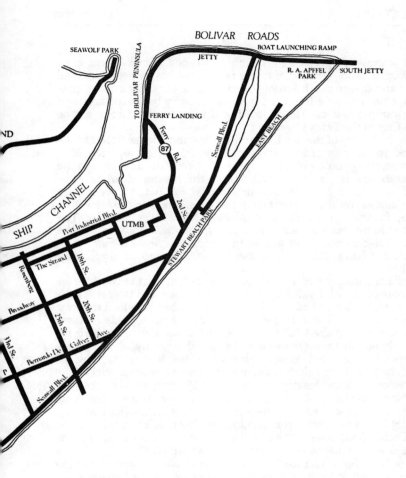

BOLIVAR ROADS

SEAWOLF PARK

BOAT LAUNCHING RAMP

JETTY

R. A. APFFEL PARK

SOUTH JETTY

TO BOLIVAR PENINSULA

FERRY LANDING

Ferry Rd.

87

Seawall Blvd.

EAST BEACH

ND

SHIP CHANNEL

Port Industrial Blvd.

UTMB

2nd St.

STEWART BEACH PARK

The Strand

18th St.

Rosenberg

Broadway

20th St.

25th St.

Galvez Ave.

33rd St.

Bernardo Dr.

Seawall Blvd.

GULF OF MEXICO

to Scale

39

bathed worthwhile projects in the money needed to make them grow and prosper. And part is due to the far-sighted city fathers, business people, and investors who have pulled the area out of its decline, prevented it from turning into a seedy resort of tacky beach cottages and fishing camps, and are slowly putting it back on the throne as the Queen City of the Texas Coast.

From the luxury of the San Luis and the Tremont House hotels to the playland atmosphere of Stewart Beach Park, this is now a place with a bit of everything you'd expect in a resort city. You can slip back into the nineteenth century; as you stroll one of the historic districts' tree-shaded streets, surf in the Gulf or waterski the bayous, wear your bathing suit as you shell and eat shrimp at a restaurant on the seawall or dress up for the *shrimp boccaccio* at the more formal Wentletrap on The Strand, admire the intricate craftsmanship of the woodwork in the Bishop's Palace, watch with glee as the dolphins spin in the air at the Sea-Arama, or do any one of a thousand other things to make your stay enjoyable.

Despite the long list of lures thrown out to visitors, the two biggest draws of the island are still the ageless ones: the sun and the sea. There are miles and miles and miles (32, in fact) of beaches on which to romp or soak up the sun. These are neither as sparkling nor as wide as those farther south on Padre Island, but they are clean and convenient no matter where you are on the island. As for fishing, why brave the discomforts of an isolated fishing camp when the fish are waiting all around the island, and all the comforts of a resort city are available?

Galveston's colorful history goes back to 1528 when it was discovered by a Spanish explorer. The discoverer, however, was shipwrecked and kept prisoner for six years by the Karankawa Indians, a fact that may belie that tribe's reputation for cannibalism. The flags changed—Spanish, French, Mexican—but the island stayed the same until Jean Lafitte came and went, and the settlers arrived in the early 1800s.

During the Texas War for Independence, Galveston was one of the temporary capitals for the provisional government, and a Galvestonian, Samuel May Williams, was a major financial backer of that revolution. After the Texans wons, Michael B. Menard bought most of the eastern end of the island from the new republic for $50,000 and laid out the townsite with the streets much as they exist today.

During the Civil War, Galveston fell to Federal troops in October 1862. But Confederate General Bankhead Magruder decided to strike back. With a force consisting of two river steamboats—converted into "Cottonclads" by piling cotton bales on the decks and around the gunwales—a couple of smaller boats, 300 combat veteran survivors of a decimated New Mexico unit, and some other riflemen, he launched a surprise land and sea attack against the Federal invaders. When the smoke cleared, the Federal ships were either sunk or run off, and Magruder and his men had Galveston back, plus 300 prisoners. A large Federal force, operating out of New Orleans, made one more attempt to get at Galveston and Houston in 1863 with a small armada of ships and several thousand men. This time the thrust led to the Battle of Sabine

Pass, which turned out to be another disaster for the Union (see Port Arthur). After that, Galveston stayed in the Confederate ranks until the war ended.

By the late 1800s, Galveston had become the third largest port in the nation, and fortunes were being made by entrepreneurs, bankers, cotton factors, and shipping firms. The Strand, copied and named after the same street in London, became known as the "Wall Street of the Southwest." And with the money and prominence came the social whirl. Elegant homes were built, and the city became a cultural center.

Unfortunately, the inhabitants forgot that Galveston is a barrier island open to the devastating whims of Nature. In 1900 disaster struck in the form of an unexpected hurricane that threw tidal waves over the low-lying island as if it had been but a tiny sandbar. Six thousand perished in what is still listed as the greatest natural disaster in American history. The flourishing port and most of the island's buildings were destroyed.

Undaunted, the survivors started to rebuild. But first they worked out a way to protect their island from future hurricanes. The plan they decided on would take heroic efforts, high purpose, perseverance, and years to complete. They started by building the seawall (originally less than 4 miles long, now almost 10). Then, behind that protective barrier, they worked for eight years dredging sand from the waterways and using it to raise, by 6 to 17 feet, the elevation of the entire city of more than 2,000 buildings. This prodigious project was severely tested by a storm in 1915 that was reportedly even worse than the one in 1900. Casualties numbered nowhere near the totals of the 1900 storm, and some buildings were lost. Overall, though, the seawall held, and the raised city survived.

It almost didn't survive the economic disaster that followed. It was just about this time that the Houston Ship Channel opened for seagoing vessels. The railroads soon decided Houston was easier to serve than Galveston, so they located their major terminals there, turning that inland city into the major port on the Texas coast and killing the economy of Galveston in the process.

The decline was halted during the thirties and forties when gambling was tolerated in the island city. When that was outlawed, there was another nosedive.

The latest upswing started when Galveston realized that visitors would be interested in the city's historical treasures as well as its beaches. Now, once again, this resort city is growing in popularity, and the economy is strongly bolstered by the rebirth of the port. The renewed faith in the future of the island is exhibited in the construction boom. In the past few years, hotels, motels, condos, restaurants, and businesses have opened at a rate comparable to the city's Victorian heyday.

As for hurricanes—Alicia roughed up the city in 1983, but once again it bounced back, bigger and better.

Average winter temperature, 50s and 60s; average summer temperature, mid 80s to mid 90s. Humidity normally high.

A GET-ACQUAINTED DRIVING TOUR

The easiest way to get acquainted with the major sights of Galveston is to take the train or the trolley tour. But if you want a wider view or prefer to go it on your own, the following tour will lead you past most of the sights on the eastern end of the island, where the majority of them are concentrated.

The place to start, of course, is the Convention and Visitors Center in the Moody Civic Center at Seawall and 21st Street. You can pick up a map and brochures that will make your tour more interesting and meaningful. But before you start, there are three things to note about the way the city is laid out. First, many streets and avenues have two names: 21st Street, for example, is appropriately also named Moody Center Street, and Avenue B is The Strand. Sometimes both names appear on street signs and in addresses, sometimes only one. Next, the numbered (and named) streets run north and south starting at the east end of the island near Ferry Road (Texas 87), and the street numbers get higher as they work west. The lettered (and named) avenues start at the bay side of the island and go down the alphabet as they work south to the seawall. And, just to make it interesting, the city fathers occasionally stick in a half avenue: like Avenue M ½ or Avenue P ½. Finally, most east-west avenues are cut up and don't continue for any distance. Broadway (Avenue J) is the best two-way east-west in the north section of the city, while Avenue O is the major one-way going west and Avenue P the major one-way going east in the center and south. Confused? You won't be once you've checked out your map and finished this tour. Here goes.

From the Visitors Center head west along Seawall Boulevard (this puts the seawall and the Gulf on your left). The first large building you encounter is the Moody House, a retirement home. Continue along Seawall, past the major hotels and restaurants, to 61st Street (Butterowe). If you continued straight you'd be heading for Sea-Arama (see Outdoors & Side Trips) and the Mary Moody Northen Amphitheatre (see Music & Theater), but we are going to turn right on 61st. There's not much to see on this street, except motels, restaurants, clubs, and small businesses, until you go about a mile, and the street cuts across Offatts Bayou. There's a little marina here and, on good days, small boats in the bayou. Just past this is the intersection with U.S. 75. To the left is the road to Houston and to the right Broadway. Galvez Mall, the city's largest (see Shopping), is also to the left. Turn right onto U.S. 75 and Broadway. Continue down Broadway to Rosenberg (25th Street). There hasn't been much of tourist interest to see since you left the seawall, but now you've pretty well boxed in the major tourist area. From here on there's lots to see starting with the Texas Heroes' Monument, a 72-foot memorial to the heroes of the Texas Revolution, that dominates the intersection of Broadway and Rosenberg like a beacon marking the area for tourists.

Turn right on Rosenberg, heading south toward the Gulf, then left in two blocks on Avenue L. The area between 25th and 23rd from Avenue L to Avenue N is called the Silk Stocking Historic District. A number of small, but historically interesting, homes in this area are being restored. One is the blue and white–trimmed Sweeney-Royston House at Avenue L and 24th. This Victorian cottage, built in 1885, is listed in the National Register of Historic Places. This home used to be open to the public and may be again. Continue to 21st Street (Moody) and turn right. The large building on the right is a senior citizens retirement home. In the next block on the right is the former Island City Protestant Orphans Home started in 1878. After the original home was destroyed in the 1900 storm, William Randolph Hearst hosted a charity affair in New York to raise money for the present building.

Right on Avenue O. The Las Palmas House on the northwest corner of Rosenberg and Avenue O has been used in several films. Garten Verein is at 27th and O. This octagonal pavilion, built in 1876, was the center for German social life at the time. It is now part of a city park. About six blocks farther on, at 3427 Avenue O, is the Syndor-Powhatan House. Built in 1847, it is now the home of the Galveston Garden Club, which occasionally has tours or other activities open to visitors (for information, 763-0077).

Turn left off Avenue O onto 37th Street. The next turn is Avenue P, but that's two blocks, not one, because they stuck in O ½. Left on Avenue P (Bernardo de Galvez). On your right at 3601 is the 1839 Williams Home (see Historic Places), built by one of Texas' earliest entrepreneurs. Continue down Avenue P to Rosenberg (25th) and turn left. At the Heroes' Monument, turn right on Broadway (Avenue J).

Immediately on your left, on the northeast corner of Rosenberg and Broadway is the Sealy Mansion, called "Open Gates." This castle-like 1889 home is now owned by the University of Texas Medical Branch and is being converted to a conference center. On the next block, also on your left, is the Ashton Villa (see Historic Places). Starting at 19th, you are entering what is called the East End Historic District, which is a residential community of about 40 square blocks listed as an entity in the National Register of Historic Places. It goes east to 11th and north about six blocks to Market (Avenue D). Just past 18th Street, on your right, is the Doll Museum. The house on your right at 1515 Broadway was built in 1871 and is notable for the porches with slender columns, arches, and imaginative gingerbread trim. At 14th, on your left is the Bishop's Palace, probably the most well-known building in Galveston. Across the street is Sacred Heart Catholic Church, built by the Jesuit fathers in 1903. The statue on the dome, added in 1950, is a copy of the famous Christ of the Andes.

Turn left on 12th Street, go one block to Sealy, and turn left again. At 1228, on your right, is the Burr House, built in 1876 in a Classical and Gothic Victorian blend. The Queen Anne–style Skinner House at 1318 is from 1895. The original iron fence still encloses the yard. The Smith-Chubb House at 1417, on your left behind the Bishop's Palace, was built in 1859 and is called the "Flat Roof House." What has been described as "the strangest house in a city of strange houses" is on your left at 1627 Sealy, on the corner of 17th Street. This is the John Clement Trube House. Built in 1890, it is a cross between Gothic and Moorish design. Note the sculptured burning torch decoration on the octagonal tower is repeated on the iron fence posts. On your right at the corner of Sealy and 19th is the Sonnentheil House. Built by one of the best-known carpenters in the area in 1886, it is notable for numerous woodworking details.

If you want to see more of the historic homes in this area, get a copy of the East End Historic District tour map from either the Convention and Visitors Center or The Strand Visitors Center. This map pinpoints and gives details on about 100 historic homes in the area.

Otherwise, turn right on 19th Street. The First Presbyterian Church is at the corner of Church (Avenue F) and 19th. This was the first church congregation in Galveston, organized in 1840. The church building was started in 1872 and completed in 1889. Turn left on Church. Behind the First Presbyterian and standing back-to-back with it is the oldest surviving church building in the city, on the corner of Church and 21st. This is St. Mary's Cathedral—also the oldest cathedral in Texas—which was built in 1847 with a half million bricks brought in from Antwerp, Belgium. In an act of thanksgiving after the church survived the disastrous flood of 1875, the tower was crowned with a statue of Mary, Star of the Sea, which has withstood all the storms since. The statue's survival has inspired the growth of a myth—as long as the statue stands, Galveston will stand.

Turn right on Moody and right again on Post Office (Avenue E). On your left is the 1894 Grand Opera House (see Music & Theater). Go back to 19th and turn left. Ahead at Market (Avenue D) is the American National Insurance Company Tower; at 20 stories high it is Galveston's lone skyscraper. Individual visitors used to be welcome on the top floor observation walk for the best bird's-eye view of the city. But after the last hurricane, the company decided that was too big a risk and that the insurance premiums to cover themselves for visitor mishaps were too high, so the walk was closed to individuals. Escorted group tours usually can be arranged. For information call 763-4661.

Go one more block to Mechanic (Avenue C) and turn left. On the corner of Moody (21st Street) is the old cotton exchange. Between 23rd and 24th is the new Tremont Hotel (see Hotels & Motels) and across the street, The Strand Street Theater (see Music & Theater).

At Rosenberg (25th Street—are you getting this dual name system now?) turn right. On your left is the Railroad Museum (see Museums) and Shearn Moody Plaza. At the next block turn right on The Strand (see Historic Places), the street of nineteenth-century commercial buildings that have been restored to their former glory and now house some of the finest shops and restaurants in the city. A left on 20th Street will take you to the waterfront where you make a right. Along here you'll see the banana boats being unloaded, the 1877 tall ship *Elissa*, and Pier

19, which is the home of the Mosquito Fleet (Galveston's shrimpers), the Galveston Party Boats, and tour boats. If you want a better view of it all, stop at Hill's Pier 19 Restaurant (see Restaurants) and climb the outside stairs to the observation deck.

Turn right on the first street past the waterfront sights and left at The Strand. Follow The Strand out of the old restored district and through the warehouse and project housing. When the road turns, you'll see the Texas Medical Center and the University of Texas Medical School on the right. Turn into the medical complex. The enormous red brick building you see is Old Red, the Ashbel Smith Building. Before the turn of the century, it housed the entire UT medical school (see Colleges & Universities). Drive back onto The Strand and turn right. On your left you can see the huge cranes at the container ship terminal. At the water tower, which is Holiday Drive, turn left. On your left is the small Port Holiday Shopping Center. At the end of this road is the Galveston Yacht Club. Turn left into the parking lot and make a loop through it to get a closer look at the large pleasure craft berthed there. Straight ahead you may see the container cranes in action. After the loop back to Holiday Drive, turn right, then left at the water tower, which puts you back on The Strand. It's one block to Ferry Road. (If you want to take the Bolivar Ferry—see Bolivar Peninsula, above—turn left.) Turn right and go down Ferry Road to Seawall Boulevard. When you reach there, on your left will be the Stewart Beach Recreation Area and the Gulf. (If you want to loop out to the east end of the island, with its south jetty and R. A. Apffel Park, take a left.) Follow Seawall west just past the Galvez Hotel to your starting point at the Convention and Visitors Center.

TOUR & GUIDE SERVICES

Galveston Island is geared for visitors. You'll find brochures popping up almost everywhere that give information on the sights to see and places to go. Detailed information is available at the Convention and Visitors Bureau, and guided tours of the historic city are available through numerous tour services. Tours may be taken by train, trolley, car, boat, or on foot, either in a group, on a custom-designed tour, or on your own.

GALVESTON CONVENTION AND VISITORS CENTER
2106 Seawall at 21st, on ground floor corner of Moody Civic Center
763-4311
Open seven days 9–5
Free
W+ back entrance
Staffed with knowledgeable and helpful people, this is where to go to find out everything a tourist would want to know about Galveston—accommodations, restaurants, sights, tours, local activities, and directions. You'll come out filled up with information, tons of brochures, a three-month activities calendar, and a useful map. This is also the place

to get tickets and board the Treasure Island Tour Train and the Galveston Flyer Trolley.

HARBOR TOURS
Pier 19 at the north end of 19th St.
763-5423
End of May until early September only
Tours seven days at 10 a.m., 2 p.m., and 7 p.m.
Adults $5, children $3
W

The *Dixie Queen* will carry you from its dock next to the Mosquito Fleet of shrimp boats out into the ship channel for a two-hour narrated tour that covers about twenty miles. Sights to be seen include the historic ship *Elissa*, the banana docks, the shipyards with the huge dry docks, the Yacht Basin, Seawolf Park on Pelican Island, the oil refineries, and the big ships in Bolivar Roads and the port. It's operated by Galveston Party Boats, which also offers day-long and overnight fishing trips. Sun deck and snack bar.

HERITAGE TOURS
Galveston Historical Foundation
2016 Strand (Drawer 539, 77553)
765-7834
Fee depends on tour details
W

Custom-designed tours for groups. The Galveston Historical Foundation, which has done such an outstanding job preserving the Ashton Villa and other historic buildings, does an equally fine job showing off the history of Galveston. And since the GHF has access to a number of historic properties, the itineraries often include dining in a private nineteenth-century home. The key here is "ask and you shall receive." If they can't get you in, no one can. The drawbacks are the tours are *only* for groups, and since they are designed for each individual group, they must be arranged well in advance—two weeks is a bare minimum. The more time the Foundation has to plan, the better the tour.

HRH CARRIAGE TOURS
112 15th St.
763-7084
$15 a half hour for couples

You can pick up one of these horse-drawn carriages or buggies near The Strand Visitors Center or the west end parking lot of the Hotel Galvez at Seawall and 21st. Slow, narrated tours through The Strand, the historic districts, downtown, or just about anywhere you want to go as long as it isn't hazardous to the horse and you're willing to pay for it. Reservations are encouraged, and you can usually find a publicity flyer in the Visitors Center or in hotels or motels that'll cut $2 from the cost of your ride.

TREASURE ISLAND TOUR TRAIN
Departs from Moody Civic Center
2106 Seawall
765-9564
Seven days a week in summer; May: departures at 9 and 11 a.m., 1:30
and 3:30 p.m.; June through August: 9, 11, 1:30, 3:30, and 5:30.
Closed Monday from September through November, March through
April; closed December, January, February
About $3.50 + tax, children $1.75 + tax
W

This is one of those pink-awninged, open-air trains that you see in
zoos and other amusement areas. It carries up to 64 passengers on a
leisurely, 17-mile, narrated trip that takes about an hour and a half. It's a
good way to get acquainted with the city since the tour covers both old
and new Galveston and includes Seawall Boulevard, the Rosenberg
Library, the business district, the historic districts, The Strand, the
shrimp fleet, Yacht Basin, and Texas Medical Center.

THE STRAND VISITORS CENTER
2016 Strand near 20th St.
765-7834
Open seven days; Summer: Sunday through Thursday 9:30–6, Friday
and Saturday 9:30–8; winter: 10–5. Closed on Christmas Day and for
hurricanes
Free
W ramp to see movie

This should be your first stop when you hit The Strand. It is another
project of the Galveston Historical Foundation and is located on the
ground floor of a restored building, below the office of that organization. It is an excellent example of how a visitors center should be run.
Given half a chance, the courteous, efficient, and knowledgeable staff
working under W. Barry Vinson, the center director who often shows
up to work in a costume, will soon have you as enthusiastic about the
area restorations as they are. There is an endless stock of brochures
covering everything about The Strand, walking tours of the other historic districts, and even costume ideas for dressing up for the annual
"Dickens on The Strand." A free, 20-minute film on the history and
restoration of the *Elissa* is rerun every 45 minutes. History and travel
guidebooks, postcards, and tickets to the Trolley, Opera House, other
Foundation properties, and historic events are for sale. You can also
pick up a map for a self-guided tour or rent a cassette player ($2) that
will guide you through a walking tour of the area.

TROLLEY TOUR/SHUTTLE
Departs from Moody Civic Center with scheduled stops at important
sights
763-0884 for groups only, otherwise Visitors Bureau 763-4311

Tours daily starting on the hour from 9 a.m. to 5 p.m. (later in summer)
Adults $3.75, senior citizens $3.50, children $2

The Galveston Flyer, a bus designed to look like a 1920s trolley, follows much the same path as the train tour. But in this case, your ticket is valid all day for one complete loop, and you can get on and off at any of the stops, all of which are located at or within easy walking distance of the major tourist attractions. The narrated tour includes stops at several hotels and motels, Ashton Villa, the Railroad Museum, The Strand Visitors Center, Yacht Basin, and the Bishop's Palace. The trolley makes this shuttle loop once an hour.

GUIDEBOOKS

BOB'S GALVESTON ISLAND READER
By Bob Nesbitt
Published by the author
$3.50

This old-time Galvestonian's inside view of the island's history and sights is told with a little irreverence and tongue-in-cheek. Available at The Strand Visitors Center.

RAY MILLER'S GALVESTON
By Ray Miller
Houston: Cordovan Press
$19.95 hardback

This book is an enlarged version of the Galveston section of Miller's *Eyes of Texas* Gulf Coast guide. A little bit of history, a little bit of gossip, and a lot of old photos bring the past to life. Available at most bookstores.

POINTS OF INTEREST

PELICAN ISLAND
Take 51st St. north over Pelican Island Causeway onto Seawolf Parkway

Largely a man-made island across from the Port of Galveston, it was developed by dredging. In addition to shipyards and other industrial sites, it is also the home of Seawolf Park and Texas A&M University's Moody College of Marine Sciences and Maritime Academy.

PORT OF GALVESTON
Along Water Street on north side of island from 9th to 41st

Banana boats, shrimpers, grain carriers, and container ships—they all use this port, which claims to have the fastest access to the open seas of any major American port. It is also unique in being the only port in the nation where all facilities, from railroad switching to crating, are coordinated under one management. The value of this highly efficient system has resulted in the title of America's "Port of Quickest Dispatch." It also helps it be the only major port in the country not supported by public funds. The port now handles close to 10 million short tons of cargo every year; almost 7 million of that is bulk grain. Historically, this was the first major port in Texas, and as long as it held that distinction, Galveston was also the state's largest city. For a better understanding of port operations, see the working scale model of the port in the Railroad Museum.

ROSENBERG LIBRARY
2310 Sealy (Ave. I) at 24th St., immediately behind Ashton Villa
Parking in rear at Ball (Ave. H) and 24th
763-8854 or 763-2526
Monday through Thursday 9–9, Fridays and Saturdays 9–6
Free
W ramp entrance in alley

The Rosenberg is the oldest Texas public library in continuous operation and one of the oldest in the Southwest. In addition to being a city library, it also houses several art and history galleries, a rare book room, and the Galveston and Texas History Center. The Galveston Art League has a gallery on the first floor featuring exhibits by local artists. On the third floor is the Harris Gallery, which features changing art exhibits; the Hutchins Gallery, a small museum presenting well-displayed exhibits on local and Texas history; the James M. Lykes Maritime Gallery with a permanent display on the history of shipping in Texas that includes large model ships from the era of sails to container ships; and the history center. The extensive archives of the history center include Galveston newspapers starting in 1844 and a letter from Andrew Jackson to Sam Houston. Among the architectural drawings on file are those of Nicholas J. Clayton who designed approximately 120 buildings in the city between 1872 and the early 1900s, including what is now known as the Bishop's Palace. The history center is open Tuesday through Saturday, 10–5. The rare book room, also on the third floor, contains a variety of properties that start with Babylonian clay tablets and go to current books from fine presses. This quietly decorated room gives the feeling of a comfortable living room—a serene place to get away from it all. It is open Tuesday through Friday 1–5 and Saturday 9–5. The library also offers lecture series and special classes, and a travel, art, and foreign film series at various times during the year (small admission charge).

THE SEAWALL
Ten miles long starting near the east end of the island

In addition to providing evidence of man's never-ending battle with nature, the seawall is also a monument to the spirit of Galvestonians who say this island city is worth saving at any cost. After the devastating hurricane of 1900, in which 6,000 Galvestonians died, it was decided to build the seawall and, using sand dredged from the bayous and waterways, raise the elevation of the entire town. Those projects took eight years, but they saved the city from the ravages of the next big storm in 1915. The first seawall was less than four miles long, but over the years it was slowly lengthened until now it protects about one-third of the island from the Gulf surf. There are also 14 granite-covered jetties built out into the Gulf between 10th and 61st streets that are designed to protect the beaches and seawall from the Gulf currents. One of the engineers who worked on the original design of the huge city-saving project was Brigadier General Henry M. Roberts, who is more famous for his book *Roberts' Rules of Order*. The solid concrete seawall was constructed to a height of 17 feet, and Seawall Boulevard, built behind it, is one of the island's best-known streets. The seawall also claims the title of being the longest continuous sidewalk in the world, great for strolling, jogging, bicycling, skateboarding, and roller skating. Bicycles—including surrey types—and skates may be rented at several shops on the east end near Stewart Beach.

TEXAS MEDICAL CENTER
Between Strand and Market from about 4th (Holiday) to 14th St.
761-1011
W
Built around the University of Texas Medical Branch (see Colleges & Universities), this medical complex includes John Sealy Hospital, Shriners Burn Institute, Graves Psychiatric Hospital, Ziegler Tuberculosis Hospital, St. Mary's Hospital, Marine Biomedical Institute, Child Care Center, and the Texas Department of Corrections Hospital.

HISTORIC PLACES

The Galveston Historical Foundation is responsible for four of the architectural treasures listed below: Ashton Villa, the *Elissa*, 1839 Williams Home, and The Strand Walking Tour. To encourage you to visit all of their historic attractions, they offer combination tickets that discount up to $2.50 off the total price. These tickets may be purchased at The Strand Visitors Center or any of the Foundation properties.

ASHTON VILLA
2328 Broadway at 24th St. (parking in the rear)
762-3933
Open every day except Thanksgiving and Christmas
Tours Monday through Friday 10–4, Saturday and Sunday 12–5
Adults $3, children $1.50, family $8
W first floor and multi-media show
This gracious mansion, with its Italianate tall windows and low roof, was built in 1859 by James M. Brown, a business pioneer and wealthy merchant, during Galveston's reign as the leading seaport of the Southwest. Brown designed and built the house himself, even making his own bricks in his brickyard. The Galveston Historical Foundation saved the house from destruction in the late 1960s, restored it to its past

splendor, and furnished the three-story structure with Brown family possessions and authentic antiques of the mid 1800s. The hour-long tour covers the dramatic history of Victorian Galveston and the part this home and the Brown family played in that era. It also includes a multimedia presentation on the 1900 hurricane and the gigantic projects of building the seawall and raising the elevation of the city. The villa is listed in the National Register of Historic Places. Gift shop.

THE BISHOP'S PALACE
1402 Broadway at 14th St.
762-2475
May 31 to Labor Day: tours seven days 10–5; rest of year: tours Wednesday through Monday 12–4
Adults $2.50; children over 13 $1.50, under 13 50¢
Beautiful examples of the attention to detail that was the hallmark of old-time craftsmen abound in Galveston, but nowhere is a greater concentration of them in one place than in the Bishop's Palace. This grandiose home is often considered the crowning achievement of the well-known Galveston architect Nicholas Clayton, whose work left a lasting stamp on the city. He designed it for Colonel Walter Gresham, a Galveston attorney who served as a representative to Congress. The house has 24 rooms—enough space even for Gresham, his wife (an artist), and their nine children—and took seven years and $250,000 to build. It was finished in 1886. The wealth of details is almost overpowering. The interior woodwork, including the imposing grand staircase, is of rosewood, satinwood, white mahogany, American oak, maple, and other rare woods. The examples of fine craftsmanship and elegance in the house include a crystal chandelier from Venice, damask wall coverings from London, and a marble fireplace from Italy. The mantle and fireplace in the downstairs music room are lined with pure silver. The massive sliding doors downstairs are unique in that the wood surface on each side of the door matches the room it faces. The American Institute of Architecture named this home on its list of the hundred most architecturally significant buildings in the United States, the only residence in Texas to receive this distinction. It is also on the carefully selected list of 14 structures included in the Archives of the Library of Congress as representative of early American architecture. Originally called the Gresham House, its name was changed in 1923, when the Catholic Diocese of Galveston-Houston purchased it for the bishop's residence, a role it still serves when the bishop is in Galveston. The remodeled basement serves as the headquarters for the Newman Club at the University of Texas Medical Branch (UTMB), and tour and gift shop income supports both the palace and the Newman Center at UTMB. The tour of the palace lasts approximately 30 minutes, and if there are enough people, a new tour group starts every 15 minutes. If weather permits, visitors are asked to wait on the huge porch until the next tour starts. Since the tour concentrates on the inside of the house, this is a good time to take a close look at the solid construction of native Texas granite, white limestone, and red sandstone, all cut and shaped on the premises. It's also a good time to take pictures.

EAST END HISTORIC DISTRICT
11th to 19th between Mechanic (Ave. C) and Broadway (Ave. J)
The best way to enjoy the architectural beauty of this tree-shaded, 40-block district near The Strand is to stop first at the Convention and Visitors Center or The Strand Visitors Center and pick up a walking tour map, which marks the significant houses and gives details on each. This area is where the well-to-do merchants, professionals, and city fathers lived from the late 1800s through the early 1900s. A few homes here date back as far as the 1850s, but most were built between 1875 and the turn of the century. They represent a hodgepodge of styles from Queen Anne and Gothic to Greek Revival, but the majority fall into an unofficial classification called Galvestonian Victorian. The entire district has been placed on the National Register of Historic Places and designated as a National Historic Landmark. As such, property owners cannot make changes to the exterior of their homes without consent of the city's Historic District Board.

ELISSA: A TALL SHIP FOR TEXAS
Pier 21 off Water (Port Industrial Blvd.)
763-1877 or 763-0027
Open seven days 10–5
Adults $3.50, children $2.50, families $10
W deck only, call ahead
The story of the search for and restoration of this iron-hulled sailing vessel is almost as interesting as a visit to the ship itself. The Galveston Historical Foundation wanted a ship to represent that city's role as an important nineteenth-century port. Many candidates were considered and rejected, some because they were too big and restoration costs would have been astronomical, but most because they had no connection at all with Galveston. The search ended in Piraeus, Greece, with the *Elissa*, a 150-foot, square-rigged barque that had called at Galveston several times in the 1880s. She was a tramp merchant ship carrying a variety of cargoes to more than a hundred different world ports from the day she was launched from a Scottish shipyard in 1877 until 1970 when she made her last voyage carrying a load of smuggled cigarettes. She was towed to Galveston in 1975, and then the search started for craftsmen proficient in rigging and other almost-forgotten maritime skills. With the aid of a few specialists, a small army of inexperienced but energetic volunteers, and more than $3.6 million in donations, she was opened to the public on July 4, 1982. *Elissa* is the oldest ship in Lloyd's of London Register of Shipping and the third oldest ship afloat, giving way in age only to England's famed *Cutty Sark* and the *Star of India* in San Diego. Not only afloat, although more than a century old, she is still sailed at least once a year, which may make her the only operational nineteenth-century sailing ship in the world. Today her hold is furnished with maritime exhibits rather than cargo. The exhibits tell the story of her career and the heyday of the Port of Galveston. To

keep the children from being bored, they can climb in, around, and over a mock-up ship on the dock. Also on the dock is the Sail Loft, a museum shop featuring nautical gifts. A free film on the restoration of the *Elissa* is shown at The Strand Visitors Center, just about three blocks away. You'll get more out of your visit to the ship if you see the film first. Parking near the *Elissa* is difficult to impossible, since the port workers need all the spaces and the railroad tracks on the street are frequently used by port switch engines moving freight. Best to park near The Strand and walk down.

1839 SAMUEL MAY WILLIAMS HOME
3601 Ave. P (Bernardo de Galvez)
765-1839
Monday through Saturday opens 9:30, Sunday opens 11, last tour at 3:30
Adults $2.50, children $1.25, families $7
W

Although a little out of the way, this home is worth a visit for several reasons. It is one of the oldest on the island and an example of a prefabricated home, built in Maine, then carefully taken apart, shipped to Galveston, and reassembled. It was also the home of a relatively unknown man who worked behind the scenes in the War for Texas Independence. Samuel May Williams was the business mind behind Stephen F. Austin's colony, and when the Texans declared their independence, he used his financial savvy and some of his own money to buy the first ships for the Texas Navy, recruit volunteers for the army, and purchase supplies and munitions for both. A venture capitalist, he is often called the "Father of Texas Banking." Another reason this house is worth a visit is the outstanding 13-minute slide show, narrated by Alexander Scourby, in which photos of actors in period costumes dramatically recount the life of this forgotten hero. There is an audio system that is activated as you enter each room so you can listen to recorded conversations that might have taken place in that room. The house has been restored and furnished to resemble what it looked like in 1854. Two points of interest are at the top and bottom. At the top is the cupola and widow's walk. It's no longer possible to see more than a sliver of the Gulf from these vantage points, but it doesn't take much imagination to picture the view as it must have been in Williams's time. At the bottom, you can see the result of the 1900 hurricane when the level of the island was raised by pumping sand from the bottom of the harbor. Many buildings were raised on jacks, and thus the effects can't be seen. But the Williams home was built on seven-foot brick piers so only the lower level of the kitchen was buried under the fill. A small example of the extent of this gigantic project can be realized by comparing the present porch and entrance to the house, which are almost on ground level, with old drawings that show the original structure with a large flight of front steps leading to the porch.

SILK STOCKING HISTORIC DISTRICT
Along 24th and 25th between Ave. L and Ave. N

Another area of historic homes. Formerly a political precinct of the city, its name supposedly came from the time when only well-to-do ladies could afford silk stockings, and this district was where they lived. This area is easier to walk than the East End since it is not as extensive. It contains some excellent examples of nineteenth-century architecture including the Sweeny-Royston House at 24th and Avenue L, another work of the most popular architect of the time, Nicholas Clayton. It was built in 1885 as a wedding gift from J. M. Brown, who built Ashton Villa, to one of his daughters. It is listed in the National Register of Historic Places and designated as a Texas Historic Landmark.

STRAND NATIONAL HISTORIC LANDMARK DISTRICT
20th to 25th between Water (Ave. A) and Mechanic (Ave. C)

Many cities have lost the battle to stop their once-flourishing downtown areas from the rot that leaves the area dominated by seedy bars and empty stores. Galveston is one city that won that battle—just as it won the battle to save its old residential areas—by playing up its history. Instead of tearing down old buildings, the civic-minded have turned the very age of the buildings into a tourist attraction. And the major symbol of victory is The Strand. The restoration of most of the iron front buildings in just a six-block section of this avenue has led to a rebirth of the whole area. When King Cotton reigned supreme and Galveston was *the* port on the Texas coast, this was the commercial heart of the Southwest, called the "Wall Street of the Southwest." No longer lined with banks, traders, and commercial houses, it is now a sightseer's and shopper's delight, offering, in a few short blocks, a fascinating group of shops, restaurants for every taste and pocketbook, and interesting galleries, all in restored buildings constructed in the mid and late 1800s. And in keeping with the restoration, the modern street lights are gas. Sure, you can just wander around and enjoy the sights, but if you want to get the most from your visit, you should start at The Strand Visitors Center at 2016 Strand (see Tour & Guide Services). From there you can venture forth armed with free maps and brochures and, if you want to go all the way, an audio cassette player that will direct your walking tour (adults $2, families $3).

MUSEUMS

ANTIQUE DOLL MUSEUM
1721 Broadway near 18th (some parking in rear alley)
762-7289
Tuesday through Saturday 10–5, Sunday 1–5; closed January
Adults $3, children $2

A fantasyland for children—and probably some adults, too—as well as a mecca for doll collectors. Every downstairs room in this restored

1850 cottage is brimming with dolls, some of which outdate the house. The oldest doll is "Queen Anne," a jointed doll from the seventeenth century. There are also contemporary dolls, including the Cabbage Patch Kids; Kewpie dolls; French dolls with beautiful fashion clothes, realistic wigs, and paperweight eyes; the famous *Bye-Lo-Baby*, known as the "Million Dollar Baby" for being the first doll to make its American distributor a million dollars; and a number of dolls by members of the National Institute of American Doll Artists, including one of Princess Grace dressed in an exact copy of her wedding gown. At any one time, there are between 700 and 1,000 dolls on display. These are the cream of the crop from the extensive collection of Mrs. H. L. Trentham, the owner. Some dolls are for sale in the small gift shop.

GALVESTON COUNTY HISTORICAL MUSEUM
2219 Market (Ave. D)
766-2340
June through August: Monday through Saturday 9–4, Sunday 1–5;
September to Memorial Day: closed Sunday
Free
W steps in front, call ahead

This small museum gained new life and perspective when the county and the eminently successful Galveston Historical Foundation agreed to joint operation. Its home is the narrow, old City National Bank Building, built in 1906 and noted for its facade featuring Classic Revival twin columns. Other architectural treasures carried over from the bank are the painted barrel-vault ceiling and impressive gilded chandelier above the gallery. The exhibits tell the story of Galveston County—a county with more history to tell than most, including that of the Karankawa Indians, Jean Lafitte, the Civil War Battle of Galveston, and the 1900 hurricane. The permanent exhibit on the gallery floor concentrates on these features, while the mezzanine is used more for changing exhibits. There are also lectures and other programs, including a musical presentation designed to add life to the museum. Parking is difficult; the easiest way is to park on the less-trafficked street to the east or near The Strand and walk down.

ST. JOSEPH'S CHURCH
2206 Ave. K at 22nd
765-7834 or 762-3933
Free

A Texas Historic Landmark building, this simple frame structure with Gothic Revival detailing was the parish church of German Catholics from its establishment in 1859 until 1968. After that it served as the German Heritage Center. Now it has been leased by the Galveston Historical Foundation and is being turned into an Ecumenical Museum to display the city's religious history. Call for details.

THE RAILROAD MUSEUM
123 Rosenberg (25th St.), free parking, entrance on Santa Fe Place
near 26th, one block south of The Strand and one block west of
Rosenberg
765-5700
Open seven days 10–5, except Thanksgiving and Christmas
Adults $4, children $2, group rates for 15 or more
W+

Located in the old Santa Fe railroad station, the museum's official
name is the Center for Transportation and Commerce. But if you ask
anyone in Galveston for directions to that mouthful, you'll probably get
a blank stare. Everyone, including the workers in the museum, refer to
it as the Railroad Museum. And that's what it is. There are some exhibits
about commerce and other modes of transportation—the excellent
working scale model of the Port of Galveston, for example (but even that
depends on an HO gauge model railroad as the "working" part)—but
the heart of the museum is the full-scale model of Galveston's station
waiting room as it was in 1932 and the 35 railroad locomotives and cars
displayed on the center's tracks. The entrance to this five-acre world of
railroading is through a replica of an 1875 depot complete with sounds
you'd be likely to hear at a station in that era. From here you are led
through a courtyard, where a fully restored 1929 steam locomotive
stands grandly, into the media rooms, where you'll progress through
five imaginative sound and light shows that cover the island's history
from its discovery in 1528 to the present. The original, large station
waiting room, its art deco splendor faithfully restored, is the setting for
the "people's gallery" where 39 life-sized travelers are frozen in a moment in time in 1932. The authentically dressed models are made of
ghostlike white plaster from original castings taken directly off live
models in casual poses. Headphones located near each grouping let you
eavesdrop on conversations that might have taken place back then. This
modeling technique was carried over into the Rail Collection. As you
clamber aboard and wander through the old cars, you'll see a child
climbing into a berth, a gentleman shaving, and other "people" on the
train. Among the 35 railway cars on display are steam locomotives, restored Pullman cars, freight cars in use from 1890 to 1930, a mail car,
and the opulent Anacapa, a 1929 private rail car. There is also a locomotive that became a TV and movie star. From 1960 to 1973, Engine
#555, built in 1922, appeared in more than a half dozen films and TV
shows. The museum is another project of the Moody Foundation. It
cost almost $7 million, and it's worth every penny even if you aren't a
railroad buff or a nostalgia addict.

GALLERIES

GALVESTON ART CENTER ON THE STRAND
2127 Strand
763-2403
Wednesday through Saturday and Monday 10–5, Sunday 1–5; gallery
closed in September, shop open year-round
Free
W steps, call ahead

The building may be old—from 1886—but the thrust of this nonprofit
exhibition space is to feature the works of emerging artists in all media
from all over the country. The center, which has been open since 1971,
operates under the auspices of the Galveston County Cultural Arts
Council. It offers 11 shows a year plus art lectures, programs, and a
spring and fall film series that is held at the Learning Resource Center at
the University of Texas Medical Branch. Artworks, the gift shop in the
Galveston Art Center, specializes in fine crafts.

HOWLAND ART GALLERIES
2314 The Strand
763-2370
Closed Tuesday
W

The works of more than 50 well-known southwestern artists are fea-
tured here. Most are paintings emphasizing the outdoors, and some are
sculpture. Owner Bill Howland also occasionally presents one-artist
shows.

DON ROUSE'S WILDLIFE GALLERY
2314 The Strand
763-1391
W

Sharing the building with Howland's, this gallery lives up to its name
by concentrating exclusively on wildlife art in just about every form, at
times lapping over into gift shop items. The favorite subject seems to be
ducks and other waterfowl, which appear on everything from doormats
to duck stamp prints. There are also pewter and porcelain sculptures,
collectors' plates, and jewelry.

MUSIC & THEATER

COLLEGE OF THE MAINLAND COMMUNITY THEATRE
Texas City
8001 Palmer Highway, FM Rd. 1764 east of I-45
(409) 938-1773 or 938-1211 ext 345
W

It's called the "Biggest Li'l Theater in Texas." During the school year, this combined college–community theater usually puts on six or seven productions covering the spectrum of musicals, classics, contemporary drama, and comedy. A musical is presented during the summer.

THE 1894 GRAND OPERA HOUSE
2020 Post Office (Ave. E) near 21st St.
765-1894
AE, MC, V
W+

The restoration goes on. This grand old building, which saw its first performance in 1895, was made even grander from May through December 1985. It is now as close in design as possible to the original house. Everything from ballet and opera to rock and pop concerts are performed here. You can walk in and look around when no show is on. Conducted tours, usually at $2 each, are available for groups if arrangements are made in advance. Parking is a slight problem during major productions. It's first come, first park on the street, or there is a pay garage at 21st and Market (Ave. D).

HOPE ARENA
2301 Hope Blvd., turn right at entrance to Scholes Regional Airport
740-HOPE
W+

A newcomer to the Galveston scene, this 30,000-square-foot multi-purpose arena, seating 3,000, plays host to concerts, expositions, and agricultural, trade, and horse shows. Part of the funds generated by these shows sponsor a therapeutic program for handicapped children in which they work with horses.

MARY MOODY NORTHEN AMPHITHEATRE
Galveston State Park, FM Rd. 3005 at 13 Mile Road
737-3440
Open end of May to mid August, Tuesday through Sunday at 8:30
Adults $5–$8, children $3–$6
W call ahead for special seating

This 1,800-seat outdoor theater is the site of the yearly Paul Green extravaganza, *The Lone Star*, in which the story of Texas' independence is told by a cast of a hundred—plus horses and cannons—singing, dancing, and fighting their way to glory. It's a lot of hokum but a reasonable theatrical version of history and fun for all ages. Generally this outdoor drama starts the season and then in late June begins to alternate with a big musical. Recently that was *Hello, Dolly!*, but it's subject to change. The restaurant is open before the shows. The amphitheater sits on the edge of the park marsh area where they spray regularly to keep the mosquito population down, but it may be a good idea to take insect repellent, just in case.

STRAND STREET THEATRE
2317 Mechanic (Ave. C) near 24th St. (since the Tremont House Hotel was built, this one block of Mechanic is now renamed Ship Mechanic Row)
763-4591
Productions year-round, normally Thursday through Saturday at 8 and Sunday matinee
$5–$7
W
Galveston's only all-year professional theater produces about seven shows a year in this small, intimate playhouse with 110 seats. Most are dramas and comedies, but occasionally there's a musical.

UPPER DECK THEATRE
See Colleges & Universities, Galveston College

COLLEGES & UNIVERSITIES

GALVESTON COLLEGE
Administration: 4015 Ave. Q near 41st St.; Fort Crockett Campus: 5001 Ave. U near 51st St. (take 53rd St. north from Seawall to Ave. U)
763-6551
W variable
A growing community college with an enrollment of over 2,400, Galveston College offers a wide range of two-year associate degree and career training courses, junior college courses, and a comprehensive program of continuing education. Most continuing education courses are held at the Fort Crockett campus, which is behind the San Luis Hotel. These courses are offered throughout the year, and some are short term enough for visitors to attend. Visitors are also welcome at choral group concerts and drama department productions given at the Upper Deck Theatre, a 150-seat arena stage theater on the third floor of the Fort Crockett building. There are usually four to five shows during the season from October to May. Nonstudent tickets are about $3. Call for schedule.

TEXAS A&M UNIVERSITY AT GALVESTON
Mitchell Campus: take 51st St. north across causeway to Pelican Island, campus on right; Fort Crockett campus: next to Galveston College campus at Ave. U and 51st
766-3200
W variable

This is one of the places where the Texas Navy (and others) gets its officers. This branch of A&M trains officers for the U.S. Merchant Marine, one of its many marine-oriented programs. Its academic programs include marine biology, marine sciences, marine transportation, marine fisheries, maritime systems engineering, and maritime administration. Enrollment is about 590, including about 270 maritime cadets. The best attraction for visitors at the 100-acre Mitchell campus on Pelican Island is the training ship *Texas Clipper*. If it's in port, you'll be able to see it on your right as you come off the causeway. Other, smaller vessels in the school's research-teaching fleet, which is one of the largest in the country, are berthed farther down the dock. The *Clipper* was built in World War II as a troop carrier. Later converted to a cruise liner by American Export Lines, she has served since 1965 as a dormitory and floating classroom in winter and the summer training ship for the school. The maritime cadets are required to complete three summer cruises in preparation for Merchant Marine licensing. The 473-foot, 15,000-ton ship is also used for a summer school program for recent high school graduates who earn freshman college credits while visiting both foreign and domestic ports. The ship is in port from early September to late April, and you are welcome aboard on weekend afternoons. For information contact the Public Information Office at 766-3359. Groups may arrange a conducted, one- or two-hour tour of the *Clipper* through that office. Two marine biology field tours, one on foot and one by boat, conducted by graduate student guides may be arranged by calling the Coastal Zone Laboratory at the school, 766-3265. These tours are for groups, but individuals may come along if there's space. Both cost $35 for the half-day trip, but the boat trip requires an additional $125 or so from the group to pay for the fuel used by the *Roamin' Empire*, the school's 44-foot, converted yacht that is used for scientific outings.

THE UNIVERSITY OF TEXAS MEDICAL BRANCH (UTMB)
Between Strand and Market from 4th to 14th St.
761-1011
W

Starting with a class of 23 in 1891, UTMB is now a $750 million health care complex. The medical branch has about 2,100 students enrolled in its four schools: School of Medicine (graduating about 200 doctors a year), School of Nursing, School of Biomedical Sciences, and School of Allied Health Sciences. The largest, as well as the oldest, medical school in the state, it offers a full spectrum of health care services in its seven hospitals and 85 specialty and subspecialty outpatient clinics. The major architectural attraction on the campus is another Nicholas Clayton structure, the Ashbel Smith Building at 916 Strand. Fondly called "Old Red" for its red sandstone exterior, it was named after the physician who is credited with having influenced the legislature to locate the state medical school in Galveston. Of particular interest are the two-story arches that are the main motif of the building. Guided tours of UTMB may be arranged for organized groups of limited size by contacting the Public Affairs Office (761-6759) at least two weeks in advance.

SHOPPING

ON THE STRAND
This famous street is not only a place to meet history firsthand, it is also a shopping area filled with fine stores. As with any shopping area that caters mostly to visitors, prices for items you can find elsewhere are generally a little higher. Then again, in most cases, so is the quality. In addition, many of the shops are truly one-of-a-kind or, at least, the best of the crop, and much of what they sell falls in one of those categories, too. The following are just a few of many shops along The Strand and on the side streets.

BASTIEN'S STAINED GLASS STUDIO
2317 The Strand
765-9394
If your appreciation of the beauty of stained glass is heightened after visiting the Bishop's Palace or some of the other Victorian homes in Galveston, this is the place to go. Usually there are only small, decorative stained glass pieces on display—among the giftware of crystal, ceramic florals, and glasswork—but larger pieces are available and can be made to order. The studio is in the rear of the store, and although you can't enter, sometimes you can watch the artists at work through the half door.

THE BOOK BAG
2021 The Strand
762-1741
Started as a children's bookstore (and its stock is still primarily carefully selected books for children), the Book Bag's adult section is growing. Browsers are welcome.

GALLERY ROSENBERG
2311 The Strand
762-5014
The owner of this elegant shop once wrote about antiques as a magazine columnist, and her selections of antique art, furniture, and appropriate accessories are witness to her expertise.

HENDLEY MARKET
2010 The Strand
762-2610
This next-door neighbor of The Strand Visitors Center is worth a drop-in when you visit there. Housed in one of the city's oldest commercial buildings, the shop inside the tall, glass-paned doors is a hodgepodge reflecting the delightfully eclectic tastes of the owners. Browsers will find Victorian clothing (a place to go for authentic costumes for "Dickens on The Strand"), tintypes and old photos, lace and linen, South American folk art, Mexican toys, antiques, old maps, books, and magazines.

OCCIDENTAL TRADING COMPANY
2119 The Strand
762-7400

If you're searching for a brass gift item, there's a good chance you'll find it here. The owners claim they have the largest stock of brass decorative accessories in Texas. There is also a collection of nautical antiques and a year-round Christmas shop in the rear.

THE OLD PEANUT BUTTER WAREHOUSE
100 20th St., one block north of The Strand
762-8358

The name dates back to the early 1900s when this was the warehouse of a wholesale grocer who painted the names of some stock items, including peanut butter, on the front of the building. You can still get peanut butter here in the Peanut Pantry, which also sells a number of other culinary concoctions. You can also buy antiques, depression glass, and other collectibles in this interesting assemblage of shops under one roof.

EIBAND'S
22nd St. and Central Plaza
765-6613
W

Central Plaza is a downtown, walking shopping street lined mostly with routine chain and local shops. But far and above the routine is Eiband's. Considered the city's grand lady of department stores and located on the same corner for over a hundred years, Eiband's continues to emphasize the marketing formula that has kept it in business when all around it failed: high fashion, quality products, and customer service. Now this locally owned store is the hub of the revitalization that is slowly turning the Central Plaza shopping area around.

GALVEZ MALL
6402 Broadway, west of 61st St.
744-5241

This is Galveston's largest air-conditioned shopping center. Anchored by Sears and Bealls, it contains the usual assortment of shoe stores, clothing stores, jewelers, fast food places, a cafeteria, and a movie theater.

NORMA'S
6019 Stewart Road near 61st St.
744-5268

Antiques, flowering plants, and gentle lighting make shopping in this women's fashion shop almost relaxing. Norma's has famous labels in everything from sport clothes to formal wear, plus hats, belts, and other accessories and cosmetics.

THE OLD BOOKSHELF
2125 39th St. at Ave. Q ½
763-8652
   This is the type of musty-smelling, used bookstore that true book-
lovers treasure. Nothing fancy, just a small corner store with thin aisles
and tightly packed shelves of both hardbacks and paperbacks. There's a
little bit of everything here including a fair collection of Texana and Galveston history.

OUTDOORS

SEAWOLF PARK
Take 51st St. causeway to Pelican Island, continue on approximately
two miles from end of causeway
744-5738
Open seven days, dawn to dusk
Parking $2; fishing: adults $2, children $1; tours of ships: adults $2,
children $1
W+ except for ships
   This peninsula, projecting from a corner of Pelican Island into Galveston Bay, has a little bit of something for everyone. Want a great view?
The best is from the upper level of the three-level pavilion. From there
you can see the Port of Galveston, the University of Texas Medical
Branch, the Houston Ship Channel, and the Texas City dike. You can
also follow the ferry all the way from Bolivar into its slip near the Coast
Guard Station on Galveston Island and the pilot boat going out to meet
the big ships in the Gulf, and you can see the *Selma*, a World War I
experimental concrete ship that sunk in nearby shallow waters. Want to
fish? You can while sunning on the large boulders that line the shore or
from the 380-foot fishing pier. And you can often wave at the fishing
party boats, which show how smart you were to pick this spot, as they
pull up and anchor just feet off the rocks. For the kids there's a playground, and—for the kids, the military buffs, and the curious—there
are the two World War II ships to explore. One of these is the *USS
Cavalla*, a submarine that includes a Japanese aircraft carrier among its
kills. Even though some parts of this ship have been removed (like the
torpedoes) to make room for touring, you can still feel the claustro-
phobic tightness of life on a World War II sub. The other is *USS Stewart*,
a destroyer escort. Snack bar and picnic areas.

The Beaches

   There are 32 miles of Gulf beaches on Galveston Island, and every
mile is public. The open-beach law means that you can claim your piece

of sand and set up your little empire for the day even if it's in front of a beachfront hotel or condo. The beach itself may not be as sparkling or wide as on Padre Island, but there's space for all, and it is well-patrolled and well-maintained. The Galveston County Sheriff's Department has lifeguards in towers at designated family recreation areas and on patrol in boats and distinctive green and white vehicles that cover the rest of the beach. The natural and man-made debris left by the tides and by the over 1.5 million visitors annually is regularly cleaned up by the Parks Department. And to make sure there's no slacking off on either of these important jobs because of lack of funding, one percent of the hotel-motel room tax is allotted to each project. From March 15 through September 15, vehicles are not allowed on the beaches except in posted parking areas. The rest of the year, driving on the beaches is permitted. The beaches farther to the west are often ideal for solitude, beachcombing, and birdwatching, in addition to the usual activities of swimming, fishing, and surfing. Stuck in along the shoreline are a number of beach parks. The important ones are covered below in their order from east to west.

R. A. APFFEL PARK
Seawall and Boddecker Dr. (extreme east end of the island)
763-0166
W variable
This 800-plus-acre park was opened in 1983 after a $1.6 million bond issue paid for site development and a new 11,000-square-foot recreation center with bathhouse, restrooms, concessions, and gift shop. The beach here is wide and sandy, and there is a boat launching area, bait camps, fishing from the jetty and in the surf, and restaurants. Pay parking near beach, free farther out.

STEWART BEACH PARK
Seawall near Broadway
765-5023
W variable
See Kids' Stuff.

SEVEN MILE BEACH PARK
FM Rd. 3005 at 7 Mile Road
W variable
Small park with boardwalk, dune bridges, and restrooms.

GALVESTON COUNTY BEACH POCKET PARK #1
FM Rd. 3005 at 7½ Mile Road
744-6750
Open March 15 through October 15, closed rest of year
Autos $3 and up
W variable
A seven-and-a-half-acre park that includes beachfront picnic area, children's playground, bathhouse and restrooms, food and drink con-

cession, and boardwalk to the beach. Ski Trek, a cable waterskiing facility, is located in the lagoon next to the park entrance (see Sports & Activities).

GALVESTON COUNTY BEACH POCKET PARK #2
FM Rd. 3005 at 9½ Mile Road
737-1544
Open March 15 through October 15, closed rest of year
Autos $2 and up
W variable
A little over 5.5 acres of beachfront. Bathhouse with restrooms, playground, sun deck, and boardwalk to the beachfront.

GALVESTON ISLAND STATE PARK
West Beach, on FM Rd. 3005 near 13 Mile Road, approximately 10 miles west of Seawall and 61st St. (entrance just past Mary Moody Northen Amphitheatre)
737-1222
Autos $2
W + but not all areas
This 2,000-acre park cuts across the narrowing center of the island from the 1.6-mile beach on the Gulf to the marshes on Galveston Bay. This provides the opportunity for a wide variety of outdoor activities: enjoy the sun and surf, cast a line in the Gulf, wade-fish in the marsh, or walk along the four miles of nature trails with observation platforms, birdwatching blinds, and boardwalks over the bayous. Park headquarters with restrooms, showers, and a concession store is on the beach side along with 150 multi-use campsites with two-way (water and electric) hookups, picnic tables with shade shelters, grills, and a dump station nearby ($6 per night), plus 60 day-use sheltered picnic sites. The bay side has 10 screened shelters with two-way hookups, lights and picnic tables inside and grill outside ($8 per night), and a group camping area with 20 two-way hookups, restrooms, and showers ($6 per night per trailer). The Mary Moody Northen Amphitheatre with its outdoor drama (see Music & Theater) adjoins the park on the bay side. Camping reservations are accepted 90 days in advance and are strongly recommended in summer. Write Rt. 1, Box 156-A, Galveston 77551.

SIDE TRIPS

Houston is right up the road. Well, to be a little more exact, it's about 40 miles or so—and another world—up I-45. And on the way you pass Texas City, which is part of Galveston County, and the Lyndon B. Johnson Space Center.

TEXAS CITY
Take I-45 nine miles northwest of Galveston
If you've never seen a refinery or a chemical plant up close, now's

your chance. Turn off I-45 onto Loop 197. Following the loop northeast will take you right past several refineries and chemical plants as you head downtown. Unfortunately, Texas City is still most famous for the 1947 ship explosions in the harbor that killed 500 and injured another 4,000 in a town of 16,000. But that was years ago, and now the city is gaining prominence for other reasons, including its famed five-mile dike and one of the largest fishing contests in the country.

TEXAS CITY DIKE
I-45 to Loop 197 to 8th Ave. N., right on 8th to the dike (alternate route: I-45 to FM Rd. 1764 to dike)
Open at all times
You've always wanted to go way out in the water to fish, but you get seasick in a boat? Here's the answer. When Texas City says the dike projects five miles into Galveston Bay, that's not hype. Five miles it is— and they also claim it's the world's largest fishing pier, since this is a wide dike, not just a walk-on jetty. There are a couple of seafood restaurants and bait shops near the beginning of the dike, and part of the local shrimp fleet is docked a short way down. Otherwise just about all you see as you drive out on the dike is fisherfolk on the boulders that line both sides. Of course, there's much more on the water: tankers, freighters, and barge tenders on the Houston Ship Channel and Galveston Bay, sailboats, shrimpers with hordes of hungry gulls and other birds shadowing the boats coming in with their catch, and windsurfers whipping along. At the end of the dike, there's a restaurant, fishing pier, and tiny beach park. But here the real reward is a great view of Galveston and Texas City. The dike road is two lane, and traffic can crawl on a summer weekend, but if you get bored you can pull off at one of the many wide spots and fish or just watch the world sail by. A word of caution: all along the dike are signs that read "WARNING BEWARE: Undertow and wake from passing ship may wash over rocks." Obviously this doesn't happen often or the road wouldn't be open, but it's something to be aware of.

LYNDON B. JOHNSON SPACE CENTER (NASA)
Take NASA Road 1 approximately three miles east from I-45 (Gulf Freeway)
1-713-483-4321
Self-guided tours seven days 9–4, guided tours hourly starting at 10, closed Christmas Day
Free
W+ call 1-713-483-4241 for information
The space shuttles may take off from Florida, but this is where the astronauts train, and this is the "Houston" you hear them talking to during the flights. There's a lot of walking involved in both the self-guided and conducted tours, so wear comfortable shoes and allow between two and three hours to tour it all at a relaxed pace. All tours start at the Visitors Center. Follow the signs from the two parking lots—the weekday visitor parking and the weekend and federal holiday visitor

parking (the latter is closer). At the Visitors Center you can see moon rocks, space hardware, and films. To take the self-guided tour, pick up a brochure with map here and follow the green arrows around the compound. Stops include the Mission Simulation and Training Building with its Skylab and shuttle trainers and the Space Shuttle Orbiter Training Building where you can view the full-scale shuttle trainer. There are also briefings lasting approximately 35 minutes in the Mission Control Center, but you have to sign up for these and for the guided tour at the information desk in the Visitors Center. And if you don't feel like all that walking, a visit here is still worth the trip just to get up close to the gigantic rockets on display near the parking lot. You'll wonder how NASA ever got them off the ground! Restaurant and gift shop.

HOUSTON
See Texas Monthly Guidebooks: *Houston*.

KIDS' STUFF

JUNGLE SURF WATER SLIDE
West Beach
9402 Seawall, just west of Sea-Arama
744-4737
Open seven days in summer from 10 a.m.
$3.25 half hour, $5.75 hour, group rates
   This is supposed to be the highest water slide in town. A lot of kids like it because no mats are required, which makes for a speedier ride. Small private beach.

SEA-ARAMA MARINEWORLD
West Beach
Seawall and 91st
744-4501
May through September, open seven days 10–9; October through April 10–dusk
Adults $8.95, children $5.50, + tax
W
   How about a show that includes performing sea lions, leaping dolphins, and a fearless diver who goes into a tank of sharks? That's family entertainment, and that's what Sea-Arama provides in its 38-acre park. The show bill also includes trick waterskiers, a lion-taming act, a snake show, and a bird show. Not all these are presented all year; no waterskiers in winter, for example, but there's always enough consecutive entertainment to fill about three hours. And you can spend as long as you like wandering around the marine and other exhibits, like the aquarium—probably the best one on the Texas coast—with dozens of tanks holding hundreds of aquatic species from all over the world and the large underwater windows that let you look into the 200,000-gallon oceanarium populated by sharks and other generally unfriendly creatures like the alligator gar. There are also exotic bird exhibits. Few know

that Sea-Arama is also a refuge for stranded and injured birds, many of which decide to stay after they've recovered. Because of this refuge program, the brown pelican and black swan, both almost extinct, are now being successfully bred and raised here. Playground, shaded picnic area, food, and other concessions.

SEAWOLF PARK
See Outdoors.

SIR GOONY MINIATURE GOLF
8910 Stewart Road, take Seawall to 89th, turn right, go two blocks
744-0181
Open seven days 11–10
$1.50
Just east of Sea-Arama, this 18-hole miniature course also has an electronic game room and concession stand.

STEWART BEACH PARK
Seawall near 4th St.
765-7424
Amusement area open summer seven days 9–9; winter: 9–dusk; closed November to mid February; beach always open
Cost of rides varies
Parking $2
W
This is the most developed of the county's beach parks—a miniature Coney Island on the beach. There's a pavilion with bathhouse (fee), chairs and beach umbrellas for rent, restaurant, and concessions. Attractions include two water slides, bumper cars, bumper boats, miniature golf, go-carts, and miniature speedboats. All at prices ranging from $2 up. In other words, fun city for the kids, and exhaustion of body and purse for parents.

SPORTS & ACTIVITIES

Birdwatching

See Outdoors, Galveston Island State Park. Also the beaches and marshes on the west end of the island and on Bolivar Peninsula are good sites for this activity.

Boating

You can boat in Galveston Bay, the bayous, or the Gulf. Boat rental firms are listed in the Yellow Pages, or contact the marinas. For the location of free boat launching sites, contact the Convention and Visitors Bureau. Commercial launching sites are also listed in the Yellow Pages.

Fishing

Any type of saltwater fishing you want, Galveston has it. There's the bay, the piers, the surf, and offshore in the Gulf. Some 52 varieties of saltwater fish populate the warm waters along and offshore from the island. Red snapper, ling, dolphin, and jackfish make up the principal offshore species. Inshore anglers are most likely to catch speckled trout, redfish, pompano, whiting, flounder, and catfish.

Bay & Gulf Fishing

A number of charter and party boats operate daily out of Galveston from the docks around Pier 19 and the Yacht Basin for both bay and deep-sea fishing. With charter boats you usually pay so much a day for the boat and guide and split the cost among the fishermen. Most of these charter boats are small with a capacity of about six. Charter companies are listed in the Yellow Pages. Party boats are bigger craft carrying a large number of fishermen at a set price. The price depends on whether it is a half- or full-day trip, bay or deep-sea fishing. Party trips cost from about $10 to $75, with $45 being an average for a day deep-sea trip on a weekend. A listing of some of the party boat companies follows.

GALVESTON PARTY BOATS
Pier 19
763-5423

REEL FUN CHARTERS
Yacht Basin
762-3319

WILLIAMS PARTY BOATS
Pier 19
762-8808

Pier Fishing

Several commercial piers and numerous rock groin piers extend well into the Gulf from the beachfront. Most are lighted for night fishing, and the commercial piers have bait and tackle shops. The usual charge is $2. If you don't have a fishing license, you can buy one at these piers.

FREE PIERS
Along Seawall Boulevard, all of the public rock groin piers
Texas City Five Mile Dike

COMMERCIAL PIERS

FLAGSHIP FISHING PIER ★ Seawall and 25th, behind Flagship Hotel ★ 762-2846

GULF COAST FISHING PIER ★ Seawall at 90th ★ 744-2273

SAN LUIS PASS FISHING PIER ★ San Luis Pass at west end of island ★ 233-6902

SEAWOLF PARK ★ See Outdoors

61st STREET PIER ★ Seawall at 61st

Surf Fishing

The relatively isolated 20-mile stretch of West Beach leading to San Luis Pass and the area around the pass itself are touted as the best for this type of fishing.

Golf

GALVESTON MUNICIPAL GOLF COURSE
1700 Sydnor Lane, west of airport, take Stewart to 99th to Sydnor
744-2366
Open seven days, 8 a.m. weekdays, 7 a.m. weekends to dark
Call for green fees
Eighteen-hole course. Lessons available.

BAYOU GOLF CLUB
Texas City, west end of Loop 197N off 25th Ave. N
948-8362
Open seven days, 7 a.m. to dark
Green fees $5−$6
Eighteen-hole public course. Lessons available.

Horseback Riding

There are two riding stables near each other on West Beach. You can ride almost a mile and a half of the beach for about $8 an hour.

GULFSTREAM STABLES
FM Rd. 3005 at 8 Mile Road
744-1004
Open seven days

SANDY HOOF STABLES
FM Rd. 3005 at 7½ Mile Road, next to Beach Pocket Park #1
740-3481

Jogging

The seawall is where joggers congregate.

Surfing, Waterskiing & Windsurfing

There are designated surfing areas along the beach at Seawall Boulevard, and windsurfing is most popular in the bay and near the Texas City Dike. Waterskiers seem to prefer the bay and Offatts Bayou. Rentals, lessons, and tows are available at the T-Marina at 61st St. and Offatts Bayou. Windsurfing and small sailboat rentals there, too. For an introduction to waterskiing, you might want to try Ski Trek.

SKI TREK
FM Rd. 3005 next to Beach Pocket Park #1
740-1347
Saturday and Sunday from Easter through mid May and after Labor Day as long as weather permits, seven days in summer 10–7, closed winter
About $10 hour

Ski Trek is a controlled waterski set-up operating with cables off tall towers with a half-mile course around a lagoon. They provide all equipment as well as instruction. Average speed of the ride is 24 mph, so this isn't kids' stuff. Rates are by number of starts—about $5 for three starts—or by the hour. No restrooms, but the Beach Pocket Park restrooms are close by.

Tennis

Free, no-reservation, lighted courts are available at:

GALVESTON COLLEGE
Fort Crockett Campus (See Colleges & Universities)
After classes have finished
Limited to 1½ hours play

LASKER PARK
Ave. Q and 43rd St.

MENARD PARK
Seawall and 27th St.

SCHREIBER PARK
81st and Beluche, take Seawall to 81st, north to Beluche

Courts for which a fee is charged are available at:

THE GALVESTON RACKET CLUB
83rd and Airport
744-3651

Reduced rates and special tennis packages are offered by a number of hotels and motels in conjunction with this club.

ANNUAL EVENTS

April

BLESSING OF THE SHRIMP FLEET AND RAINBOW FESTIVAL
Near Pier 19 and on The Strand
First or second Sunday following Easter
W variable
Decorated with banners and flowers, the boats of the Mosquito Fleet cruise up and down the ship channel as everyone afloat and ashore celebrates the blessing. What has become known as the Rainbow Festival, a Galveston Arts Council celebration of the arts, is held in conjunction. Overall, it's boats, arts, crafts, food, and entertainment.

May

HISTORIC HOMES TOUR
765-7834
Two weekends early in month
$10–$12
W variable
This annual tour usually includes visits to six restored nineteenth-century homes, selected by the Galveston Historical Foundation, that are not normally open to the public. Tied in are a variety of special events, such as architectural lectures and art exhibits. For your money you receive a handsome illustrated booklet explaining the history of the homes on the tour and a map to guide you to them. You must get from home to home on your own. At each home you'll be given a guided tour. Most other activities are free to tour ticket holders.

June through August

THE LONE STAR
See Music & Theater, Mary Moody Northen Amphitheatre.

December

DICKENS ON THE STRAND
The Strand between 20th and 25th
765-7834
Usually first Saturday and Sunday in December, 10 a.m. to 8 or 10 p.m.
Adults $5, children over six $2 (cheaper if purchased in advance)
W

A pre-Christmas street festival in which a five-block section of The Strand is turned into an authentic re-creation of The Strand in London as it was during the nineteenth century. There are English bobbies chasing pickpockets; street performers and street vendors; food booths selling pigeon pie, plum pudding, fish 'n chips, and other Victorian victuals; parades; strolling carolers; hand bell choirs; Scrooge and the other characters from Dickens's stories; Queen Victoria; and even the master himself, Charles Dickens. Want to get in FREE? All you have to do is wear a Victorian costume. Caution: it can be cold on The Strand in December. A number of activities take place the Friday "Night Before Dickens" at the various Galveston Historical Foundation properties and places like Ashton Villa, the Railroad Museum, and The Strand Street Theatre. This has grown into a major festival in the city, and a number of hotels and motels offer special packages in connection with it.

HOTELS & MOTELS

As a prime resort city on the Texas coast, Galveston offers a wide range of accommodations running from old motels that have gone seedy with age to sumptuous new hotels in the grand tradition. And the prices have a wide range too. They also go up and down with the seasons.

Rates for a double in the high summer season:
  $: under $45
  $$: $45–$55
  $$$: $56–$80
$$$$: over $80

AIRPORT RESORT INN
2525 Jones near the Galveston Municipal Airport watertower
744-5331
$
W+ two rooms

One of several new economy motels. Even though not on the beach, this one stands out because each of the 69 rooms includes a small kitchen and because of the number of extras available to guests, including free passes to fish from the 1,200-foot Gulf Coast Pier and reduced rates at the nearby Galveston Racket Club. A small coffee shop serves breakfast and lunch, and snacks and drinks are available after that at The Squadron Club, which faces the sun deck and pool.

THE COMMODORE ON THE BEACH
3618 Seawall at 37th St.
763-2375 or outside Texas 1-800-231-9921
$–$$$
W

Most rooms on the beachfront have some Gulf view, even though it may be restricted. This is one of the few in which even the people in the lowest priced rooms can look out squarely at the beach. The view is made more accessible by balconies on all upstairs rooms, and perhaps to compensate for not having as good a vantage point, the ground floor rooms open onto the pool. The 91 rooms are on the small side but are more than adequate. Lounge. 24-hour coffee shop next door.

THE FLAGSHIP HOTEL
2501 Seawall at Rosenberg (25th St.)
762-8681 or in Texas 1-800-392-6542, outside Texas 1-800-231-7128
$$$–$$$$
W
  The Flagship occupies a truly unique position in the world of hotels and motels along the Texas coast—over the Gulf. This seven-story hotel is solidly anchored on a steel-and-concrete pier. So solidly, in fact, that the hotel lost part of a wall in the last hurricane, but the pier didn't budge. About half the rooms face east and half toward the west, so you get either a sunrise over the surf or a sunset room. Let them know if you're an early riser or a sunset romantic, and they'll try to match you to that side. But if that doesn't work out, you can still catch the glory of the sunrise, or moonrise, in the Reef Dining Room, which opens at 7 a.m. Or drink a toast to the setting sun in the Lookout Lounge. Both have window walls with wonderful views. About two-thirds of the 225 rooms have small balconies that expand the view. So if the ambience of the room is important to you, also ask for one of those. Aside from the dazzling vistas, you'll get a typical hotel room with typical hotel furnishings, a swimming pool, fishing pier, reduced rates for golf, and lounge entertainment.

GAIDO'S MOTOR INN
3800 Seawall at 38th St.
762-9675
$$–$$$
W + one room
  There's nothing Gaido's offers that is much different than any other medium priced motel on the seawall, except guests receive a pass that moves them to the head of the line at the immensely popular Gaido's restaurant next door. This may not sound like much, but if you talk to people who have waited in that line you'll probably find many who think that privilege alone is worth the price of the room. Just in case you don't, the motel does have 108 rooms, a swimming pool, lounge, package store, room service, golf privileges, and a restaurant that serves breakfast and lunch.

HOLIDAY INN ON THE BEACH
5002 Seawall at 50th St.
740-3581 or 1-800-465-4329
$$$
W + two rooms
  Another motel with a view. All 180 rooms face the Gulf, and those above the first floor have balconies. This is not your run-of-the-mill Holiday Inn. The rooms are a little classier, the Jetty Restaurant a little flashier and fernier, and the B. Jigger Lounge's piano bar more popular.

There is also a large, ragged-L-shaped swimming pool and sun deck to help set it aside from the ordinary.

HOLIDAY INN–YACHT BASIN
600 Strand near Holiday Dr.
765-5544 or 1-800-465-4329
$$$
W + two rooms

Another upscale member of the chain. As the name implies, it's convenient to the Yacht Basin, but it is also across the street from the Texas Medical Center–University of Texas Medical School and a short drive from the historic district on The Strand. And if you still hanker for the beach they'll provide transportation to get there. Golf membership is available, and public tennis courts are just a block away. There are 244 rooms, in-room movies, pool, sauna, and restaurant, plus Checkers Lounge that is one of the choice night spots on the island. Checkers has a DJ, neon decorations, a "must be 21 to enter" rule, and $2 cover on Friday and Saturday nights.

LA QUINTA MOTOR INN
1402 Seawall near 14th St.
763-1224 or 1-800-531-5900
$$$
W + one room

Part of the growing Texas-based chain of moderately priced motels. Across from the seawall and within easy walk of Stewart Beach Park. Behind the Spanish decor are 115 rooms, a pool, and the La Quinta Cantina. A 24-hour restaurant and lounge are close by.

MARRIOTT'S HOTEL GALVEZ
2024 Seawall at 21st St., entrance on Ave. P (also called Bernardo de Galvez Ave.)
765-7721 or in Texas 1-800-392-4285, outside Texas 1-800-228-9290
$$$–$$$$
W +

The grand old lady of the seawall has had a face-lift in the last few years and regained at least part of her renown. Built in 1911, the Galvez was the center of Galveston social life for close to 40 years. Then old age and poor economic conditions started to have their effects. Fortunately, the Marriott chain took over, and after extensive and expensive renovations, it was reopened in 1980. Old-timers may say some of the former elegance lost out to the new indoor swimming pool that now adjoins the main lobby, but there is still a feeling of luxury and spaciousness as you stroll around the ground floor. That lavish use of space doesn't always carry over in the 228 rooms. Although tastefully decorated, some are rather small. Many have a Gulf view. Its location across the street from the Moody Convention Center means large groups often book here. In addition to the indoor pool, there's an outdoor one, a sauna, a gift shop, and golf, tennis, and racketball club membership privileges available. There is also limited covered parking. The still elegant Galvez Dining Room lists prime ribs, steaks, and seafood on the menu. The Saturday cookout on the terrace and Sunday champagne brunch are popular. For a casual setting for drinks, there is the Veranda, and for live music, the Galvez Lounge.

RAMADA INN
Seawall and 59th St.
740-1261 or 1-800-228-2828
$$$
W+ two rooms

Another new Galveston entry across from the seawall. The 151 rooms are in an L-shape around the sun deck and pool. Poolside and room service are available. You can see the Gulf from about half the rooms. Covered parking under the buildings is a real plus when the summer sun is blazing. Periwinkles, the restaurant, serves all meals but is known locally for its weekend buffet breakfast. Lounge.

THE SAN LUIS ON GALVESTON ISLE
Seawall and 53rd
765-8888 or in Texas 1-800-392-5937, outside Texas 1-800-445-0900
$$$$
W+ six rooms

From the valet parking and the tiered pool with waterfall and swim-up bar in front to the intimate dining in Maxmilian's inside, this hotel epitomizes gracious living. Built on the hilltop site of old Fort Crockett, all 244 rooms in this 15-story luxury hotel have small, private balconies that overlook the Gulf. In-room movies, hydrotherapy pool, sauna, specialty shops, and golf, tennis, and racketball club membership privileges are available. In addition to Maxmilian's (see Restaurants), there is the Waterspout Lounge and the Spoonbill, another restaurant that overlooks both the Gulf and the pool garden. The San Luis Condominium is attached, and some of the units there eventually (perhaps by the time you read this) may be available for rent.

THE TREMONT HOUSE
2300 Ship's Mechanic Row between 23rd and 24th St. (Mechanic St. renamed for this one block)
763-0300
$$$$
W+ two rooms

If this was Hollywood, everyone would be ballyhooing this hotel as "another George Mitchell extravaganza." Mitchell is the developer who has helped provide Galveston with the ingredients for elegant living: first the Wentletrap, his continental restaurant on The Strand; then the San Luis Hotel on the seawall; and now, working with his wife Cynthia, this renaissance of a grand hotel from Galveston's past. The guest register of the original Tremont Hotel, built in 1839, includes the names of General Sam Houston, Ulysses S. Grant, Clara Barton, Anna Pavlova, and Buffalo Bill. That hotel, on a nearby site, was destroyed by fire in 1865. The second Tremont was opened in 1872, just in time to be part of one of the grandest periods in Galveston's history. It fell on hard times and was leveled in 1928. The third Tremont is in a restored 1879 building that started out as a wholesale dry goods concern and later was the 40-year home of the *Galveston Tribune*. Most of its 125 large, airy guest rooms have 14-foot ceilings, 11-foot windows with lace curtains, and furnishings reminiscent of the Victorian era. A four-story, white stucco atrium greets guests entering the building, and bird-cage elevators take them to the upper levels where ironwork bridges connect the halls. The small Merchant Prince Restaurant specializes in French cuisine, and a walkway connects the hotel with the Wentletrap Restaurant. The rosewood bar in the Toujouse Lounge is from the 1860s.

OTHER ACCOMMODATIONS

Condominiums

Condominium rentals also have high and low seasons, and the price ranges of most are equal to the cost of a luxury hotel. However, you get an apartment instead of a room. Rates per day for a one-bedroom apartment (which may sleep four to six) in high season are:

$: under $50
$$: $50–$70
$$$: $71–$100
$$$$: over $100

Most require two nights minimum stay. Weekly and monthly rates may be substantially lower.

BY THE SEA CONDOMINIUMS
7310 Seawall
744-5295
$$$; MC, V
W

All the apartments in this 12-story building have balconies large enough to sit on with an unobstructed view of the Gulf. Out of 104 units, there are usually about 40 in the rental pool ranging in size from efficiencies to three bedroom, two bath. Pool and tennis court. Maid service available at additional cost.

THE GALVESTONIAN CONDOMINIUMS
1401 East Beach Blvd. off Seawall Blvd. east of Stewart Beach
765-6161
$$$$; AE, MC, V
W

If you want to be just minutes away from activities along the seawall and still out of the heavy traffic and wall-to-wall development, the East

Beach is the place to go. It also has the best views of the large ships entering the port. The only thing between the condo and the wide beach is the sun deck and heated pool. There are also two lighted tennis courts and a Jacuzzi. Apartments are large. Usually about 20 percent of the 180 units are in the rental pool, from efficiencies to three-bedroom, two-bath units. All have large balconies with an unobstructed view of the beach and the Gulf.

ISLANDER EAST CONDOMINIUMS
915 Seawall (actually on East Beach with Seawall address—after Ferry Road intersection, take second road to right off Seawall)
765-9301
$$$$; AE, MC, V
W

These condos offer the quiet of East Beach, a pool, and tennis courts. About 45 units are available for rent: from efficiencies up to two bedrooms, some with kitchenettes and some with full kitchens, all with private balconies and a good view. Maid service is available at additional cost. Three-night minimum on major holiday weekends.

SEA SCAPE CONDOMINIUMS
10811 FM Rd. 3005 (this is the continuation of Seawall Blvd. going west)
740-3561 or in Texas 1-800-392-0075
$$$$; AE, V, MC
W

These condos are in the relatively undeveloped area several miles to the west. The beach here is wide, and there's nothing between these low-rise, grey and white–trimmed wooden buildings and it. A heated pool and one for the children, spa, and a tennis court are available. All the apartments have balconies facing the Gulf, but some views are better than others. About 75 percent of the 135 units are in the rental pool. Covered parking under the buildings.

THE VICTORIAN CONDOTEL
6300 Seawall, just west of Texas Spur 342 (61st St.)
740-3555 or in Texas 1-800-392-1215, outside Texas 1-800-231-6363
$$$
W

These low, white buildings give the image of coolness even on the hottest day. One-bedroom apartments are available. All 231 rental units have private balconies with some sort of Gulf view, but it's best from the two-bedroom units. Maid service is included. Two pools (one heated), three whirlpools, snack bar, lighted tennis courts, and some covered parking are available.

Bed & Breakfast

The bed and breakfast phenomenon, which is spreading throughout the United States, has taken hold in Galveston's historic districts. Until recently there were only two, but now the city has granted additional permits, and a B&B organization has been formed. For information call Galveston Island Bed and Breakfast Inns, 762-9001, or the Galveston Convention and Visitors Center, 763-4311.

Rates for a double during the summer:
  $: under $60
 $$: $61–$85
$$$: $86–$100
$$$$: over $100

THE GILDED THISTLE
1805 Broadway
763-0194
$$$–$$$$; No cr. (takes checks)

Three rooms are available in this two-story home near the East End Historic District. Built in 1893, it has been included in the Galveston Historic Homes Tours. One room has a private bath, and two share a bath. For the breakfast part, there is coffee and juice at the door and a full breakfast at the guests' convenience until noon. Cheese and fruit trays with wine are served on fine china with sterling silver in the evenings. Parking is around the corner on 18th Street and in the rear. It's an easy walk to Ashton Villa and the Bishop's Palace (see Historic Places).

THE VICTORIAN INN
511 17th St. and Post Office (Ave. E)
762-3235
$$; AE, MC, V

This is Galveston's original B&B inn. Built in 1899, this restored historic home is furnished with turn-of-the-century pieces. The four available guest rooms are named after the four children of the original owner, Isaac Heffron. Mauney's Room is the only one with a private bath, and the rule on that is "first come first gets." This rule also applies to the garage. The others get street parking, which is at the door. A continental breakfast and evening hors d'oeuvres are served. Two-night minimum on weekends. Close to Texas Medical Center.

Beach Houses

Most house rentals are located on the island west of 100th Street. Usually they come fully equipped with maid and linen service. Some of

them can be rented for as short a time as two nights, but most are
rented by the weekend or the week. Everything from one-bedroom to
five-bedroom houses is available, but the average is two or three bedrooms, which will sleep four to ten people. These are located on the
beach and on the bay. Some are simple beach houses, others are beach
houses and town homes decorated by high-priced interior designers
with all the luxuries built in. Prices depend on the size, location, and
amenities and, in the summer high season, range from about $150 to
$700 for a weekend and $300 to $1,800 for a week. Some of the agencies
that rent these homes are:

LELIA WOLVERTON REALTY
P.O. Box 5255 (77551)
737-1430

PIRATES BEACH AND PIRATES COVE
Rt. 1, Box 149B (77551)
737-2771

SAND 'N SEA PROPERTIES
P.O. Box 5165 (77551)
737-2556

SEA ISLE
Rt. 1, Box 178 (77551)
737-2750

RESTAURANTS

Galveston has a wealth of restaurants, including several that are close
to being great. In fact, it has probably the largest selection of fine restaurants in one city on the Texas coast. And fortunately, most of the
good ones are responding to the growing competition by working to
become better. Let's hope that the long waiting lines and need for reservations won't encourage them to slack off in their quest for culinary
perfection or tempt them to raise their prices to a point that the bill
spoils the meal.

Putting on the Ritz

MAXIMILIAN'S
San Luis Hotel, 5222 Seawall at 53rd
765-8888 or in Texas 1-800-392-5937
Dinner only, closed Monday
Reservations recommended
$$$$; Cr.
W+ rear entrance to hotel
You walk through the hotel's casual Spoonbill Restaurant, through
etched glass panel doors into this plush, intimate inner salon. The

menu offers selected entrées emphasizing seafood, veal, and lamb. The service is prompt but pleasingly unobtrusive. Jackets required for men. Another Mitchell creation, along with the Wentletrap and the Tremont. Valet parking in front. Bar.

THE WENTLETRAP
2301 The Strand at Tremont (23rd St.)
765-5545
Lunch Monday through Friday, Sunday brunch, dinner seven days
Reservations recommended for dinner
$$$–$$$$; Cr.
W+

"Mitchell's Wentletrap" is a rare Texas seashell prized by collectors. And for a time, until the competition grew up around it, this fine restaurant exemplified that type of rarity in Galveston. George Mitchell, the developer after whom the seashell was NOT named, restored the 1871 T. J. League Building as the home for a superb dining establishment. The three-story atrium with overhead skylight adds a bright and airy feeling to the white iron columns, brick wall with arches, and ornately carved nineteenth-century bar. The seafood entrées include filet of trout with sautéed crabmeat and mushrooms in wine sauce. And in a world of steaks, it's hard to beat the *filet mignon* topped with shrimp in garlic and wine sauce. Valet parking and jackets required for men at dinner. Bar.

Dinner for Two

BALINESE ROOM
2107 Seawall near 21st St., on a pier over the water
763-8516
Usually open seven days for lunch and dinner, but call
$$$; Cr.
W

It's a long stroll along the corridor from the entrance to the main rooms near the end of the pier. Things keep changing here—the decor, the names of the rooms, the days open, the menu, the management— but through it all the view remains constant and is worth a stop if there's any romance in your soul. Once the most famous dinner club and gambling casino on the island, it is striving mightily to regain some of the prestige of the former and a little more of the rakishness of the latter. Unfortunately, the kitchen is sometimes erratic, but sticking to the simple dishes can be rewarding. Lunch buffet generally good. Informal, but no swimwear. Music and dancing at night. Valet parking. Bar.

CAFE TORREFIE
The Strand and 22nd St.
763-9088
Lunch and dinner; closed Sunday

$$$; AE, MC, V
W call ahead
A quiet fern restaurant with a Belgian pelican on the sign outside, and mostly French cooking inside. It claims to specialize in seafood, but the omelets and quiche are worthy of notice. The wine cellar was once the vault of the Mensing Brothers wholesale grocery business. Generally live entertainment, jazz groups and others, from Wednesday through Saturday. Bar.

American

DONNA'S DOWNHOME DINER
The Strand and 21st St.
763-4535
Open seven days for lunch and dinner
$$; Cr.
It doesn't look much like a 1940s diner, but some of the dishes on the blue plate special, like the pot roast and the catfish, come right out of that era and are just as hearty and filling. Checkered tablecloths and the open kitchen also add to the aura of days gone by. Eat in or take out. Bar.

Barbecue

WAREHOUSE BARBECUE AND SANDWICH SHOP
101 14th St. between Water (Ave. A) and The Strand
765-9995
Open seven days for lunch and dinner
$; AE, MC, V
W
The barbecue sauce may not win any prizes with true-blue barbecue fanciers, but you do get a heap of meat under it for your money. Lots of links, ham, ribs, beef, and chicken pit-cooked over oak and pecan wood. Also BIG hamburgers and loads of other sandwiches. The decor is almost all beer ads, but they sell wine, too. Take out.

Chinese

JANE'S CAFE
1902 31st St. and Ave. P (Bernardo de Galvez)
763-9545
Lunch and dinner in spring and summer, dinner only in fall and winter, closed Sunday and Monday
$; MC, V
W

No gaudy red dragons here. Just an unpretentious cafe, differing from every other cafe only in that there are a few Chinese prints on the walls, teapots on the shelf behind the counter, and plenty of Chinese culinary skills in the kitchen. The ingredients are fresh and oriental—like meaty Chinese black mushrooms instead of the delicate white ones. Most entrées are stir-fried leaving the vegetables crisp and the seafood and meats loaded with flavor. The Chinese mustard is so hot that a whiff will clean out your sinuses. American food is also available. It's good, too, but why waste an opportunity for an oriental treat? If you want atmosphere, go elsewhere; if you want good Chinese food, try Jane's. Beer. Street parking.

French

LE PAYSAN
2021 The Strand
765-7792
Open seven days for lunch and dinner
$$$; Cr.
W side entrance
This restaurant is located in the restored Galveston Common Building across from The Strand Visitors Center. Even though the tables are crowded together, the tall windows all around make the room seem larger and brighter. The food carries out that feeling with country French cuisine as light, but satisfying, as the semi-classical music played in the background. Fresh baked, crusty rolls served with the meal come from the French bakery tucked in a corner of the restaurant, luring you to its display of tempting pastries. A good time to sample these is during the three to five o'clock afternoon tea time. Beer and wine.

Italian

CANDY'S
2112 Mechanic (Ave. C) near 21st St.
765-5323
Lunch and dinner, closed Sunday and Monday
$$; No cr.
With a bar running along one side of the small room, soft lighting, and nautical decorations, this looks more like a plush bar than an Italian restaurant. But don't let it fool you. Candy is famous for her hearty, home-style Italian dishes cooked from scratch in her open kitchen. And if the atmosphere is subdued, Candy makes up for it. She's even more famous for her overwhelming personal attention to her customers. From almost anywhere in the room you can see into her kitchen as she prepares each meal, popping out at every chance to meet and loudly

greet diners, often with a hug, and frequently shooing away the wait-ress as she advises and takes orders. Since Candy is head waiter, menu advisor, and cook, the service can be slow. So relax, have some wine from the large selection available, and enjoy. Bar.

Mexican

APACHE TORTILLA FACTORY AND MEXICAN FOOD
511 20th St. near Post Office (Ave. E)
765-5646
Sunday breakfast and lunch, Tuesday through Saturday all meals, closed Monday
$; No cr.
W

Another cafe where the attention is given to the food not the decor. A few bullfight posters and Mexican records on the jukebox are all the atmosphere you get, but menu items like a lunch special of *papas con carne* or a breakfast of eggs and *chorizo* more than make up for that. Look for the daily specials on the board. Take out available. There's street parking, and some of the nearby side streets aren't metered. Beer.

EL NOPALITO
614 42nd St. between Church (Ave. F) and Winnie (Ave. G)
763-9815
Breakfast and lunch only, closed Wednesday
$; No cr.
W

Definitely not in the tourist area, and since 42nd is not a through street, it's a little hard to find. But the Martinez family cooking makes it worth the effort if you like Tex-Mex food. Want to start off your day with a little fire in your soul? Try the *huevos rancheros*. They really aren't too spicy, just enough to give you that warm feeling all over. However, if you want to start a bonfire, there are hot items on the menu like the *carne con chile*. If that still isn't enough, a bowl of chili is always on the table.

Sandwiches

OLD STRAND EMPORIUM
2112 The Strand near 21st St.
763-9445
Open seven days 10–6
$; AE, MC, V

The gourmet grocery items in the old-time grocery store setting makes this a great place to browse while you listen to the clinky music from the coin player piano. And when the sights and smells hike up your appetite, you can get a large po'boy or any other delicatessen sandwich to take with you or eat at the tables in back or the barrel tables on the sidewalk in front. Beer and wine.

Seafood

BENNO'S ON THE BEACH
Seawall at 12th St.
762-4621
Open seven days for lunch and dinner
$; MC, V
W

It looks like a casual, fast food place, but the emphasis here is on the feed not the speed. For one thing, they avoid the common fault of over-cooking the seafood, even when frying. One of the best buys on the beachfront is their boiled shrimp. You get a plate full. But watch out—they're boiled Cajun style and have a peppery bite. Ask about their "Off the Wall Menu." Take out available. Beer and wine.

CLARY'S
8509 Teichman across from the *Galveston Daily News*
740-0771
Monday through Friday lunch and dinner, Saturday dinner only, closed Sunday and last two weeks in November
Reservations recommended
$$–$$$; Cr.
W

Another hard-to-find restaurant that's worth looking for. Going to-ward Houston on I-45, take the Teichman exit past Galvez Mall, go under I-45 and turn right. There's a Cajun touch to many of the seafood dishes, like *shrimp au seasoned*, that makes them distinctive without being overpowering. Clary Milburn usually lets his chef prepare most of the menu items now, but he still likes to try the recipes for the not-on-the-menu specials and insists his waiters know how to describe them to his customers. This restaurant is a favorite with locals. Some tables in the rear dining room have a view of Offatts Bayou. Jackets suggested for men. Bar.

GAIDO'S
3828 Seawall at 39th St. (Mike Gaido Blvd.)
762-0115
Tuesday through Sunday lunch and dinner, closed Monday December through February
$$–$$$; AE, MC, V
W

Not many restaurant founders have a street named after them, but Mike Gaido does on 39th Street, and he earned it. The family restaurant he founded is still going strong after more than 70 years. The weekend lines to get in, which seem longer every year, are testimony that the Gaido family must be doing something very right. The lure, of course, is using fresh local fish instead of the frozen or processed product. The freshest catch is always listed on the typed sheets inserted in the menu. The menu itself is long but uncomplicated, and the dishes are reliable so you get what you expect, usually in large portions. The best deals in the house are for the young and the old. The complete children's dinner (under 12) is only $4.95, and the senior dinner (over 65), which runs from appetizer to dessert or an after dinner liqueur, is just $10.95. The beverage list from the Grog Shop bar is even longer than the menu and includes vintage wines, choice spirits, and over a hundred imported beers.

HILL'S PIER 19
Wharf near 20th St.
763-7087
Open seven days 11 a.m.–9:30 p.m.
$$; AE, MC, V
W downstairs only
A little expensive for cafeteria style, but this place has two things going for it. The first is not great, but good seafood. And the second is the view from the enclosed upstairs room or the outdoor decks—worth whatever little extra it costs. This is the closest thing to a bird's-eye view of the port you can get from The Strand area. Part of the shrimp fleet is always docked across from the restaurant, with the cranes and gulls using the empty boats as perches, and you'll probably see at least one large banana freighter being unloaded behind them. From the top deck you can see over to Pelican Island. The fish is fresh, but if you want, you can pick out your fish at the market in the building and have the restaurant cooks prepare it. Or the market clerks will pack it in ice for a long trip home. Beer and wine.

JOHN'S OYSTER RESORT
7711 Broadway near Teichman, across I-45 from Galvez Mall on the access road
744-1617
Lunch and dinner Tuesday through Saturday in summer, lunch and dinner Saturday and Sunday, dinner only Tuesday through Friday in winter, closed Monday
$$–$$$; Cr.
The old white stucco building, which dates from 1917, has been given a face lift that makes it look swanky, but the seafood retains its old-fashioned goodness. Oysters are still the house specialty. One of the few seafood places around that gives you the choice of broiled rather than fried on the seafood platter. The parking lot and the broad flight of entrance steps, beneath the two-story porte cochere, is at the rear on the bayou side. You can eat on the porch with a good view of the water, or inside with ceiling fans gently swishing the air-conditioned coolness off the white walls. Reservations are suggested for summer weekends or if you want a spot on the porch. Bar.

TUFFY'S SEAFOOD HOUSE
South Jetty on East Beach, take right at east end of Seawall Blvd.
763-9280
Open seven days, lunch and dinner
$$–$$$; Cr.
W

Perhaps it's because Tuffy's is off the beaten track and the food is only a little above the ordinary that this restaurant has lost some business to the new competition in town. But it can't lose the view. Tuffy's South Jetty location's walls of windows at the water's edge give diners a clear view of everything coming in and out of the ship channel. This is a casual place to spend an afternoon watching the ships go by as you satisfy the inner you with boiled shrimp and a cool drink. Bar.

Sweet Stuff

LA KING'S CONFECTIONARY
2323 The Strand
762-6100
Open seven days 10–10
$
W

This Gay Nineties ice cream parlor and candy factory is complete with metal frame sweetheart chairs, ceiling fans, wooden floors, and a soda fountain. Come at the right time, and you can see them making candy in the rear of the store.

CLUBS & BARS

More and more the night life in Galveston is gravitating to the plush hotel night spots (see Hotels & Motels). However, there are also a few other places to go on the town. Like most clubs, these come and go in response to the fads followed by their fickle customers.

SEABREEZE
1721 61st St., near Offatts Bayou
744-5717
Open seven days
AE, V
W

You better call ahead if you have distinct musical likes or dislikes because the management rotates the bands, and you may get anything from rock or reggae to jazz or the sounds of the fifties, all live in the Upperdeck Lounge. You can also eat lunch or dinner here. Full bill of fare emphasizing seafood and steaks. Before dark you can watch the windsurfers and waterskiers on the bayou. Bar.

OFFBEAT

COLONEL BUBBIE'S STRAND SURPLUS SENTER
2202 The Strand, entrance on 22nd St.
762-7397
Monday through Saturday 10–4 "usually"
It seems appropriate that architect Nicholas Clayton (who else?) was commissioned by a colonel, W. L. Moody, to do this building back in 1884, because now, more than a hundred years later, it is the headquarters of another colonel—Colonel Bubbie. This warehouse-type building is stacked with surplus from the armed forces of more than 50 different countries. It's a REAL military surplus store—no fakes here—filled with treasures like Civil War and Spanish-American War memorabilia for the collector or Spanish Army leather ammunition pouches for those who want to start a new fashion. But the heart of the matter is that this is a great place for the bargain hunter. Few countries skimp on quality in military uniforms, so all-wool or 100 percent cotton items abound. One section, for example, has crate-type shelves filled with wool sweaters from the British army, navy, and police, the Spanish army, and the U.S. Air Force and all at prices that you'd expect from a surplus operation. Colonel Bubbie buys and sells worldwide, so the selections are always changing. There's not much space inside; the aisles are narrow and twisting, and you may have to wait in line to get in on a summer Saturday and wait again to use the dressing room in the old vault. But a visit to Col. Bubbie's is an experience every shopper should have.

GALVESTON TO BRAZOSPORT
The drive from Galveston to Surfside in Brazosport parallels the Gulf the whole way. From Galveston on FM Road 3005 behind West Beach to San Luis Pass is about 21 miles. As you drive west, you can see the island narrowing in width, the distance between developments getting longer, and the number of grazing cows increasing. It costs a dollar to cross the causeway at San Luis Pass. Immediately on the other side is Follett's Island. To your left is the San Luis Fishing Pier. From here it is about 14 miles on County Road 257 to Surfside, one of the communities making up Brazosport.

★ BRAZOSPORT ★

★★
BRAZORIA COUNTY   ★   67,000   ★   (409)

Brazosport is not a city itself but a made-up name for a loose confederation of nine cities clustered on the coast near the mouth of the Brazos River. Interlocking like pieces of a jigsaw puzzle are Brazoria, Clute, Freeport, Jones Creek, Lake Jackson, Oyster Creek, Richwood, and the beach communities of Quintana and Surfside. The boundaries between the cities are marked, but most visitors won't realize—or care—which city they are in most of the time.

Geographically, Brazosport is unique in that it occupies the only "frontal mainland coastline" in Texas. That's coastline that does not have a barrier island, bays, estuaries, or tidal marsh. There is only about 20 miles of it in Texas, and it's all here.

As a recreational area, Brazosport appears to have one big drawback. It is home to Texas' fastest growing industrial complex, the heart of which is a grouping of the plants of Dow Chemical and 55 other companies mostly engaged in the production of basic chemicals used as raw materials by others in the industry. The stretch of this complex is nine miles long and averages a mile and a half in width. Other coastal cities have large industrial complexes, but they are usually not right in the

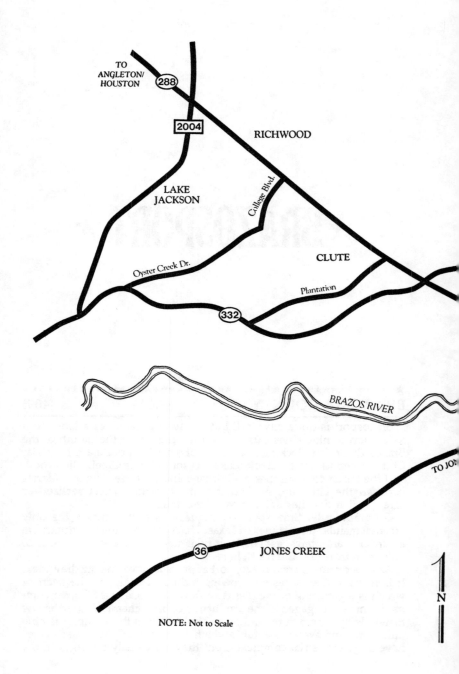

NOTE: Not to Scale

OYSTER CREEK

332

523

SURFSIDE
BRIDGE

Ave. A

SURFSIDE BEACH

INTRACOASTAL WATERWAY

TO GALVESTON/
SAN LUIS PASS

SURFSIDE

rt Blvd.

Velasco Blvd.

BRAZOS RIVER

OLD

Second

Pine

BRAZOS
HARBOR

QUINTANA

Lamar

GULF
OF
MEXICO

EEPORT

288

1495

BRYAN BEACH

AZORIA

CR 723

INTRACOASTAL WATERWAY

STATE PARK
BRYAN BEACH
AREA

center of everything. This one runs down to the Intracoastal Waterway, which backs the beach communities. The complex is the backdrop for everything you see or do in the area. That's the bad news for the recreation-minded visitor. The good news is that most visitors won't even notice it after the first day or two.

Brazosport is a relatively undeveloped recreational area with a lot to offer. You can drive on the more than 20 miles of accessible, mostly empty beaches to find your own private spot. And if you tire of the sameness of sea, sand, and surf, this mainland coastline offers variety in the form of cool woodlands that come almost to the water's edge. A short drive and you're in groves of live oaks and pecans. It is also a birdwatchers' paradise, flanked on one side by the Brazoria National Wildlife Refuge and on the other by the San Bernard National Wildlife Refuge. For ship watchers, large cargo vessels are always docked at Freeport, and a large shrimp fleet has this port as its home base.

Perhaps Brazosport's biggest draw for anglers is that it is an excellent jumping-off place for deep-sea fishing. From the Freeport jetties to the 100-foot depth where the big ones bite is less than two hours by boat. It also harbors one of the more luxurious marina-yacht clubs on the Texas coast. Surf, jetty, and small boat inshore fishing are also popular as is crabbing in the more than hundred miles of waterways in the area.

All this at prices generally lower than those at the more famous coastal resorts. In sum, Brazosport is a low-key, generally low-cost vacation area.

Brazosport also figures prominently in Texas history. It was here in Brazoria County that Stephen F. Austin and his colonists landed; it is also where the Texans first fought the Mexicans (in 1832, four years before the Alamo) and where Santa Anna was brought after his defeat to sign the treaty that gave Texas its independence. And here the new government of the Republic of Texas sat for the first time.

That first battle with the Mexicans came about when the Mexican government built a one-cannon fort at Velasco commanding the mouth of the Brazos River. The site is no longer visible today, but it was just behind the Coast Guard station in what is now Surfside. The commanders of Fort Velasco, and another fort at Anahuac to the east of Galveston Bay, irritated the Texans when they started charging customs and clearance duties that the Texans considered close to outright piracy. The situation came to a head when the commander at Fort Anahuac imprisoned several Texans, including William B. Travis. The men of the illegally formed militia at Brazoria decided to level the fort at Anahuac. Their plan was to load two cannon and about 120 men aboard the tiny schooner *Brazoria* and sail down the Brazos and across the Gulf to Anahuac. But when the commander of Fort Velasco refused to let the ship pass, the Texans decided to level that fort instead.

Late on the night of June 25, 1832, about a hundred Texans stole ashore from the ship and surrounded the fort, intending to attack at dawn. That plan was spoiled when one of them tripped and accidentally fired his rifle. For the rest of the night both sides fired at each other in the dark, doing little damage. With daylight, however, the Texan sharpshooters took command of the battle. The Mexicans' only cannon was on an exposed mound in the center of the fort so it could shoot over the walls in all directions. This arrangement was good for controlling the river, but unfortunately for the Mexicans, it also meant the walls got in the way for close-in shots. The Texans stayed below the angle of fire, picking off any soldier who exposed himself on the mound. After a few hours of fire from the sharpshooters, the fort surrendered.

Naturally, the Texans expected retribution from Mexico for this act of rebellion, and it wasn't long in coming in the form of five Mexican gunboats. But the whims of politics saved the day. The Texans considered President Bustamante a tyrant, so not long before, they had pledged their support to a Mexican general who was trying to overthrow the president. As it turned out, the commander of the gunboats was also a follower of that general. So instead of a bloodbath, there was a fiesta that ended with the Texans handing back Fort Velasco.

The general they favored did become the leader of Mexico. His name? General Antonio López de Santa Anna. And in another twist of fate, the colonel who surrendered Fort Velasco to the Texans also became a follower of Santa Anna and later led the Mexican troops in what is known in Texas history as the "Goliad Massacre."

The humidity can get high in this area, but it is usually tempered by Gulf breezes. The average winter temperature ranges from 45 to 60, and the average summer temperatures are in the 80s and 90s.

A GET-ACQUAINTED DRIVING TOUR

Pick up a map at the Chamber of Commerce office (see Tour & Guide Services) and start from there. Get back on Texas 332 and drive west (away from the Gulf). The Dow Chemical plant will be on your left and the city of Clute on your right. At just about the point the Dow plant ends, you'll cross into Lake Jackson.

During this drive you'll be going in and out of seven of the nine cities that make up Brazosport. Probably the only reason it will make any difference which city you're in is if you want to buy an alcoholic drink. Then the patchwork makeup of this composite city could be frustrating. Under the Texas local option laws, some of the cities are wet and some dry, and wet and dry can coexist on each side of a boundary street.

If you ever felt you didn't know whether to go this way or that way, then the place for you may be Lake Jackson where there are streets named This Way, That Way, and Anyway. And there's a story that a church on one of these Ways has a driveway named His Way. As you approach the road to the airport on your left, check the street signs on the right for one of these Ways.

At the end of Lake Jackson you'll come to Brazos Mall. Just past this is FM Road 2004. Turn right. For the next few miles you'll be in woodlands. Continue on until you reach Texas 288. If you went left you'd be on your way to Houston. But we're going to turn right and go east on

288. For the next mile or so you'll be in Richwood. After you go about a mile and a quarter, start looking on your right for College Boulevard. When you find it, turn right. This will take you to Brazosport College (see Colleges & Universities) and the Brazosport Center for Arts and Science (see Museums, Galleries & Theater). Drive around the campus, then loop back, and retrace your route to Texas 288 where you'll turn right and continue on.

Shortly you'll be back in Clute. (Have you ever traveled through so many cities in such a short time?) It's about two miles to the cloverleaf intersection with Texas 332. This is almost back where you started, having circled Clute, Lake Jackson, and Richwood, but there's more. About three miles farther on, after the road cuts through the Dow plant and you're in Freeport, the Mystery Monument (see Points of Interest) will be on your left. This restored shrimp boat is set up in the city park at the head of the Old Brazos River. The gaily painted root beer stand near the boat is Antonelli's River Inn (see Restaurants). Stay on 288, skirting Freeport, until you come to FM Road 1495, then turn right. This road takes you across the drawbridge over the Intracoastal Waterway to Bryan Beach, Quintana Beach, and the tiny city of Quintana. You can't see it, but off to the right before you cross the Intracoastal is the U.S. government's oil storage facility in huge underground caverns at Bryan Mound. FM Road 1495 turns into a county road ending at the beach. If you take a right on the beach, you can follow it to Bryan Beach State Recreation Area. But the tides sometimes make this beach route impassable, so turn back the way you came to the first crossroad, County Road 723, and go right to Quintana Park (see Points of Interest). From there or from the nearby jetty, you can look across at Surfside Beach.

When you finish exploring this little island, double back to FM Road 1495 and head back to Freeport. Just after you get into town, the port, with its more than 1,500 feet of docks, will be on your right. This port is growing and will become a major factor in Gulf shipping upon completion of an improvement program to deepen the harbor and put in a 1,200-foot turning basin that will enable Freeport to handle the largest cargo ships.

Turn left at Second Street, just before the bridge. Among the places you'll pass on the street are Girouard's General Store (see Offbeat), the Cock of the Walk (see Restaurants), and Captain Elliott's Party Boats (see Sports & Activities). Turn right at the light at Velasco Boulevard, just past the party boats. As you cross the bridge, look to your right for a view of the shrimp fleet. If you look farther down in that direction, you'll see a large metal rectangle sticking up above the river. This is the Velasco Memorial Tide Gate. When a storm tide warning is given, the small boat owners drive their craft up the Old Brazos River, the tide gate is lowered, and there the boats ride out the storm safe and secure in the sealed-off waterway.

Continue on Velasco Boulevard for about two miles, through the chemical plants, until you reach Texas 332, then turn right to Surfside. To your left as you start to cross the steep Surfside Bridge, you can see the Bridge Harbor Yacht Club, a luxury marina-condominium resort.

At Surfside (see Points of Interest), you can drive on the beach and stop at one of the beachside stands for a snack. County Road 257, which runs behind the beach, is the road you'd take north to go to San Luis Pass and Galveston.

This Get-Acquainted Driving Tour ends here.

TOUR & GUIDE SERVICES

BRAZOSPORT CHAMBER OF COMMERCE
Clute
420 Texas 332, approximately half a mile from Texas 288 interchange
265-2505
Monday through Friday 8:30–4:30
Free
W variable

The large sign makes it easy to find, but its location on the access road makes it a little hard to get to. The trick is to turn north at Main, then immediately right on the access road. They'll provide you with maps, brochures, and general information about all the cities that make up Brazosport and the surrounding area.

CAPTAIN ELLIOTT'S RIVER CRUISE
Freeport
1010 West 2nd at Velasco Blvd. (Texas 523)
233-1811
Friday and Saturday 7:30 p.m. and 9:30 p.m., April through September usually (more often if there is a demand, call)
Adults $8, children $4
W

A one-and-a-half-hour narrated tour of the calm waters of the Brazos River and the Intracoastal Waterway. Inside and outside seating. Snacks available or bring your own.

FREEPORT CITY DOCK TOUR
1001 Pine
233-2606
Monday through Friday 8–5
Free

This half-hour tour normally requires reservations at least a week in advance. It can be interesting, especially if a lot of port activity is going on at the time, but otherwise it's hardly worth the trouble of advance reservations.

POINTS OF INTEREST

THE MYSTERY MONUMENT
Freeport
On Texas 288 (400 block of Brazosport Boulevard) at head of Old
Brazos River
Open at all times
Free
W

Forty tons of wood, iron, and rigging, proud bow still held high, this shrimp trawler looks eager to return to the Gulf waters that were her home for almost three decades. This 60-foot craft was once the undisputed wood-hull queen of the Gulf shrimp fleet from the Mississippi to the Mexican border. There are no records to prove it, but experts estimate *The Mystery* had a career catch of close to 3.5 million pounds of shrimp. Now a monument to the pioneers of the Texas shrimping industry, she got her name when her first owners thought it a mystery how they'd pay for her.

Possibly as interesting as her life at sea is the story of the Chamber of Commerce's project to transform *The Mystery* into a monument. It started with the trawler abandoned and sunk at her berth. Moving her proved to be about as simple as moving the first space shuttle from its hangar to the launch pad. She was refloated, towed to another dock, hauled out of the water, cleaned up, and returned to her original mooring where she promptly sunk again. That, plus the fact that she would almost have to be turned into a submarine to pass under a railroad bridge on the water route, encouraged the committee to decide on an overland move.

Raised again but threatening to go under at any moment, she was carefully towed across the water to the site of a 100-ton crane and lifted onto a trailer. The trailer's center beam immediately sagged to about an inch off the ground. On the move, the trailer hung up on a levee and, when finally worked loose, chased two winch trucks down the other side, tied up traffic, got stuck again on a railroad track, and in two hours had moved a grand total of half a mile.

Finally, *The Mystery* was hoisted onto her permanent resting site. It was then that the movers discovered they had moved her with a couple of tons of water in her hull.

MUSEUMS, GALLERIES & THEATER

BRAZOSPORT CENTER FOR ARTS AND SCIENCE
Clute
400 College Drive on campus of Brazosport College
265-7661
Closed Monday, different hours for various sections, see below
Free
W+

This center is a cultural complex containing the Brazosport Museum of Natural Science, the Nature Center and Planetarium, Art Gallery, Little Theatre, and Music Theatre.

MUSEUM OF NATURAL SCIENCES, NATURE CENTER, AND PLANETARIUM
265-3376
Tuesday through Saturday 10–5, Sunday 2–5
The cornerstone of this museum is its seashell collection, which is reputed to be the most comprehensive on the Gulf Coast. There are also sections devoted to area archaeology, fossils, and rocks and minerals. Children will be especially fascinated by the Touch Tables. The museum has a gift shop. The new Nature Center offers both displays and classes on plants and wildlife, while the planetarium presents a variety of shows and classes on subjects ranging from astronomy to navigation. Call for times.

ART GALLERY
265-7971
Tuesday through Sunday 2–5
This is the gallery of the Brazosport Art League. The exhibits, which are changed every four to six weeks, are in a variety of media and include traveling exhibits as well as the work of local professional and amateur artists.

LITTLE THEATRE
265-7731
This local group usually presents about three major productions and a children's program each year in its 199-seat arena theater.

MUSIC THEATRE
265-7051
Usually two or three major musicals are produced by this local organization each year in a 399-seat theater. There are also traveling shows and musical movie classics.

COLLEGES & UNIVERSITIES

BRAZOSPORT COLLEGE
Lake Jackson
500 College, off Texas 288
265-6131
W
This community college offers mostly vocational programs in almost 40 fields including a unique junior college program in offshore marine technology. Occasionally, lectures and other programs are open to the public; call for information. The Brazosport Center for Arts and Sciences is on campus (see Museums, Galleries & Theater).

SHOPPING

BRAZOS MALL
Lake Jackson
Texas 332 at FM 2004
297-8001
W
   This, the only indoor shopping center in the area, contains Joske's, Penney's, Sears, B. Dalton Bookstore, and more than 90 other stores, fast food places, and a cafeteria.

OUTDOORS

BRYAN BEACH STATE RECREATION AREA
Take FM Rd. 1495 to end at Bryan Beach, then right and down beach approximately two miles
Open daylight hours
Free
   This undeveloped, almost primitive peninsula park is bordered by the Gulf, the Brazos River, and the Intracoastal Waterway. It offers a quiet beach and fishing and self-sufficient camping areas for those who want to get away from it all. There are no roads into the area. The surest way in is by small boat because the tides, when particularly high, can cover the beach route and dictate whether cars can get in or out.

QUINTANA PARK
Take FM Rd. 1495 across Intracoastal Waterway, then left on County Road 723 to Quintana and right to beach
Free
W variable
   It's a small park, but there's a large deck with picnic tables, a snack bar, bathhouse, and boardwalk down to the beach. Just north, behind the beach toward the jetties, you'll find earth mounds, which are all that remains of emplacements for cannon that guarded the harbor during the Civil War.

SURFSIDE BEACH
Follow Texas 332 to its eastern end
Free
W variable
   Located on the site where Santa Anna signed the treaty that gave Texas its independence, this is the major beach community in Brazosport. Swimming, sailing, surfing, sunning, fishing, and all the other beach activities are available here. It's also a magnet for high schoolers and other young people from as far away as Houston who enjoy cruising their cars and motorcycles up and down the beach. Cars are often parked hub-to-hub on summer weekends—with their sound systems

on full. Because of the storm tides and beach erosion, most of the bars, fast food stands, surfboard rentals, and other honky-tonk structures are built on tall pilings that make the beachfront look like it might fold up and steal away overnight. Fun for kids and teenagers, but if you like your beach activities more sedate, try going farther up the beach to the north past the crowds and the car parade. Beach houses for rent (see Other Accommodations).

SPORTS & ACTIVITIES

Birdwatching

The Freeport Christmas Bird Count, sponsored by the National Audubon Society, has ranked first or second in the nation since 1970. The record count is 226 different species and it usually averages more than 200 species. Although access is difficult, two of the best places for birding are the nearby national wildlife refuges.

BRAZORIA NATIONAL WILDLIFE REFUGE
Approximately four miles east of Surfside
849-6062
Access difficult
This 10,361-acre refuge is open for wildlife studies, observation, and photography; however, the roads into the area are often impassable, and the only sure way in is by boat. Call first. You can fish or crab in much of the refuge, but hunting is restricted to designated areas, requires a permit, and is only allowed by boat. For information write the Refuge Manager at P.O. Box 1088, Angleton 77515.

SAN BERNARD NATIONAL WILDLIFE REFUGE
Approximately 10 miles west of Freeport off FM Rd. 2918
849-6062
Easier to get to than Brazoria, this 24,454-acre refuge is one of the winter homes of the blue and snow geese. Possible activities include hiking as well as wildlife studies, hunting, and fishing. For information write the Refuge Manager at P.O. Box 1088, Angleton 77515.

Boating

A map indicating the location of small boat launching ramps is available from the Brazosport Chamber of Commerce (see Tour & Guide Services).

BRIDGE HARBOR YACHT CLUB
Freeport
From Texas 288 at west end of Surfside Bridge on the Intracoastal

Waterway
233-2101
The old Bridge Harbor Marina has been completely razed and from its remains has risen a $28 million, Mediterranean-style resort. When all construction phases are completed, it will include over 300 deep water slips, 80 condominium homes, swimming pool, tennis courts, and a restaurant. Some of the condos are available for daily rental from $150 a day up, which, of course, includes all the privileges of club membership. The slips will accommodate craft of nine-foot draft or less in lengths to over 100 feet and are equipped with hookups for everything from water to cable TV. Fuel dock and ship's store.

Fishing

Deep-sea fishing is the sport that visitors seem to prefer here, but there's also pier and jetty fishing. The closest large pier is the San Luis Fishing Pier (233-9381), located about 14 miles north of Surfside on County Road 257 at the causeway to Galveston. As for jetty fishing, there are the long jetties at Surfside and Quintana. (A word for the wise from local anglers: tennis shoes are fine if you're close to shore on a jetty, but if you're going out far, the wet moss is hazardous. They recommend golf shoes for more secure footing.) You can also crab at almost any one of the many creeks in the area. The major catch for offshore fishing is red snapper, but there's also ling, king mackerel, and amberjack. A number of charter boat outfits are listed in the Yellow Pages, but the only party boats are operated by Captain Elliott's Party Boats at Velasco and 2nd in Freeport (233-1811). A 12-hour deep-sea trip costs about $45.

Golf

FREEPORT MUNICIPAL GOLF COURSE
830 Slaughter Road off Texas 36
233-8311
Open seven days from dawn until dusk
Green fees $5.30–$7.90
Eighteen-hole public course. Slaughter Road is off the old route of Texas 36 that parallels north of the new route at this point.

Tennis

Lighted courts are at Brazosport College on College Boulevard and Lake Jackson and Brazosport High School on Texas 36 and 228 in Freeport.

ANNUAL EVENTS

April

BLESSING OF THE SHRIMP FLEET
Freeport
Old River Harbor
233-0651
Usually late in month
    This weekend includes a parade of the shrimp boats and onshore festivities ranging from a seafood cooking contest to a street dance.

July

FISHING FIESTA AND JULY 4TH CELEBRATION
Fiesta at Freeport
Headquartered at Freeport Municipal Park
233-7695
July 4th Celebration at Lake Jackson
Dunbar Park
265-6633
    Freeport's Fishing Fiesta runs about four days around the Fourth of July. In addition to fishing tournaments, it includes boat races, a shrimp festival, and other activities. The biggest fireworks display in the area is usually at Lake Jackson's Old Fashioned Fourth.

HOTELS & MOTELS

    The motels in Brazosport seem more oriented toward visitors interested in fishing or business than those interested in a beach holiday, because most beach-goers are day-trippers from the area or from Houston. As a result, only a few motels are at Surfside Beach, and a half dozen other small- to medium-sized motels are scattered along Texas 288 and Gulf Boulevard in Freeport, while the better-known chain motels are concentrated in Clute and Lake Jackson, about eight miles from the beach. Unfortunately, the quality of the smaller motels varies dramatically from one to another and sometimes from season to season. Some are clean, comfortable bargains; some are not. Unless you are either adventurous or already familiar with one of them, it might be a good idea to make reservations at one of the chains for the first night or two. Then, if you decide you must be on the beach, you can check out the others to find one that suits.

If you plan to stay for a weekend or longer, especially if on a family holiday, it could pay you to look into reserving a beach house (see Other Accommodations).

Hotel-motel rates for a double during the summer:

$: under $30
$$: $30–$45
$$$: $46–$65
$$$$: over $65

BRAZOSPORT HILTON INN
Lake Jackson
925 Texas 332, two miles west of Texas 288 interchange
297-1161 or in Texas 1-800-442-7260
$$$
W + two rooms

This 150-room hotel has an indoor pool in the lobby-like center of the building, which can be a boon especially on a rainy day. The restaurant offers an imaginative and wide-ranging list of entrées that usually can be counted on to live up to the menu-writer's descriptions. Because Lake Jackson is a dry city, membership cards are required at the disco club. These cards are complimentary for guests and available at a small fee for others. The disco seems to attract singles of all ages, which can make for a lively but crowded club on weekends. You won't feel out of place if you dress up.

HOLIDAY INN
Lake Jackson
915 Texas 332, two miles west of Texas 288 interchange
297-3031 or 1-800-HOLIDAY
$$–$$$
W + one room

Nothing spectacular, just 112 rooms living up to this chain's reputation for dependability, a large pool, and a small restaurant. Services include an airport courtesy car—or you can land your helicopter on the front lawn—and in-room movies. The small club-bar (free membership for guests, fee for others) offers live entertainment nightly.

LA QUINTA
Clute
1126 Texas 332, one and a half miles west of Texas 288 interchange
265-7461 or 1-800-531-5900
$$
W variable

This chain offers moderate prices while cutting only a few of the frills. Just like higher-priced competitors, it offers color TV in all 136 rooms, complimentary coffee in the lobby, a small pool, and clean, comfortable rooms. But there's no restaurant (a Denny's is next door) and no bar.

MOTEL 6
Clute
1000 Texas 332, one mile west of Texas 288 interchange
265-6766
$
W variable

Now this is part of the chain that believes that no frills means just that. If all you want is a clean, simple room for the night at a reasonable price, that's what they offer. Everything, including TV, is extra—not much extra but not included in the room price. If you don't plan to spend much time in your room and would rather have the dollars to spend elsewhere, this could be the answer. No restaurant, of course, but a number of them are nearby.

SOUTHERN EXECUTIVE INN
Clute
805 Texas 332 at South Main, approximately half a mile west of Texas 288 interchange
265-3301
$$–$$$
W+ two rooms

One of the newer motels in town, just up the highway from the Brazosport Chamber of Commerce. Though not a chain, it offers chainstyle accommodations in its 105 rooms, complimentary continental breakfast, small pool, airport transportation, and a small (membership fee) club-bar. No restaurant, but other restaurants are close by on the Texas 332 strip.

OTHER ACCOMMODATIONS

There are close to 200 beach houses in the Surfside Beach area with rents starting at about $325 a week for a two bedroom, one bath at the low end of the location and frills scale (stark simplicity) during high season from mid June to mid August. They drop as low as $200 a week at mid winter. But don't hold your breath while trying to reserve one of these low renters. There are only a few, and they're booked early. Most houses rent for $450 to $700 a week in high season. These usually have two or three bedrooms, sleeping up to 15 people, with central air, a covered porch, maybe a washer and dryer and other amenities, and a location very near or directly on the beach. On the top end of the scale, it'll cost $1,000 or more a week for a three bedroom, two bath that sleeps 10 in the lap of luxury: fireplace, dishwasher, microwave, two TVs, hot tub, beautiful interior design, and even a burglar alarm system. They chop off a couple of hundred dollars immediately before or after high season and several hundred off the rest of the year.

Details and current rates can be obtained from the following rental agents. All addresses are: Rt. 2, Surfside Beach 77541.

Brannan Realty ★ Box 1115 ★ 233-1812
Haygood Properties ★ Box 1087 ★ 233-6734
Resort Rentals ★ Box 1195 ★ 233-3155
Sand Castle Rentals ★ Box 1155 ★ 233-7879
Tarter Real Estate ★ Box 1090 ★ 233-7063

RESTAURANTS

American

PORT CAFE
Freeport
216 West Park (between 2nd and 3rd)
233-9217
Open seven days 7 a.m.–3 p.m.
$; No cr.
W

In a world where too many cooks know only how to thaw and serve, it's a pleasure to find a kitchen staff that works from scratch—even for the hamburgers. The menu isn't large, but catering to a trade of fishermen and port workers with hearty appetites means the portions are. Nothing fancy—seafood, steaks, and chicken—but when owner Judy Travis says "home cooking," she means it. A typical lunch special, which goes for under $5, is baked chicken with green beans, a mildly spiced dressing, and giblet gravy.

Seafood

COCK OF THE WALK
Freeport
920 W. 2nd St.
233-7715
Open seven days for lunch and dinner
$–$$; AE, MC, V
W

In an area where saltwater catches abound, this restaurant specializes in freshwater catfish. All portions for your table are served on one platter that is heaped with catfish, hush puppies, fries, and coleslaw to be eaten off tin plates. Waiters dress in old-time sailor suits wearing hats that commemorate the toughest man aboard each boat who wore a red turkey feather in his hat and was called the "cock of the walk." From a window seat you can see the shrimp boats anchored nearby. Bar.

Sweet Stuff

ANTONELLI'S RIVER INN
Freeport
420 Brazosport Blvd. (Texas 288) behind *The Mystery*
239-1983
Open weekends in spring and fall, seven days in summer, 11–7,
closed October through March
W

Keg root beer and ice cream are the main items here, and they are
treats enough to lure people from miles around. This root beer stand
was originally a popular spot in downtown Freeport. When Mr. Antonelli died it fell into disrepair. Finally the owner's son, a San Antonio
doctor, donated it to the Freeport League, and they moved it to its
present spot where it is now once again gaily painted and enshrined in
a circle of colorful flowers.

OFFBEAT

GIROUARD'S GENERAL STORE
Freeport
626 Second
233-4211

It's a local landmark with cluttered aisles where you can find an anchor or a can of beans. It appears that everything you've wanted but
couldn't find in stores anymore is stashed away someplace here, all giving support to Girouard's slogan, "If we don't have it, you don't need it."
The butcher shop is set in the midst of rows of hardware, and scattered
around the store, you'll find Japanese saki wine, brass coatracks, handmade furniture, antiques, small handmade fishing nets, a wealth of
enameled cast-iron cookware, a passport photo set-up, and everything
else you'd expect in a combination general store and ship chandler's
shop. Girouard's is reportedly also the only grocery store in the country
certified as a government agent for marine charts.

BRAZOSPORT TO PORT LAVACA

There are a couple of small beach communities on stilts and a few
fishing camps holding on against Gulf storms and beach erosion between Brazosport and Port Lavaca, but the only two developed towns
equipped to handle visitors are Matagorda and Palacios. The easiest
route from Brazosport to Matagorda starts with Texas 36 from Freeport
through Jones Creek to Brazoria. About two miles of this road between
those two cities passes through the neatly tended fields of one of the

Texas Department of Corrections prison farms. At Brazoria, turn west on FM Road 521 and follow it about 30 miles to Wadsworth. Then turn south on Texas 60 and stay on it for eight and a half miles to where it ends at Matagorda.

★★★

MATAGORDA

MATAGORDA COUNTY   ★   605   ★   (409)

Matagorda was established in 1829. At one time this was a major Texas port, but those days are long gone. Now its claim to fame rests more on the controversial nuclear power plant being built nearby than on the city itself. The city is on East Matagorda Bay, about eight miles from the Gulf. To get to the beach, take FM Road 2031 down the strip of land that runs between the bay and Colorado River. Even though this isn't a great beach, it's just about the only accessible beach on the Gulf between Brazosport and Port Aransas, which means summer weekends of bumper-to-bumper traffic and shoulder-to-shoulder suntanners.

CHRIST EPISCOPAL CHURCH
Cypress and Lewis
Christ Church was organized in 1838, and the congregation built its first house of worship in 1841. After the hurricane of 1854 destroyed that, church members salvaged as much of the cypress timbers and other parts of the building as they could and used them to build anew in 1856. Services are still held in this simple wooden building. This is reportedly the oldest Episcopal church in Texas.

Retrace your route back on Texas 60, and turn left on FM Road 521 where it goes off to the west just south of Wadsworth. From this turn-off it's about six miles to the nuclear power plant.

SOUTH TEXAS PROJECT
FM Rd. 521 between Texas 60 and Texas 35
Visitors Center: (512) 972-5023
Tuesday through Saturday 9–5, Sunday 1–5, closed Monday
Free
W
Although the nuclear power plant itself is still several years away from completion, the twin-geodesic domed Visitor Center is open. The exhibits and films here are, naturally, nuclear-friendly. They are designed to acquaint you both with nuclear power, in general, and this generating plant, in particular. Plant tours are available for groups, but advance reservations are required. Even if you can't tour it, a telescope in the center will give you a close-up look of Unit One of the plant, which is under construction just across the highway.

Continue on about 11 miles more on FM Road 521 until it dead-ends into Texas 35. A left turn will take you to Palacios, but if you're a hearty eater and in this neighborhood around lunchtime, you might want to detour a few miles for some home-style cooking. If so, turn right and go north on 35 about six miles, and just where that road starts to bend to the east, take FM Road 616 on your left into Blessing. At the first (and only) stoplight is the Blessing Hotel, built in 1907.

BLESSING HOTEL COFFEE SHOP
FM Rd. 616 at Ave. B
588-6623
Seven days for breakfast and lunch
$
W

It's called a coffee shop, but it's really a ballroom converted into a dining room with old cook stoves. It is also usually packed, because this coffee shop is famous for its family-style meals in which you dish out your own servings from pots and pans lined up on the old iron stoves. There are usually two meats and several vegetables, and this is rice country, so you can expect that with every meal.

If you don't want to detour to Blessing, turn left from FM Road 521 and go about six miles to Palacios.

★★★
PALACIOS

| MATAGORDA COUNTY | ★ | 4,667 | ★ | (512) |

Fishing, both for sport and for livelihood, is the main occupation in this area. There's a beach on the bay, a pleasant park, and free lighted fishing piers.

LUTHER HOTEL
408 S. Bay Blvd.
972-2312
Doubles from $20

Built on the bay in 1903, this rambling, white-frame building with a large porch and manicured lawn remains one of the few surviving grand old dames of the coast. It offers 15 large, high-ceilinged rooms and apartments without air conditioning and 11 newer motel-style apartments with it.

PETERSEN'S RESTAURANT
416 Main
972-2413
Open seven days for all meals
$–$$; Cr.
W

Most customers say they come to eat the seafood, but deep in their hearts they know they come for the homemade pies.

TO PORT LAVACA
From Palacios, get back on Texas 35 and continue west about 30 miles to Port Lavaca.

★ PORT LAVACA ★

★★★

PORT LAVACA

CALHOUN COUNTY SEAT ★ **12,818** ★ **(512)**

In the 1840s, this thriving port shipped thousands of bales of cotton from seven large wharves. It also exported large quantities of cattle, hides, and tallow, which led to it being known by the Spanish word for the cow, "la vaca." Today it is still a port, serving such major area industries as the country's largest bauxite refinery, owned by Alcoa, which is located at Point Comfort across the bay. It is also the base for commercial and sport fishing. Its location on protected Lavaca Bay attracts boating and waterskiing enthusiasts while nearby beaches round out the opportunities for water sports.

TOUR & GUIDE SERVICES

PORT LAVACA–CALHOUN COUNTY CHAMBER OF COMMERCE
2300 Texas 35, one block west of causeway
552-2959

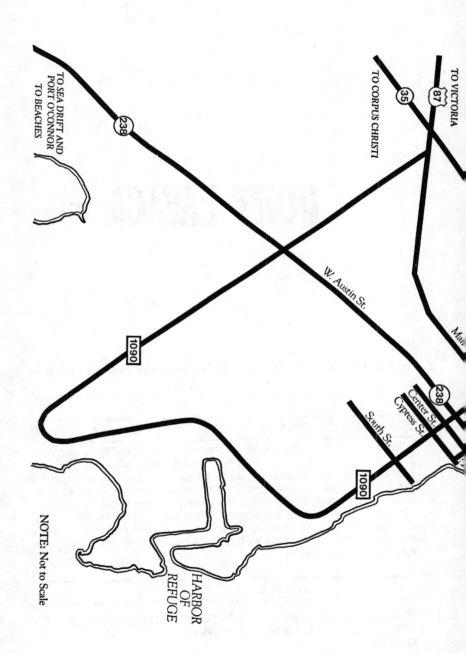

TO VICTORIA

TO CORPUS CHRISTI

TO SEA DRIFT AND
PORT O'CONNOR
TO BEACHES

W. Austin St.

Main

Center St.
Cypress St.
South St.

HARBOR
OF
REFUGE

NOTE: Not to Scale

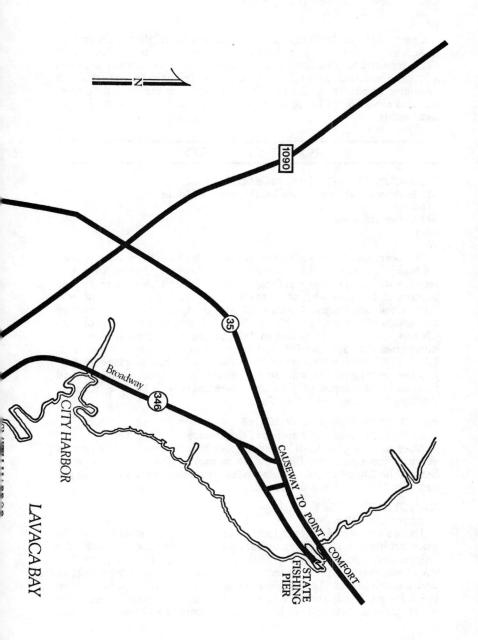

N

1090

35

Broadway

346

CITY HARBOR

LAVACA BAY

CAUSEWAY TO POINT COMFORT

STATE
FISHING
PIER

111

Open Monday through Friday 8:30–5
Free
W
One thing to get for sure is the free map that has all the details on Port Lavaca on one side and a map of the whole county, which includes Port O'Connor and Seadrift, on the other side. The county side also includes a lot of information for anglers and boaters. It's not quite a chart, but it does give depths for all the local bays and out into the Gulf. Brochures are also available on Indianola (see Outdoors & Side Trips) and other local sights.

POINTS OF INTEREST

CALHOUN COUNTY JAIL MUSEUM
301 S. Ann St. at Leona, two blocks south of Main
552-2661
See below for hours
Free
W
The permanent home of this museum is a turn-of-the-century county jail building that resembles a small castle. However, that building was recently declared unsafe, and while it goes through the long and costly process of being rehabilitated, the museum collection is located next door in the Courthouse Annex at 201 W. Austin. Among the displayed mementos of the county's history is a 4×8–foot model of the old Indianola townsite as it looked in 1875 before the second of the three hurricanes that destroyed it. The museum in the annex is open from 1:30 to 4:30 Tuesday through Friday. When the jail building is reopened, you can once again climb the spiral iron staircase to see the tiny second floor cells. It's expected that the hours there will be 2–6 Tuesday through Thursday and 9–1 on Saturday.

HALFMOON REEF LIGHTHOUSE
2300 Texas 35, behind Chamber of Commerce
After surviving the Civil War, a number of hurricanes, and 90 years of service, this squat little lighthouse was moved to its present location behind the Chamber of Commerce a few years ago. It's not open, so you can only look at it from the outside.

RANGER CEMETERY
Harbor St. off Broadway
There's a hundred years of local history in the gravestones here. The main problem is finding the cemetery because it's tucked in behind a fish cannery on the north side of the street. Harbor is a short, commercial street, and parking is restricted. It may be best to park on Broadway and walk the block. This site was named after the 1850 burial of Margaret Peyton Lytle, the wife of the "poet" of the Texas Rangers. The oldest grave is that of Major James Watts, victim of a Comanche raid on

the nearby community of Linnville in 1840. Watts and his recent bride fled at the first sign of the Indians, but Mrs. Watts insisted on returning to their home for a gold watch left behind. The Comanches were waiting, killed Watts, and captured his wife. A posse later caught up with the Indians and rescued Mrs. Watts, but not before an Indian shot an arrow at her. It was deflected by the steel stays in her corset. Among the others buried here are 10 Federal soldiers who died in an epidemic during the Civil War. The last burial occurred in 1941.

SHOPPING

The major shopping area is concentrated at the intersection of Texas 35 and FM 1090. Here one small covered mall and two large strip centers occupy three of the four corners with everything from discount stores and supermarkets to an ice cream shop and restaurants.

MELCHER'S HARDWARE
203 E. Main (U.S. 87) at Colorado
552-9224
W

It's a walk back in time, with worn wooden floors and that musty, old-time hardware store smell. The wall shelves reach all the way to the ceiling and are crammed full of everything from nails to TVs.

WHATNOT SHELF
137 E. Main (U.S. 87) at Colorado
552-4322

Across from Melcher's, the Whatnot Shelf looks out of place almost surrounded by run-down buildings and seedy downtown bars. But this is where the local shopping experts say you can buy the most interesting gifts in town. There's the usual stock of shells and brass items you'll find in any gift store, but among the items that distinguish it from most of its competitors is the selection of dolls, doll furniture, and elaborate kits for building doll houses.

OUTDOORS & SIDE TRIPS

BAYFRONT PARK
Extension of Main St. east of Broadway
552-9798
Free
W

This landfill park juts out into the bay making it a nice place for fishing or boat watching. A children's playground, which resembles a fort, and a few picnic tables are all that is here now, but a marina and other attractions are in the works.

INDIANOLA
From Port Lavaca, take Texas 238 (Austin St.) approximately two miles to where it goes right at fork with Texas 316; continuing straight puts you on 316, go a little over eight miles to beach

What you can see here is a historical marker, a monument, and a beach park. What you can't see is the ghost of a town that once was one of the most bustling ports on the Gulf.

In the 1840s huge concrete and wooden piers stretched out half a mile into the Gulf, and this was a main port of entry for new colonists coming to Texas, including the Germans who arrived with Prince Carl zu Solms-Braunfels to found the inland cities of New Braunfels and Fredericksburg. In the 1850s it was the main army supply depot for the western frontier, and here Jefferson Davis, then U.S. secretary of war, shipped Arabian camels as an experiment to replace army horses in the western desert. The town survived Union shellings and capture and recapture during the Civil War, yellow fever epidemics, and two hurricanes (in 1866 and 1875) that partially destroyed it and killed more than 900 people. But it couldn't survive the third hurricane in 1886 that leveled it to the ground.

The 22-foot granite monument here is not to the people who withstood three lashings from the elements before they gave up, but to La Salle, the French explorer who landed here in 1685.

There are covered, concrete picnic tables, barbecue pits, a boat ramp, restrooms, hookups for campers, plus an assortment of bait shops, rental cabins, and taverns along this shallow beach. If you follow the beach road north, it leads to Magnolia Beach where the beach gets wider and there are more picnic tables, a couple of restaurants, and fishing piers.

PORT LAVACA STATE FISHING PIER & PIER PARK
Texas 35 at the causeway over Lavaca Bay
552-4402
Fishing pier open seven days, summer 6 a.m.–midnight, winter 8 a.m.–midnight; park always open
Fishing $1 per device + tax, park RV spaces $6.50–$7.50
W variable

This lighted fishing pier is built on the pilings of the old causeway from Port Lavaca to Point Comfort. It extends more than 3,000 feet into the bay, and local anglers claim this is a great place to catch speckled trout, flounder, and redfish. A fee is charged for fishing, but if you just want to stroll out and sightsee, that's free. The bait shop concessionaire handles both the state pier, the boat launching site, and the adjoining city park. The park has a swimming pool (fee), playground, restrooms, and showers. There are 19 waterfront RV spaces with two-way hookups and TV cable ($1 extra) plus 34 pull-thru spaces with two-way hookups only. The entrance is on the road parallel to Texas 35. To reach it, turn off Texas 35 on the street next to the swimming pool, just east of the Chamber of Commerce building, then turn toward the bay on the first street on the left.

SPORTS & ACTIVITIES

Fishing

Landlubbers can fish off the lighted state pier or from the many beaches. Or you can go out in a boat in the bay or the Gulf. Most of the area guides and charter boats operate out of nearby Port O'Connor. Check the Yellow Pages or the Chamber of Commerce for those.

Hunting

Port Lavaca is on a peninsula so there's lots of water around to lure the waterfowl migrating south for the winter. Its proximity to Aransas National Wildlife Refuge makes it even more attractive to these sport birds. There's also deer hunting in season.

ANNUAL EVENTS

April

LA SALLE DAYS
Indianola and Port Lavaca
Call Chamber of Commerce for details
Usually last weekend in month
Admission
W variable
France in the 1600s is the background theme of this festival that only recently became an annual event. Activities at Indianola include a re-enactment of La Salle's landing.

September

JAYCEES' FISHING TOURNAMENT
Calhoun County waters
Call Chamber of Commerce for location of headquarters
Labor Day weekend
Approximately $20 entrance fee
This three-day tourney starts at 6 p.m. the Friday before Labor Day and ends at noon on the following Monday. Fish must be taken from Calhoun County waters, which include Lavaca, Matagorda, Espiritu Santo, San Antonio, and Guadalupe bays. For details write the Port Lavaca Jaycees, P.O. Box 92, Port Lavaca 77979-0092.

HOTELS & MOTELS

A number of small motels are scattered around the city, but the major ones are located at the northeastern end of the city on Texas 35 leading to Pier Park and the causeway that crosses the bay to Point Comfort. Rates for a double:

$: under $30
$$: $30–$40
$$$: over $40

BEST WESTERN SHELLFISH INN
Texas 35 at the causeway
552-3723
$$–$$$
W

This motel is located on the water, so you can walk out of your room and look out at the bay or at Pier Park, which is just across the highway. Some of the 49 rooms have small refrigerators—a plus for keeping the fishing catch. All have free HBO, and there's a pool, hot tub, and small children's playground.

CHAPARRAL MOTEL
2086 Texas 35, two long blocks west of causeway
552-7581
$
W+ two rooms

This is a new, inexpensive, 53-room motel with swimming pool and free HBO. No restaurant, but the Kettle Kitchen and Holiday Inn restaurants are right next door.

HOLIDAY INN
2100 Texas 35, two long blocks west of causeway
552-4511
$$$
W+ one room

Recently refurbished, there are 99 rooms, the chain's free in-room movies, and a pool. The Gazebo Restaurant offers an all-you-can eat buffet as well as specials for lunch and a variety of seafood, steaks, and other standard menu items for dinner. The lounge has a DJ for dancing Monday through Saturday.

VIKING INN
150 Texas 35 next to Viking Mall
552-2981
$–$$
W

The 60 motel rooms are partly shielded from traffic noise by their location around the pool behind the lobby-restaurant building. The restaurant offers lunch and dinner specials and a selection of nonfried seafood. Live entertainment in the lounge Monday through Saturday.

RESTAURANTS

Chinese

CHINA KITCHEN
309 Calhoun Plaza Shopping Center, Texas 35 and FM 1090
552-1520
Lunch and dinner
$$; MC, V
W

The traditional Americanized Chinese restaurant decor complete with gilt and red screens, lantern lights, and large wood carvings seems more subdued and authentic because of the Chinese background music. The menu lists seafood, beef, and chicken dishes, and fortunately, most of these rise a little above the standards of the usual Chinese restaurant. Bar.

Mexican

EL PATIO
534 W. Main (U.S. 87) at Trinity
552-6316
Open seven days for breakfast, lunch, and dinner
$; No cr.
W

A good place to start the day with a hot and hearty Mexican breakfast as you watch a steady stream of locals go from table to table exchanging greetings and gossip.

Seafood

OCEAN INN
116 Commerce at Main
552-7650
Open seven days for breakfast, lunch, and dinner
$$; MC, V
W

Hurrah! Another seafood restaurant where they know that frying is not the only way to prepare fish. In addition, this one doesn't serve seafood as if it was scarce in the area—portions are generous, and prices, while a little higher than others, are at least in line with the chef's culinary skills. And in a world where salad bars are often more hype than selection, this one's variety makes you want to belly on up. If you can get a window seat, you'll have a good view of the bay. Oyster bar and lounge open in the evenings.

PORT LAVACA TO PORT O'CONNOR
Take Texas 238 from Port Lavaca approximately three miles to FM Road 1289. Then take that road southeast for 11 miles to where it ends at Texas 185; then left eight miles to Port O'Connor.

★★
PORT O'CONNOR

CALHOUN COUNTY ★ 810 ★ (512)

Located at the southeastern tip of the peninsula that makes up most of Calhoun County, this village has Matagorda Bay to the east, Espiritu Santo Bay to the south, and Cavallo Pass to the Gulf between them. It all adds up to one of the prime fishing spots on the coast. Port O'Connor is so small and unspoiled that fishermen tend to treat it like an old fishing hole that they keep secret from all but their best fishing buddies—and often even from them. As one angler put it, "If the fish are biting anywhere along the coast, it'll probably be at Port O'Connor."

GALLERIES

OUTSIDER'S ART GALLERY AND SHOP
4th and Main
983-2296
Tiny, but packed with works, mostly wildlife and seascapes in watercolors and prints, by some well-known Texas artists. Also fish-rubbings and hand-thrown pottery.

SIDE TRIPS

MATAGORDA ISLAND
Want to roam an undeveloped barrier island for shell collecting, bird-watching—loads of pelicans and sometimes peregrine falcons—picnicking, or fishing? Several of the local charter boats will take you there. Contact the Chamber of Commerce at 983-2870 or 983-2731 for information.

FISHING

That's what it's all about here. There's a free pier on the water near Adams Street, or go out in your own boat or one of several charter boats. See the Yellow Pages for listings. The richest fishing tournament on the Gulf is held here each year in July—the Poco Bueno Invitational Offshore Fishing Tournament, a deep-sea contest in which prizes can reach over half a million dollars. But it is invitational, and the hundred or so invitees all have big boats and big money or big money backers. The Chamber of Commerce also sponsors an annual fishing event, which doesn't require an invitation (see Annual Events).

ANNUAL EVENTS

CHAMBER OF COMMERCE FISHING TOURNAMENT
Local bays
Memorial Day weekend
Call Chamber of Commerce for details, 983-2870 or 983-2731
Entrance fee $5
Three-day tourney with prizes for the biggest trout, redfish, flounder, and other catches from the local waters. Also a one-day children's tournament, usually off the pier. Street dance and other activities.

HOTELS & MOTELS

TARPON MOTEL
Maple and 14th
983-2606
Winter $30, summer $30–$50
W
The largest motel in town, it offers 37 motel rooms, plus 12 apartments and 12 RV spots. The apartments are usually filled by long-term renters, but when available they run from $35 to $95 a day depending on the season. RV spaces come with three-way hookups and cable at $10 a night. Pool, dry boat stalls, and package store.

OTHER ACCOMMODATIONS

There aren't many of them in this small town, but occasionally beach houses or condominium apartments are available that rent for $60–$100 a night. For information call Coastal Real Estate at 983-2296 or the Chamber of Commerce at 983-2870 or 983-2731. (The Chamber of Commerce number is part-time, so don't be confused by the way they answer the phone.)

PORT O'CONNOR TO SEADRIFT
Take Texas 185 west a little over 19 miles to Seadrift.

★★
SEADRIFT

CALHOUN COUNTY   ★   1,277   ★   (512)

Residing on the other side of the peninsula from Port O'Connor, the people of this village also earn their living from the sea.

ANNUAL EVENTS

June

TEXAS WATER SAFARI
City pier
Call City Hall for information, 785-2251

This is the finish line for the grueling annual canoe race that starts in San Marcos. Contestants come from all over the country to paddle for up to eight days down the San Marcos and Guadalupe rivers to the Seadrift public pier on San Antonio Bay.

July

SHRIMPFEST
City Park
Call City Hall for information, 785-2251

The Blessing of the Shrimp Fleet, boat parade, shrimp eating contest, boat races, and a street dance are just a few of the activities that more than triple the population of the town for this festival usually held on July 4.

RESTAURANTS

BARKETT'S
On Texas 185 at north end of town
785-2441
Lunch and dinner; closed Monday
$-$$
W

Barkett's is not what could be classed as a seafood lover's find, but they do things just different enough here to put it a notch above many of the other seafood restaurants on the coast. For example, on the seafood platter—that staple of every seafood menu—the shrimp are jumbo, the taste of crab in the stuffing is actually detectable, and the fish, although fried, isn't overcooked. Plus the portions give good value for your money. Beer and wine. Gift shop.

SEADRIFT TO ROCKPORT

Go north out of Seadrift on Texas 185. The intersection with Texas 35 is a little under 10 miles. Turn left (west) to head for Fulton and Rockport.

Shortly after you make the turn, Green Lake will be on your right. There are larger man-made lakes in Texas, but this one, covering 10,000 acres, is the largest natural freshwater lake in the state. About 10 miles farther on you'll come to Texas 239 going southeast to Austwell. Take this road if you want to visit the Aransas National Wildlife Refuge.

ARANSAS NATIONAL WILDLIFE REFUGE
From Texas 35 take Texas 239 to FM Rd. 2040 (from Rockport take FM Rd. 774 off 35 to 2040), headquarters seven miles southeast of Austwell
(512)286-3559 or 286-3533
Open seven days sunrise to sunset, Visitors Center 8–5, Sunday 9–5
Free
W

With almost 55,000 acres, this is the largest national wildlife refuge in Texas. It is also famous as the winter home of the whooping crane. These birds, which stand over five feet tall, migrate in October or November each year from their summer home in the Canadian Wood Buffalo National Park in Alberta, Canada. Only 21 whoopers were known to exist in the world when the U.S. and Canada started a joint program in the early 1940s to save this bird from extinction. Slowly the efforts are paying off. Though still an endangered species, more than 80 whooping cranes are now in this colony alone. The best ways to see these birds are through the telescopes in the refuge observation tower or on one of the tour boats (see Rockport, Tour & Guide Services). But there's a lot more to see here than just the whoopers. On the 16-mile-loop drive that winds through meadows, thickets, and marshes, and along the shore and tidal flats, you may see many other species of birds, plus deer, coyotes, javelina, wild turkeys, armadillos, and alligators. You must register at the headquarters before starting the tour, and you can pick up guide maps at the same time. According to the park rangers, the most rewarding time to visit is from November through March when the migratory waterfowl and the whoopers are there.

TO ROCKPORT-FULTON
It's about 38 miles from the Aransas refuge to Rockport. To get back on the route, take FM Road 2040 to FM Road 774 to Texas 35. Turn left

on 35 and continue southwest.

As you approach the causeway over Copano Bay, you'll see the Sea Gun Resort Motel on your left. The road on the north side of that resort is Park Road 13, which leads to three local sights: Goose Island State Park, the Big Tree (see Rockport, Outdoors & Side Trips), and Our Lady Star of the Sea Chapel (see Rockport, Historic Places).

★ ROCKPORT ★ & FULTON

★★

ROCKPORT

ARANSAS COUNTY SEAT	★	3,686	★	(512)

★★

FULTON

ARANSAS COUNTY	★	725	★	(512)

These neighboring towns have grown together until most visitors now think of them as one. Located on a peninsula that rivals anything on the coast for natural beauty and protected by the barrier of San José Island, both are important commercial and sport fishing centers and increasingly popular resort communities. Perhaps drawn by the rugged beauty of the area, a large number of artists have settled in Rockport and Fulton. Also considered part of this resort area is the small town of Lamar, just north of the Copano Bay causeway.

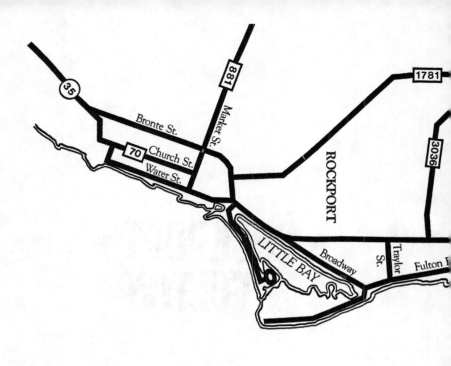

NOTE: Not to Scale

N

Aransas Bay

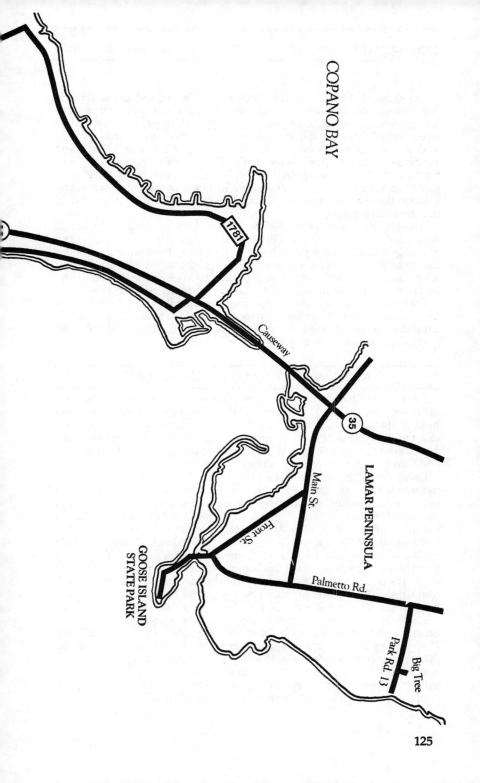

COPANO BAY

1781

Causeway

35

LAMAR PENINSULA

Main St.

Front St.

GOOSE ISLAND
STATE PARK

Palmetto Rd.

Park Rd. 13

Big Tree

The fame of these hospitable, picturesque fishing villages is spreading. Many "winter Texans," who annually make their pilgrimage from colder climes, discovered years ago that here was an inexpensive seaside alternative to driving the extra hundreds of miles to the Rio Grande Valley. Summer vacationers are finding it a simple, rustic area that offers all the amenities for anglers and families. And with a preserve right in town, it is also an ideal place for birdwatchers, especially those who prefer to watch with all the comforts of home immediately available. Despite these lures, however, this area is still relatively quiet, even during the tourist season.

It wasn't always so. From the late 1860s to 1875, packing plants in this area were the destination for huge herds of cattle that were processed and shipped out of the ports here. At that time, the demand from the East was for hides for shoes and leather goods, tallow for candles and soap, and horns for buttons and combs. The meat was almost a by-product. What couldn't be sold to the army was thrown into the bay.

Fortunately for the environment, the packing industry here had an early death. Then these two towns almost died, too. But the people turned their eyes to the bounty in the waters of the bays and the Gulf, and fishing became the major industry.

A GET-ACQUAINTED DRIVING TOUR

Start at the Chamber of Commerce building, between the harbor and Little Bay, on Texas 35. The Cape Cod–style home across from it was built in 1868. From the rear of the Chamber of Commerce building you can see the Rockport Art Center in its blue and white Victorian home near the harbor (see Galleries). If you look to the left you'll see Little Bay and One Mile Beach on Aransas Bay.

Drive down the road to One Mile Beach. This road runs along the peninsula between the two bays. On your left (west) is Little Bay, a small, enclosed bay used for waterskiing and sailing. On your right is Aransas Bay. If you clock it, you'll find that One Mile Beach is almost exactly a mile long. It ends at the small channel that leads from Little Bay to Aransas Bay. Across the channel is Key Allegro. Where the road ends is the usual site of Rockport's annual SeaFair festival. The sandy beach along here is narrow, with the grass growing almost to the water's edge. It's an ideal beach for children (and nonswimmers) since the bottom drops off so gradually that you can go out several hundred yards into the bay before the water is over three or four feet deep.

Retrace your route and turn left to go past the harbor and downtown on Austin Street. The large building marked RYSCO on your left is the Rockport Yacht and Supply. Odds are you'll be able to see them building at least one boat here because this company is a world supplier of crew and supply boats, fishing trawlers, and specialty vessels. Along Austin Street are several good restaurants, art galleries, bookstores, and gift shops (see listings below). Turn right on Market (FM Road 881) and left on Church (FM Road 70, sometimes called Business 35). Going south on Church, you'll be able to see several of the historic homes in town. At 621 is the Mathis Home built in 1869–1870 by T. H. Mathis, one of the founders of Rockport. It is still owned by a descendant. Farther along on Church, the gray house at 712 was built in the early 1890s, and the blue house across the street at 717 was built a few years before that. A block west of this house is a city park where General Zachary Taylor's army camped in 1845 en route to Mexico. There are also several other historic homes on Live Oak and Magnolia streets, which are just east of Church.

Turn right on King. The sprawling white block building with the pond behind it at 501 King is the Simon Michael School of Art and Gallery (see Galleries).

Where King ends at Bronte Street (Texas 35), turn right. Follow 35 past all the small businesses, gas stations, and fast food places back to the Chamber of Commerce building at the harbor. Then continue on along the west side of Little Bay on Broadway. Don't be surprised if you see a large number of unusual birds along here, perhaps even the endangered brown pelican, because this area has been designated the Connie Hagar Bird Sanctuary, named after a well-known Rockport birdwatcher.

At the fork, about three quarters of a mile from the Chamber of Commerce building, stay on Broadway as it goes to the the right toward Fulton Beach. From here on until you cut back to Texas 35 near the causeway, you'll be seeing more and more of the wind-sculptured, leaning live oaks that huddle together in twisted groups lining the road (see Outdoors & Side Trips). On your left, just past the fork, is the Spice o' Life (see Restaurants), and there are several good motels on this stretch of about a mile along Little Bay. From here on you'll also see that almost every motel and private home has a private fishing pier, each one sticking out into the bay like a long, thin finger.

After about a mile you'll go over a small bridge and come to another fork. To the left is Fulton Beach Road. You'll come back to that, but for now, continue on straight over the next little bridge to Key Allegro. The expensive homes on this small peninsula offer examples (good or bad) of just about every beach house style from Thailand to Disneyland. Make a loop through the area and when you're finished satisfying your architectural curiosity, go back over the first bridge and turn right on Fulton Beach Road.

About half a mile down, on your left, is the Fulton Mansion (see Historic Places). A little farther on, on your right, you'll come to Schrenkeisen's and then Charlotte Plummer's, two of the more interesting restaurants in the area (see Restaurants). Next, on your right, is the small Fulton harbor with its commercial shrimp boats and pleasure craft intermixed. The Fulton Fishing Pier is at the north end of the harbor. The Paws and Taws building next to it is used mainly as a recreation center for winter Texans.

Fulton Beach Road goes along the water for about three more miles before it butts into Texas 35. There are a couple of motels along this stretch, but mainly there are private homes and fascinating groups of the leaning trees. Just before the road turns inland you'll pass the Racket Club Condos on your left and then the Kontiki Beach Condos on your right.

Take Texas 35 to the right and go over the causeway that spans the dividing place between Copano Bay and Aransas Bay. Locally this is just called the Bay Causeway, but officially it's the Lyndon B. Johnson Causeway. The ends of the old causeway can be seen next to it. Both are now lighted fishing piers. As you leave the causeway, the Sea Gun Resort is on your right (see Hotels & Motels). This is also the home dock for the *M. V. Whooping Crane*, the excursion boat that runs tours to the Aransas National Wildlife Refuge (see Tour & Guide Services). Make a right just past the Sea Gun on Park Road 13 to the community of Lamar.

As you drive through the grove of trees that line this road, look for Front Street at a fork going off to your right. About a quarter of a mile down Front, on the right, is the parking lot for Our Lady Star of the Sea Chapel and the Schoenstatt Convent (see Historic Places). The pleasant, shaded grounds here are a good place to take a break and relax. When you're ready to go on, retrace your route back to Park Road 13, turn right, and continue. The first major (if you can call it that) crossroad is Palmetto Road. Signs here point to Goose Island State Park to your right and the Big Tree to your left (see Outdoors & Side Trips). The park entrance is just a short drive, but because there is an entrance fee and since this is just a get-acquainted tour, it has served its purpose by making you acquainted with its location—which leaves the turn to the left.

Drive carefully here. Palmetto is not only a narrow road, but the brush and trees come right up to the edge of it, and so do the deer. In fact, unless there's a lot of traffic scaring them away, chances are you'll see some deer along here. Stay on this road when it takes a turn to the right and follow the signs—they're small, but they're there—to the 1,000-year-old Big Tree.

Once again retrace your route back to Texas 35 by the Sea Gun. When you go back over the causeway, keep straight on 35. Along this road you'll pass the airport, a couple of shopping centers, trailer and RV parks, small businesses and fast food places, and wind up back on Broadway at your starting point.

TOUR & GUIDE SERVICES

ROCKPORT-FULTON AREA CHAMBER OF COMMERCE
Rockport
404 N. Broadway (Texas 35) near harbor (P.O. Box 1055)
729-6445 or 729-9952

Open Monday through Friday 9–5, Saturday 9–1
Free
W
   Along with information and the many brochures and other goodies
available here, you can get a sketch map and instructions for a self-
guided driving tour of the major sights of Rockport, Fulton, and Lamar.

M. V. WHOOPING CRANE
Lamar
Sea Gun Resort, Texas 35 just north of the Copano Bay causeway
(Star Rt. 1, Box 85, Rockport 78382)
729-2341
Mid October to mid April Tuesday through Sunday
Adults $15, children under 10 years $10 + tax
   If you want to see the big birds that this boat is named after, the most
comfortable way to do it is on an excursion to the waters bordering the
Aransas National Wildlife Refuge. And, since the cranes nest close to
the water, you'll probably get a better view of them from the deck of this
65-foot vessel than from land in the refuge itself. You can board the boat
at 7:30 a.m., and it leaves for the three-and-a-half-hour excursion at
8:00. Dress warm, bring binoculars and a telephoto lens for your camera
if you want pictures of these rare birds or any of the hundreds of other
bird species (and perhaps even porpoises) you may see on the voyage.
Early reservations are advised, especially from about January on when
all of the whoopers have arrived from their northern home in Canada.
The rest of the year the boat makes occasional moonlight sails and half-
day party fishing trips starting at 7:00 a.m. every day but Monday.

HISTORIC PLACES

THE FULTON MANSION
Fulton
Fulton Beach Road at Henderson (P.O. Box 1859, Fulton 78358)
729-0386
Open Wednesday through Sunday 9–12 and 1–4, last morning tour at
11:30, last afternoon tour at 3:40
Adults $1, children 25¢
W first floor and basement only, lift in rear
   When cattle baron George Fulton built this 30-room mansion in the
mid 1870s, he used his engineering background to make it what we
would now call "state-of-the-art." The exterior style is of the French
Second Empire, but inside, the house has a central heat and ventila-
tion system, hot and cold running water, flush toilets, gas lights, and

crushed seashell insulation. In the larder, water was circulated through concrete troughs to cool perishable food. The mansion has been restored to its original splendor by the Texas Parks and Wildlife Department. An exhibit on the second floor shows the house's deterioration before its restoration, photos of the restoration, and a cut-away of the room's solid underlying construction, which helped it survive several hurricanes. Visitors are requested to wear flat, soft-soled shoes to prevent damage to the carpets and floors. Tours take about an hour, but since you can tour the mansion only with a docent guide, you might call first and see if it's crowded to cut down your waiting time in summer. Groups of 10 or more are requested to book in advance.

OUR LADY STAR OF THE SEA CHAPEL AND SCHOENSTATT CONVENT
Lamar
Front Street off Park Road 13
Open seven days
Free
W

This chapel was built in 1858 of cement made from oyster shells taken from the bay. The motherhouse of the Roman Catholic Schoenstatt Sisters of Mary and their shrine, which is an exact replica of the original shrine in Schoenstatt, Germany, are also here.

MUSEUMS

TEXAS MARITIME MUSEUM
Rockport
Texas 35 at the harbor
To open in 1986

The plan is to open this museum in time for the 1986 Texas Sesquicentennial. Exhibits will stress the maritime history of Texas going back to the days of the Texas Navy and up to the modern fishing and petroleum industries. If it turns out the way it was represented on the drawing board, it will include an observation tower with a completely equipped ship's bridge, a working model of an offshore drilling rig, and art with marine themes. Outside the building there will be a genuine tugboat and a shrimp boat—both fully-equipped, but grounded.

GALLERIES

ROCKPORT ART CENTER
Rockport Harbor, off Texas 35
729-5519
Tuesday through Saturday 10–5, Sunday 2–5, closed Mondays and major holidays

Free
W ramp in rear

This attractive 1890s house set against the background of the colorful harbor could itself be a subject for the artist's brush. Opened in 1984, it is the home of the Rockport Art Association. There is no permanent collection, and exhibits usually run three to five weeks with an emphasis on regional art. The association also offers about 20 three- to five-day workshops a year. These are conducted by well-known artists from all over Texas and the South and cost from $30 to $150.

ESCONDIDO GALLERY
Rockport
300 S. Austin
729-0261

Original paintings in various media by Texas artists. Also some sculpture and limited edition prints.

ESTELLE STAIR GALLERY
Rockport
406 S. Austin
729-2478
W

Estelle Stair is one of the founders of the Rockport Art Association as well as one of the magnets that have drawn so many artists to settle in this area. There are paintings displayed and for sale throughout the spacious 1892 building that houses her gallery, but there is no glitter or fancy lighting. This is a working gallery, so almost half the space is devoted to classes and rental places for artists who want to come in and paint.

SIMON MICHAEL SCHOOL OF ART AND GALLERY
Rockport
510 E. King
729-6233

Simon Michael gave his first one-man exhibition at the St. Louis Museum of Fine Arts in 1923 when he was 18, and he is still painting and teaching. As a result, most of the works that are on display and for sale here are his. However, among the antiques and works by Michael, there are also a number of paintings and pieces of sculpture by other American and European artists. At one end of the gallery is an aviary for his collection of cockatoos, doves, and parakeets, all of which, according to gallery manager Zona Chilcoat, often serve as subjects for both the artist and his students.

THEATER

Rockport is the home of the Repertory Theater of America. The company is comprised of three separate touring units made up of two men and two women each who put on plays for various groups and dinner theaters all over the United States and Canada. They have four different plays in their repertoire each year and rehearse in Rockport between seasons. The RTA usually puts on three or four shows a year in Rockport under the sponsorship of local groups. For information call 729-6274.

SHOPPING

If you want convenience, a couple of strip shopping centers in Rockport are across the street from each other on Texas 35 about a mile north of the Broadway–Fulton Beach Road fork. There you'll find a variety that includes a supermarket, bank, hardware store, cafeteria, travel agency, delicatessen, and even a nightclub (see Clubs & Bars). But Rockport's conversion from simple fishing village to resort has also brought some interesting specialty shops to the area.

BOOKSHELF
Rockport
1005 Concho near Austin St.
729-9801
Closed Sunday and Monday
W

This bookstore sells mostly used books and offers a wide selection of paperbacks and some hardcovers. In other words, a place to find something inexpensive to read at the beach or on a rainy day. There are sections for romances, science fiction, Texana, and other genres, plus children's books and comic books.

THE COLLECTOR AND STEINER STUDIO
Rockport
111 N. Austin
729-9561
W

It's not mass-produced decorative glass, it's sculpture in crystal. That's what Bradley Steiner does. How well he does it is evidenced by the fact that an oriental dragon he sculptured in glass is in the permanent collection of the Corning Museum in Corning, New York. In his shop you'll find some small pieces for as low as $20 or a crystal rattlesnake for $2,400. If you think that's high priced, consider that Steiner worked longer than five weeks to make that rattlesnake. Why? Because he uses a rare and dangerous technique called lamp-working in which he subjects special glass rods to such intense heat and pulling and twisting that only 2 percent of his work survives the process without shattering.

GALLEY GADGETS
Rockport
1012 North St., near Austin St.
729-4229
A small shop crammed full of kitchenware: cookware in French porcelain, aluminum alloy, and enamelware; fine cutlery; and all the little essentials the gourmet cook can't do without.

MOONSHELL
Rockport
409 S. Austin
729-7155
W
It looks like a well-stocked gift shop, but it's really a potpourri. Mixed among the usual gift items and jewelry is the unusual, like a longhorn fireplace set, a large leather-covered wood parrot on a perch, hand-woven Peruvian rugs, and Amish-made mailboxes. There's also a section called "Grandma's Corner," stocked with a den of children's bears and other toys.

PAT'S PLACE
Rockport
504 S. Austin
729-8453
W
The books in this bookstore are displayed on a rolltop desk, rocker, chest, and other old furniture as well as on standard shelves. The emphasis is on Texana and bird, fish, and wildlife field guides, but there's a good selection of other hard- and softcover books, including those on the best-seller lists. Adding to the browsing ambience is a section of the store called Driftwood Cay Designs devoted to needlepoint.

SHELLCRAFT BY BETTY
Rockport
1048 N. Magnolia (north end of street)
729-1710
There are lots of shell shops around selling mass-produced items, but this one is a one-woman show. Betty Gifford works in her own home with shells from all over the world to make each piece distinctive. To find her house, turn north on Magnolia off Texas 35 and go almost to the dead end. There's no sign, but you shouldn't have any problem spotting the house on the east side of the street because everything from the mailbox to the porch is decorated with shells. She sells shell magnets for under a dollar, shell Christmas trees for about $150, and shell lampshades for up to $200. Betty's almost always at home working in winter, but she's also enthusiastic about fishing, so call before you come in summer.

SUNDIAL
Rockport
105 S. Austin at North
729-3373
W

The main stock of this store is carpet, drapes, and wall coverings. But there is also a large selection of woven straw products and rattan and wicker furniture that caters to the informal coastal look. Watercolors and paintings by local and regional artists are for sale.

SWISS CHOCOLATE VILLA
Rockport
Texas 35 north of fork with Fulton Beach Rd. (H.C.R. Box 358K, Rockport 78382)
729-8009
W

This heaven for the chocolate cravers is owned by a couple who came from Switzerland by way of East Africa and Kenya. Marie-Claire Herzog's background in candy-making goes back to her grandfather who was one of the founders of a Swiss chocolate factory that has been in operation since 1898. Her husband, Peter, ran a safari business in the Serengeti National Park and learned the chocolate cooking secrets from her. Now they both turn out European-style candies in their shop kitchen. In addition to producing the rich chocolate that sells for an average of $2 a quarter pound, they also make dietetic chocolate and sell other imported and specialty candies, such as jelly beans from Germany.

OUTDOORS & SIDE TRIPS

ARANSAS NATIONAL WILDLIFE REFUGE
See Seadrift to Rockport

THE BIG TREE
Lamar
Take Texas 35 north across Copano Bay Causeway to Park Rd. 13 then east to Palmetto Rd. and follow signs

This Texas Champion Live Oak has branches as big around as many other large tree trunks. But then it has had a longer time to grow than most other trees since estimates on its age start at 1,000 years and go up. It sits majestically in a grove of its much smaller and younger relatives, like a gentle giant watching the world go by. It is said that this tree was both a council place and execution site for the Karankawa Indians, and it was also used as a hanging tree when white men later dispensed frontier justice. Not the biggest tree in the state—that title goes to a bald cypress in East Texas—it is still impressive with a trunk that measures 35 feet in circumference, a height of 44 feet, and a crown that shades a large area with its 89-foot spread.

FULTON BEACH
At Fulton Harbor
Open at all times
W variable

A small swimming beach next to the harbor and public fishing pier. Restrooms at the fishing pier.

GOOSE ISLAND STATE RECREATION AREA
Lamar
Take Texas 13 across Copano Bay to Park Rd. 13, then east to recreation area entrance (Star Rt. 1, Box 105, Rockport 78382)
729-2858
Open seven days 8–8 for day use, all times for camping
Autos $2
W + but not all areas

This 307-acre park starts on the mainland and then extends out onto a peninsula and several small islands between Aransas Bay and St. Charles Bay. Possible activities include birdwatching—the great blue and Louisiana heron and the snowy egret are among those frequently seen here—and nature studies, boating, fishing, swimming, and water-skiing. Day-use facilities include a 1,620-foot lighted fishing pier, boat launch, restrooms and shower units, a recreation hall, and 23 picnic sites. There are 102 RV sites in the park—45 on the waterfront with water and electrical hookups and 57 in the wooded area. Twenty-five tent camping sites are located in the woods. Reservations are accepted for all sites, which cost $3–$5 a night.

THE LEANING TREES
Mostly along Fulton Beach Road

This is just about the last outpost of the woodlands going south along the coast, and the live oaks here appear to be hanging on in a fight with the elements for survival. Sculpted into bent and twisted shapes by the constant winds off the Gulf, at times they look like creatures bowing gracefully toward the earth and, at other times, more like a Disney version of a witch's forest.

ROCKPORT BEACH
North of Rockport Harbor off Texas 35
Open at all times
Free
W variable

Immediately behind this mile-long swimming beach on the shallow waters of Aransas Bay is Little Bay, which offers a free boat launch, waterskiing, and fishing. The seashell band shell near the entrance is used for entertainment. Rockport Beach is adjacent to the Connie Hagar Wildlife Preserve, which is the winter home of thousands of birds. Site of Rockport SeaFair (see Annual Events).

KIDS' STUFF

GO KARTS
Rockport
Texas 35S, just south of Rockport on road to Aransas Pass
729-8259
Open 10–10 or 11 in summer season only, closed Monday
Not just go-karts, but also bumper boats, mini-golf, game room, and snacks.

SPORTS & ACTIVITIES

Birdwatching

See Aransas National Wildlife Refuge, the *M. V. Whooping Crane*, and Goose Island State Park.

Over 400 different species of birds have been spotted in the Rockport area. For in-town birding try the Connie Hagar Preserve around Rockport's Little Bay. The Chamber of Commerce has a free, self-guided tour with sketch map of the best places for birdwatching in the area.

Boating

For boat launching sites contact the marinas or the Chamber of Commerce or look in the Yellow Pages. Small boating is excellent in all the area bays. The Gulf is just a short trip away.

Fishing

Bay fish include redfish, speckled trout, catfish, flounder, and drum. Depending on how far you go out and the season, Gulf catches may include red snapper, tarpon, ling, king mackerel, and a number of top-water game fish. You can bay fish from the jetty at Rockport, the fishing pier for guests of the motel you're staying in, the Fulton public pier, or the state's Copano Bay Fishing Pier. If you want to fish from a boat and don't have your own, party boats are available. The *Pisces* (729-7525) is a 58-foot party boat that makes two four-hour trips daily, morning and afternoon, from Rockport Harbor for bay fishing. It costs $25 for adults and half price for under 12. The *Lucky Day* (729-4037), a 65-footer, operates out of the Sandollar Marina on Fulton Beach Road. It also makes a four-hour trip morning and afternoon, plus occasional night trips. Fare is $15 each with half price for under 13. The *M. V. Whooping Crane* also runs fishing parties during the summer when it's not making the excursions to the wildlife refuge (see Tour & Guide Services). For charter boats and guides for both bay and offshore fishing, check the Yellow Pages. Another excellent source of information about fishing, hunting, and guides is Larry Hoffman at Larry's Tackle Town in Rockport Plaza on Texas 35 north of Rockport (729-1841).

COPANO BAY STATE FISHING PIER
Texas 35N at the causeway, approximately five miles north of Rockport
Memorial Day through Labor Day: open at all times; rest of year: open seven days from dawn until early afternoon
Adults $1 per fishing apparatus; children over 13, 50¢
W

Waste not, want not. That seems to be the excellent policy followed by Texas Parks and Wildlife Department when it comes to salvaging the old remains after a new bridge or causeway is built. Once again Parks and Wildlife has turned an old causeway scheduled for destruction into lighted fishing piers. In this case they saved pieces on both sides of the bay. Snack bar, bait and tackle shop, restrooms on both sides. Boat launch on south side.

Hunting

Duck hunting is excellent, which is to be expected since this is the winter home for many waterfowl and other game birds. For information contact the Chamber of Commerce. You can also get information on hunting and guides from Larry's Tackle Town (see Fishing, above).

Jogging

Try Rockport's One Mile Beach. Off-season this is usually traffic free anytime, but during the summer the best time is before the morning beach-goers arrive.

ANNUAL EVENTS

March

FULTON OYSTERFEST
Fulton Park at harbor on Fulton Beach Road
First weekend in month
Free
W variable

Oyster shucking and oyster eating contests are just two of the activities in this two-day event. It also includes a Saturday morning parade, kiddie rides, arts and crafts booths, and lots of food booths including those selling—guess what?

July

ROCKPORT ART FESTIVAL
Near the Art Center at the harbor, just off Texas 35
Early in month, usually weekend nearest to July 4th
Free
W variable
There are usually well over 100 booths set up in tents at which artists from all over the Southwest display and sell their works created in a variety of media. The two-day event is sponsored by the Rockport Art Association.

October

ROCKPORT SEAFAIR
North end of One Mile Beach at Little Bay, just off Texas 35
Weekend preceding Columbus Day
Free
W variable
A land parade and a boat parade, water shows, arts and crafts booths, crab races, a beauty pageant, a Gumbo Cookoff, and a variety of exhibits are always on deck to entertain visitors. But as far as most fair-goers are concerned, that's all just background. The biggest draw remains the fresh shrimp, oysters, and fish cooked up and sold by local civic groups.

HOTELS & MOTELS

The major chains haven't invaded yet, so this remains an area of Mom-and-Pop motels. At times it resembles a large fishing camp slowly entering the resort age. Don't expect anything luxurious, but plenty of clean, no-frills accommodations are available at reasonable prices. Many of these motels grew like Topsy as owners reinvested their earnings to improve a room here or add one there. So it's not unusual to find a 20-room motel in which no two rooms are alike. Some have tiny bathrooms, some commodious ones. Some rooms are small enough to give a large person claustrophobia, while others appear big enough to host a football team.

A few motels are furnished throughout with the same motel-modern furniture, but in most cases, the owners gathered the furniture piece by piece, like the rooms, and uniformity is not the order of the day. Many near the water don't have rugs, since the sand and debris tracked in by fishermen and beach-goers can be cleaned off bare linoleum more easily.

This all adds up to one caution: ask to see what's available before you register.

Rates for a double in summer:

   $: under $30
   $$: $30–$40
   $$$: over $40

HARBOR LIGHTS COTTAGES
Fulton
Fulton Beach Road across from harbor pier (P.O. Box 513, Fulton 78358)
729-6770
$$$; No cr.
W

The 12 units are set up so they are almost like small, two-bedroom apartments with kitchenettes. Carports, pool, but no room phones.

OCEAN VIEW MOTEL
Rockport
1105 E. Market at Water (office)
729-3326
$–$$$
W

This is really three small motels with a total of 30 units scattered along the waterfront but under one management. Three of the units are apartments, and 22 have kitchenettes. Two private, lighted fishing piers extend 600 and 1,000 feet into Aransas Bay. Swimming pool.

ROCKPORTER INN
Rockport
813 South Church (Business 35S)
729-9591
$$
W

A little away from the water and downtown, this small motel has an unhurried, cool look about it. The exterior is a refreshing yellow and white, and each of the 11 units has a tiny patio with wrought-iron furniture. Four units have kitchenettes, and three are two-bedroom apartments. Pool. Lighted fishing pier available.

SANDOLLAR RESORT
Texas 35, approximately five miles north of Rockport (Star Rt. Box 30, Rockport 78382)
$$
W

This combined motel and trailer park is located in a live oak grove that runs from Texas 35 to Fulton Beach Road. There are 76 full hookup RV spaces on the highway end ($10 a day) and 49 motel units, including 20 with kitchenettes and two small suites, on the beach road end. Some of the second story units overlook both the pool and the bay. One of the two restaurants is among the motel units and the other is across Fulton Beach Road on the bay. Lounge, two swimming pools, children's playground, lighted fishing pier, and marina.

SEA FOAM RESORT MOTEL
Fulton
Fulton Beach Road, next to Fulton Mansion (Star Rt. 1, Box 16, Rockport 78382)
$$–$$$; No cr.

The 26 units all have kitchenettes. Pool, rec room (winter only), lighted fishing pier, boat launch, and boat slips. No room phones. There are four RV slots with full hookups.

THE SEA GUN RESORT
Lamar
Texas 35 just north of Copano Bay causeway, approximately nine miles north of Rockport (Star Rt. 1, Box 85, Rockport 78382)
729-2341
$$$
W

Pink is the dominant color here on both the motel buildings and the cottages among the green lawns and palm trees. There are 26 motel rooms, including four with kitchenettes, and usually about 6 to 10 one- and two-bedroom cottages for rent. The others are privately owned or part of timeshare programs. In addition to the Sea Gun Restaurant and Reef Club lounge, there is a liquor store, tennis court, heated swimming pool, lighted fishing pier, and a marina that is also the home of the *M. V. Whooping Crane*, the boat that runs excursions to the Aransas National Wildlife Refuge (see Tour & Guide Services).

SPORTSMAN MANOR
Fulton
Fulton Beach Road (Star Rt. Box 35, Rockport 78382), also access from Texas 35
729-5331
$$–$$$
W

With 62 units—all have kitchenettes—this is one of the larger motels in Fulton. Two large suites overlooking the bay go for about $65 a day. Pool, lighted fishing pier, and rec room with pool table.

SUN TAN MOTEL
Rockport
1805 Broadway
729-2179
$–$$$
W

The 23 units include several two-room cottages that rent on the high end of the scale. All rooms have large kitchenettes. Its location on the edge of the bird sanctuary at Little Bay makes this a good place for birdwatching in the winter. Pool and lighted fishing pier. No room phones.

SURF COURT MOTEL
Rockport
1204 Market at Water
729-3249
$–$$$
W

The more expensive rooms here are six cabanas with kitchenettes, built out over the water with porches facing the bay. There are also 18 regular motel rooms, of which 13 have kitchenettes. Pool and lighted fishing pier.

SURFSIDE MOTEL
Rockport
1809 Broadway
729-2348
$$
W

Its location on Little Bay makes this 36-unit motel another fine spot for birdwatching in the winter. And in the summer, an added attraction on the motel's fishing pier is paddle boats you can rent to cruise in this protected bay. Eighteen of the units have kitchenettes, and there's a pool and playground.

TROPICS MOTOR HOTEL
Rockport
1212 Laurel off Broadway
729-6379
$$
W

This two-story motel is located near the Chamber of Commerce and across from Rockport Beach. Nine of the 29 units have kitchenettes, and the pool is heated. The Duck Inn restaurant is next door, and several other downtown restaurants are within easy walking distance (see Restaurants).

VILLAGE INN
Rockport
503 N. Austin on Texas 35
729-6370
$$–$$$
W

This is an example of the local motels' growth in bits and pieces. There are 28 units in a cluster of eight buildings. These range from simple motel rooms to four large two-bedroom apartments. Pool with small cabana. Its location on the edge of downtown (on the street behind the HEB Superstore) makes it an easy walk to Rockport Harbor and Beach and many restaurants and shops.

OTHER ACCOMMODATIONS

The condominium boom has hit. Fortunately no high rises spoil the simple beauty of this area, at least not yet. But a number of condo apartments, townhouses, and individual homes can be rented for one night or longer. The smallest apartment in most of the condos in this area is a two bedroom. Some have a minimum rental of two nights. Weekly and monthly rates are usually substantially lower.
Summer rates for a two-bedroom for one night are:
  $: under $75
  $$: $75–$100
$$$: over $100

KEY ALLEGRO RENTALS
Rockport
1800 Bayshore Dr.
729-2333
$$
W

Key Allegro itself is an island marina community of luxury homes that encloses the north and east sides of Little Bay. Some of these homes are available for short-term rental at higher rates, but over a hundred two- and three-bedroom condo and townhouse units on Fulton Beach Road just off the island also are for rent. Many of these overlook the water, and some include docking space for a boat. Pool, tennis courts, beach.

KONTIKI BEACH CONDOMINIUMS
Fulton
Fulton Beach Road (Star Rt. 1, Box 330, Rockport 78382)
729-4975 or in Texas 1-800-242-3407
$$
W

These condos are located on Aransas Bay at the north end of Fulton Beach Road where it turns west to Texas 35. The 62 units available include one, two, and three bedroom. All have large decks overlooking the water. Some have boat slips. Pool, tennis court, and beach.

RACQUET CLUB CONDOMINIUMS
Rockport
Texas 35 approximately one mile south of causeway (H.C.R. Box 69, Rockport 78382)
729-0880
$$-$$$
W

These condos are really on Fulton Beach Road. The entrance is through the adjoining Rockport Racquet and Yacht Club on Texas 35, but most of the 35 or so units in the rental pool are on Fulton Beach Road. Two pools, four lighted tennis courts, lighted fishing pier, and marina.

Some local realtors also handle condo and vacation home rentals. One of these is the Landlord Resort Property Management at 729-0223 or in Texas at 1-800-242-1071.

RESTAURANTS

Putting on the Ritz

SCHRENKEISEN'S
Fulton
Fulton Beach Road at Broadway
729-3332
Open seven days, lunch and dinner
Reservations recommended
$$$-$$$$; Cr.
W

From the outside it looks like a small town seafood house, but inside is a comfortable restaurant that rates with the top ones on the coast.

Texas Monthly magazine recognizes this by consistently including it in
the listings for Corpus Christi, which is more than 30 miles away and
has its own share of fine restaurants. The lighting is soft but directed so
you can read the menu and see what you're eating. There are fresh
flowers on the tables, and the service is friendly and caring. The cuisine
is classic continental, and the chef does not believe in shortcuts. The
menu includes such seasonal delicacies as fresh Alaska salmon poached
in white wine, truffled pheasant with wild rice, and rack of spring
lamb–tarragon for two. Bar.

Dinner for Two

SPICE O' LIFE
Rockport
1405 Broadway
729-4044
Lunch and dinner; dinner only on Saturday, closed Sunday
Reservations suggested on weekends
$$$; MC, V
W ramp
   The chef-owner, Kirk Von Brueckwitz, has cooked all over the world,
and the menu shows it. Among the listings of the usual American
dishes you'll also find *Gazpacho Andalusia, Australian Orange Roughy,
Filet of Flounder Française, Bengal Duck Curry,* and *Sauerbraten.* The nau-
tical theme, accented by polished brass items like a ship's searchlight, is
pleasantly done. The dining room looks out on Little Bay and Key Alle-
gro. Bar and large selection of imported beers.

American

CORKY'S
Rockport
503 Austin
729-5161
Open 6 a.m.–9 p.m. (10 p.m. in summer), closed Tuesday
$–$$; MC, V
W
   Cora (Corky) Agler opened this no-frills, downtown restaurant close
to 40 years ago, and it's still going strong. The menu includes a little bit
of all the standards, but the favorite seems to be the seafood. Among
the reasons the customers keep coming back are her all-meat crab cakes,
large portions of everything, and the fact that the kitchen doesn't use
prebreaded seafood, which means more fish and shrimp and less
breading. Wine and beer.

KLINE'S CAFE
Rockport
106 Austin, just south of the harbor
729-8538
Open 5:30 a.m.–9 p.m., closed Thursday
$–$$; No cr.
W

There's a display of Shorty and Gloria Kline's collection of old clocks on one wall and good old-fashioned cafe cooking in the kitchen. Steaks and chops, fried chicken, sandwiches, seafood, and Mexican dishes are all on the menu, and they come with homemade bread or corn bread. Wednesday night features all-you-can-eat fried fish. Beer.

Seafood

CHARLOTTE PLUMMER'S SEAFARE
Fulton
Fulton Beach Road and Cactus at the harbor
729-1185
Open seven days 7 a.m.–9:30 p.m.
No reservations taken
$$; AE, MC, V
W+

If you have three or more in your party you might want to try Charlotte's Seafare Special, which includes shrimp steamed in beer, fish, oysters, crab cakes, hush puppies, potatoes, and salad—all served family style for $11 each. The specialty is broiled and baked seafood. Frying is pretty much confined to some of the seafood platters, and then it's done better than most. There are also steaks and burgers, including oyster, fish, crab, and shrimp burgers. Extras are homemade biscuits, rolls, and cheesecake, plus a good view of the boats in Fulton Harbor. Breakfast selections are hearty and inexpensive. The clientele can crowd up at times, and when this happens the line is comfortably set up across the street at Charlotte's Party House. There you can munch on light snacks until they call you for a table. Wine and beer.

DUCK INN
Rockport
701 Broadway (Texas 35) across from south end of Little Bay
729-6663
Lunch and dinner, closed Monday
$$; MC, V
W

The same family has operated this restaurant since 1960 carrying on with the recipes from the original owner who opened it right after

World War II. Nothing extraordinary on the menu, which is heavily weighted toward seafood but includes steaks and chicken, but the old recipes seem to hold up well. Lounge.

OLIVER'S SEAFOOD HOUSE AND OYSTER BAR
Rockport
207 Austin
729-4550
Lunch and dinner, closed Monday
$$; MC, V
W

There are Louisiana-style oyster or shrimp po'boys (lunch only), seafood gumbo, and other recipes with a Cajun flavor. There's also an oyster bar. A section on the menu offers fried seafood, but all of the dinner seafood entrées are broiled, boiled, or baked. Bar.

CLUBS & BARS

DALLAS
Rockport
Texas 35N and Bay Wood Dr., Harbor Oaks Village Shopping Center
729-1424
Cover ladies night and weekends

An uptown Country and Western dance hall and bar with a canopied entrance, carpet on the floor, neon wall decorations, and upscale prices to match. Dress code says no gimme hats, T-shirts, or tennis shoes— this last because they lift the wax off the oak dance floor. The music is provided by a DJ. It's definitely not for "kickers." Steaks, hamburgers, and snacks are available.

OFFBEAT

BIG FISHERMAN RESTAURANT
Rockport
FM Rd. 1069, take Texas 35 six miles south toward Aransas Pass, then west about half a mile on 1069
729-1997
Open seven days, lunch and dinner
$–$$; MC, V
W+

The expression "that place is a zoo" fits this seafood restaurant. The Stevens family probably has as many birds and other animals in the glassed-in aviaries and cages scattered throughout their several dining rooms as they have plates stacked up in their kitchen. Almost every room in this rambling building contains a collection of such birds as toucans, macaws, and peacocks. Some people call it the Restaurant of the Five-Hundred Parakeets. And for a change of pace, there are also a couple of young mountain lions. Take a tour of all the rooms to see the whole show, then go out back to see the menagerie there. Seafood, steaks, and chicken are all on the menu. The food isn't extraordinary, but it is reasonably priced; and eating is something to keep you occupied while you watch the bird and animal antics. Bar.

TO ARANSAS PASS

To continue down the coast, take Texas 35 south 11 miles to Aransas Pass.

★ ARANSAS PASS ★

Despite its name, this city is not located on the pass between Mustang and San José islands (the entrance to Corpus Christi Bay) but on the more sheltered mainland facing the pass. The main industries in the area are shrimping and commercial and sport fishing, tying the city directly to the sea. Almost every port on the Texas coast has its shrimp fleet, but Port Aransas' central location on the coastal bend has helped make Conn Brown Harbor here the home port for one of the largest fleets on the coast, about 500 Gulf and bay shrimp trawlers.

The city had an unusual beginning in 1909 when T. B. Wheeler and his partner, Russell Harrison, son of former President Benjamin Harrison, decided to hold a lottery to sell their 12,000 acres on Red Fish Bay, which included the townsite of Aransas Pass. Interest was high because the U.S. government was about to finance the dredging of a port in this area, and it was assumed Aransas Pass would be chosen over Corpus Christi or Rockport. Lottery tickets were sold for $100 each, and special trains brought buyers from as far away as Kansas and Nebraska for the drawings. The nicest thing about the lottery was there were no losers. Only 6,000 tickets were sold for 6,000 lots. The chance part consisted of

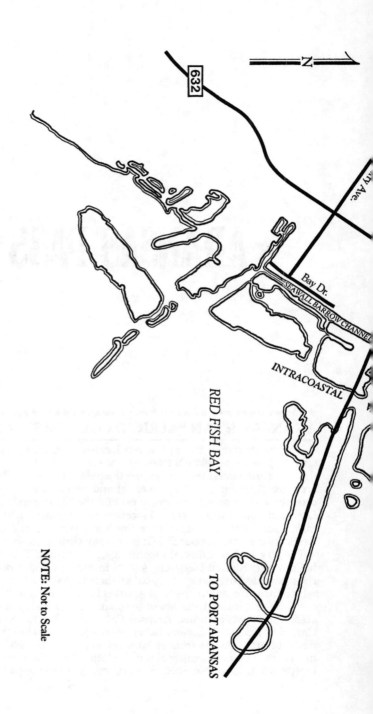

NOTE: Not to Scale

RED FISH BAY

TO PORT ARANSAS

INTRACOASTAL

SEAWALL BARROW CHANNEL

Bay Dr.

632

150

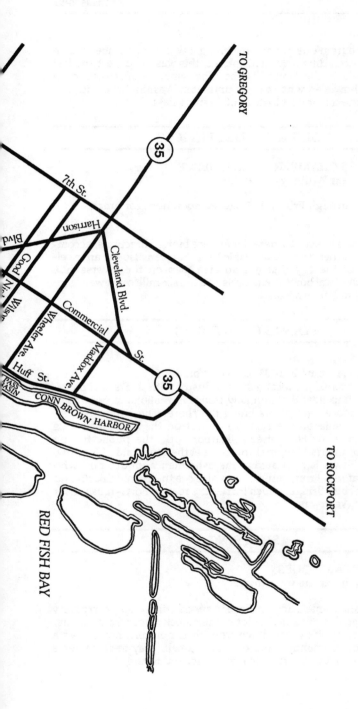

TO GREGORY

35

7th St.

Harrison

Blvd

Cleveland Blvd.

Good N...

Wilso...

Commercial

Wheeler Ave.

Maddox Ave.

St.

35

Huff St.

PASS
BASIN

CONN BROWN HARBOR

RED FISH BAY

TO ROCKPORT

151

drawing a name from one pot and matching it with a lot number drawn
from another. According to local historians, this was the largest and last
land lottery held in the United States. The winners must have been
disappointed, however, when a short time later, Washington decided to
make Corpus the major port instead of Aransas Pass.

TOUR & GUIDE SERVICES

ARANSAS PASS CHAMBER OF COMMERCE
452 Cleveland near Whitney (Texas 35)
758-2750
Open Monday through Friday 9–5, closed noon hour for lunch
Free
W

Inside information about where the fish are biting, directions, accommodations, and other data are available here. You can also get an excellent free map of the city that has an area map on the reverse side
showing both the local boating channels and the six-mile causeway leading to the ferry to Port Aransas.

POINTS OF INTEREST

CONN BROWN HARBOR
North end of city; from Texas 35, turn east on Staff

This is the center of the local fishing industry with docks and moor-
ings for the shrimp fleet that annually brings in millions of pounds of
shrimp to the processing plants lining the shore. The harbor is sheltered by a peninsula on the east. To go out on the peninsula, take
Bigelow from Staff or Huff streets. Harbor Park, the public fishing
piers, and the Seamen's Memorial Tower are at the south end of Bigelow.
The Memorial Tower is dedicated to the fishermen from this port who
lost their lives at sea. From here you can also see the Turning Basin and
the Dale Miller High Bridge, which carries the road to Port Aransas over
the Intracoastal Waterway.

SHOPPING

DANIEL'S DEN ANTIQUES
315 E. Wilson, under the watertower
758-5189

Chic and Diana Daniels don't believe in specializing—they carry "any
antique or collectible of value." A lot of their stock comes from "winter
Texans" who bring the items down from their northern homes. As a
result, this shop is crammed full of mostly small, easy-to-carry items
such as antique silver, linens, china, art glass, and toys.

OUTDOORS & SIDE TRIPS

WELDER WILDLIFE REFUGE
Sinton
Take Texas 35 to U.S. 181 northwest to Sinton approximately 27
miles, then U.S. 77 northeast about 8 miles
364-2643
Tours Thursday only at 2:55, closed holidays
Free
W variable

This refuge is unique in that it is a working ranch and is said to be the largest privately endowed refuge in the world. More than 400 species of birds have been seen on the 7,800-acre sanctuary, which was established by provisions in rancher Rob Welder's will. Deer, bobcats, javelinas, and other wildlife also roam the area. Tours normally take about two and a half hours and include a visit to portions of the preserve and the museum. When they say be there at 2:55 on Thursday, that's exactly what they mean. The gates are opened at that time, everyone waiting drives in (you tour in your own car), and then at 3:00 the gates are closed and not opened again until the end of the tour. Groups of 15 up to 72 can arrange tours at other times by calling the tour director. The best time to take the tour is in winter after the northern birds migrate to the preserve.

SPORTS & ACTIVITIES

Birdwatching

In addition to the Welder Wildlife Refuge in nearby Sinton (see Outdoors & Side Trips), birdwatching for shorebirds is usually good to excellent along the Texas 361 causeway to Port Aransas, especially in winter.

Fishing & Hunting

You can get a line in the water from dozens of places along the shore, the jetties, or the public piers at Harbor Park on the end of the Conn Brown Harbor peninsula (see Points of Interest). The catch here may include flounder, redfish, speckled and sand trout, and drum. Or, if you prefer Gulf fishing, it's just six miles away through the pass. Out there wait tarpon, red snapper, warsaw, mackerel, ling, and many other species. Duck hunting in the bay and the marshes is also good. See the Yellow Pages or call the Chamber of Commerce for information on charter boats and guides for bay and deep-sea fishing and duck hunting.

ANNUAL EVENTS

SHRIMPOREE
Roosevelt Stadium on Texas 35 near 7th, and downtown
Weekend in middle of October
Free
W

There are champion shrimp eaters here, so if you want to win the shrimp eating contest you'd better be prepared to eat at least three and a half pounds in thirty minutes. Or, if you're not into competitive gobbling, there are stands where you can buy more routine portions of this tasty crustacean or other fresh seafood dishes. Other events during this weekend include an outhouse race, men's sexy leg contest, beauty pageant, parade, street dance, concerts, contests, and a fun run.

RESTAURANTS

BAKERY CAFE
434 S. Commercial, downtown
758-3511
Opens 5 a.m., serves all meals, closed Sunday
$–$$; MC, V
W

It started out as a bakery in 1926 and slowly expanded into a small restaurant that became widely known in the area for simple, good food at reasonable prices. Seafood, steaks, chicken, and the like are all on the menu—plus fresh bakery goodies.

CRAB-N
Texas 35, approximately four miles north
758-2371
Open seven days for dinner only
$$–$$$; Cr.

You can drive here or tie your boat to the landing and go in for dinner. This restaurant overlooks one of the canals in the City by the Sea, a housing community on the Rockport road that's built on canals. Seafood is the major item, some of it with a Cajun touch, but there are also steaks on the menu. Lounge.

LA COCINA
Texas 35, approximately four miles north
729-4934
Open seven days, lunch and dinner
$–$$; Cr.
W

Most of the dishes are Tex-Mex, but there are also American-style steaks, fish, and chicken on the menu. You can, for example, order red snapper with spicy Veracruz sauce, Spanish rice, and salad from the Tex-Mex section of the menu or fried Gulf fish with potato and salad from the American section. Lounge.

UNCLE SLICK'S EATERY
Texas 35, approximately half a mile north
758-9941
Lunch and dinner, closed Sunday
$$; Cr.
W ramp
　　The dining room in this Cape Cod house is decorated with everything from old children's books and toys to quilts, and the lower walls are covered with corrugated tin. Somehow that combination works to make a bright and pleasant dining environment. The menu emphasizes seafood—try the entrées with Veracruz sauce—but also includes a variety of other choices.

HOTELS & MOTELS

TROPIC MOTEL
412 W. Harrison (Business 35), downtown
758-5333
Double $30; AE, MC, V
W
　　Tree-shaded grounds surround 16 units, some with kitchenettes. Small pool and cable TV.

OFFBEAT

THE BIG FISHERMAN
　　See Rockport, Offbeat

WALLACE MARINE BOOKS
452 S. Commercial, downtown
758-5946
W
　　Want a book on making ships in bottles or other books, charts, or publications concerning life at sea? Wallace's will either have it in stock or know where to get it. This all started when Eugene Wallace, who is an active commercial sailor, couldn't find the marine books he wanted in any bookstore. So he and his wife, Yolanda, started their own. Their large store looks a little barren when you first walk in, but actually it's well stocked. While there are many technical books on such topics as marine license preparation courses, yacht designing, and seamanship, there are also log books, books on sport and commercial fishing, books on scuba diving and other water recreation, and novels with nautical themes or settings for both children and adults.

ARANSAS PASS TO PORT ARANSAS

Texas 361 hops from island to island on the six-mile causeway that connects the mainland city of Aransas Pass with Port Aransas, which sits on the northern shoulder of Mustang Island. But it stops just short of its target, and you have to take a free ferry across the Corpus Christi Ship Channel for the last thousand yards.

From the mainland, the road first goes across the Intracoastal Waterway and then crosses Red Fish Bay and runs parallel to the ship channel from Aransas Pass, the city, to Aransas Pass, the water passage between Mustang and San José Islands that leads to the Gulf. So, on your left as you drive, you will probably see shrimpers and other boats keeping you company as they head out to sea and others heading in to their berths on the mainland. Since the causeway is built on islands, there are plenty of places to pull off and fish—and plenty of anglers who do it.

About two miles from the ferry, there is a warning sign. This one doesn't warn about tides or undertow or anything so dramatic. It says that if the line of cars waiting for the ferry is backed up to that point you can expect to wait 120 minutes to board. Then it politely notes that if you turn around and take the land route looping through Corpus Christi and out Mustang Island from the southern end to Port Aransas, you should be able to make it in about 80 minutes. If you think that sign is pessimistic, be aware that during the annual invasions of high school and college students—spring break and Easter holiday—the wait has been much longer than two hours. But at other times, the wait usually is about 15 or 20 minutes, and even on a summer weekend, the line rarely backs up to that 120-minute sign.

If you look off to the left as you approach the ferry slip, you should be able to see the Aransas Pass Lighthouse on the flats of Lydia Ann Island. Built in the mid 1850s, the lighthouse was partially destroyed in the Civil War and rebuilt in 1867, making it the oldest surviving structure in the area. Nature had the last laugh when it destroyed the usefulness of the light, which had withstood the fury of several hurricanes, by eroding away the land from the tip of Mustang Island on the south side of the pass and shifting it at a rate of more than 200 feet a year to the tip of San José Island on the north side. This erosion was stopped with the building of the jetties, but by then the pass had moved a mile south, and the light was abandoned since it could no longer guide ships to the safe passage.

The industrial area around the ferry slip on Harbor Island includes the Brown and Root facility, on the right side of the road, where they construct the steel framework for offshore oil well drilling rig platforms. These usually weigh about 8,000 tons, but in 1983 they put out a 27,000-ton giant.

The first commercial ferry started operating here in the mid 1920s, carrying six cars a trip. The present free ferries, operated by the Texas Department of Highways and Transportation, don't carry many more than that—only nine cars each—but there are six ferries, and at least one is in service 24 hours a day, every day. At peak times all six hustle back and forth in such a continuous stream they almost seem to be hooked in tandem. And flying over or bobbing in their wake, like sight-seers watching the human comedy, are the pelicans, cormorants, laughing gulls, and other shorebirds.

★ PORT ARANSAS ★

Located on the northern tip of Mustang Island, one of the chain of barrier islands that protects the coastal mainland from Galveston to the Mexican border, Port Aransas is actually one shoulder of Aransas Pass, the outlet to the sea for Corpus Christi. Fishermen, including President Franklin D. Roosevelt, discovered this rustic fishing village many years ago, but it's only within the past 20 years or so that the developers have discovered it. The result is a condominium boom that is changing the face and character of the only town on Mustang Island. Right now it is a town with a split personality—an unsophisticated fishing camp with its bait shops and run-down taverns intermingled with luxury condo buildings and some of the better restaurants on the coast. While fishing is still a principal lure, the number of visitors who come to luxuriate in the sun and the surf on its miles of sandy beaches has been going up— and up.

The Karankawa Indians were the first real settlers here. They lasted through unfriendly visits by the Spanish, French, and pirates but finally succumbed to the onslaughts of the Comanches and the Texan colonists. Lots of people passed through, but the first recorded permanent residents arrived in the mid 1850s. These were an Englishman,

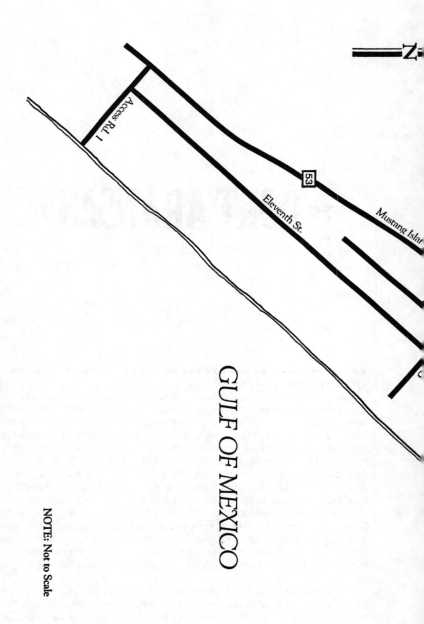

GULF OF MEXICO

Access Rd. 1

Eleventh St.

Mustang Island

53

NOTE: Not to Scale

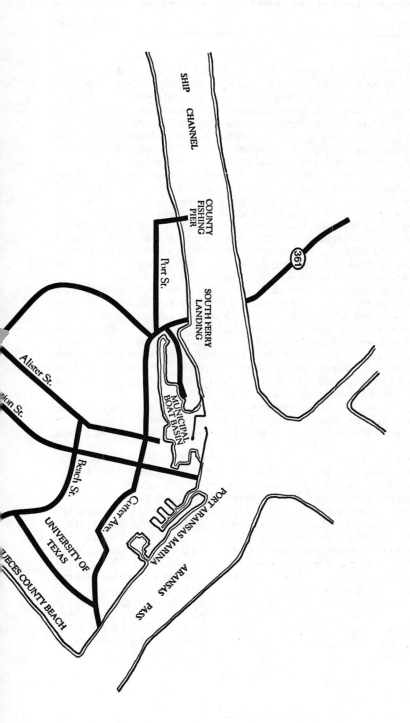

SHIP CHANNEL

COUNTY FISHING PIER

Port St.

SOUTH FERRY LANDING

361

Alister St.

ion St.

MUNICIPAL BOAT BASIN

Beach St.

Carter Ave.

PORT ARANSAS MARINA

UNIVERSITY OF TEXAS

ARANSAS PASS

UECES COUNTY BEACH

R. L. Mercer, and his family. They fished, raised cattle, and operated a small dock and warehouse for servicing visiting ships. They were soon followed by others, and a tiny community was established. In 1870, a New Yorker bought St. Joseph's Island (now known as San José), and many of the settlers left there and moved to join Mercer's settlement.

In addition to fishing, the turn-of-the-century villagers also made money catching and selling sea turtles. Some of these weighed up to 500 pounds and were shipped to market live, on their backs.

The rock jetties, which stopped the southward advance of Aransas Pass, were built in 1909 and 1910. The base rocks were hauled in from a quarry near San Antonio, and the huge granite blocks, which can be seen above the water, came from Granite Mountain near Marble Falls.

During this time the village had several names, including Tarpon, named after the popular sport fish that was prime catch in the area. It wasn't until 1912 that its present name became official. (Unofficially, most locals shorten it from Port Aransas to Port A.) Shortly after that, in 1919, a hurricane all but leveled the town, but it was rebuilt.

For a long time the only way to get to Port A was by boat or train. If you wanted to drive on the island you had to take your car on the car-train, a railroad flatcar pulled by a truck mounted on train wheels. The train ran from the town of Aransas Pass to the ferry at Harbor Island. The ferry then transported the cars across to the island where a ramp was lowered and the cars drove off through the shallow water to the beach. When the new port at Corpus Christi killed business at Port Aransas, the railroad paved its roadbed with asphalt, planked the bridges, and opened a toll road.

One of the reasons anglers love Port A is the many fishing tournaments held here. The first one, called the Tarpon Rodeo, took place in 1932. Of the 22 contestants, about half were women, and they won most of the prizes.

The island was really opened up for visitors when the Mustang Island Highway was built in 1954, linking the town with Corpus Christi. The present causeway from the city of Aransas Pass to the ferry landing was opened in 1960, and the first condo soon followed in 1965.

There's no university on the island, but at spring break in March and on Easter weekend, the number of college students in Port Aransas usually is higher than the total enrollment of the University of Texas. This influx is so overwhelming that the Chamber of Commerce keeps track of which schools break when and notifies its members who then can decide to either capitalize on the invasion or board up and hide out. It's not unusual for 100,000 students to hit at one time for one big, unruly beach party—quite a mob for a town with a population of a little over 2,000. So unless you enjoy long, long lines for ferries, restrooms, and everything else, and fender-to-fender parking on the beach, thousands of blaring radios, beer brawls, and general rowdiness, plan your visit for other times.

TOUR & GUIDE SERVICES

PORT ARANSAS AREA CHAMBER OF COMMERCE
421 W. Cotter near Cut-Off Rd.
749-5919
March until Labor Day, Monday through Saturday 9–4:30; rest of
year, Monday through Friday 9–4:30
Free
W

If you want to set yourself an impossible task, try coming up with a
question about Port Aransas that Lanette Nolte, the Chamber of Commerce manager, can't answer. Lanette's accomplishments as a one-
woman tourist bureau have been recognized by the Texas Tourist Development Association with its annual Texas Hospitality Award. The
Chamber of Commerce office is one of the first buildings on your right
as you drive off the ferry. Information on fishing, local events, where to
eat and sleep, and brochures, maps, and seafood recipes are just a few
of the things you can get here.

WHOOPING CRANE BOAT TOURS
Fisherman's Wharf, off Cotter St.
749-5760
December 26th through March, call for hours
Adults $15 + tax, children half price

This five-hour trip aboard the *Wharf Cat* to see the whoopers at the
Aransas National Wildlife Refuge also includes sightseeing and birdwatching along the way as well as a commentary on the history of Port
Aransas, Aransas Pass, and Rockport. In the summer, sunset boat
cruises run every evening from 7:30 to 9:00 ($5).

POINTS OF INTEREST

CIVIC CENTER HISTORICAL EXHIBIT
Cut-Off Rd. at Ave. A
749-4111
Monday through Friday 8–5
Free
W +

This visual recap of the history of Port A includes a model of the town
in the old days when the lighthouse and the Tarpon Inn were in their
prime. The original lens from the lighthouse is also here, complete except for a chip knocked out of it when the Confederates tried to blow up
the lighthouse to prevent its capture by Union hands. There is also a
collection of objects discovered by beachcombers, not just seashells, but
many fascinating items washed up from shipwrecks.

UNIVERSITY OF TEXAS MARINE SCIENCE INSTITUTE
End of Cotter St., at the beach
749-6729
Visitors Center open Monday through Friday 8–5, organized tours
available for groups of 12 or more by calling ahead
Free
W+

From its start in an unofficial research lab in a fisherman's shack on
the beach back in 1935, the UT Marine Science Institute has grown into
an 80-acre complex on the northeastern corner of Mustang Island. The
research interests at the institute delve into every science connected
with the sea from algal physiology to zoology. A good way to do a self-
guided tour is to start in the downstairs exhibit area in the Main Research Building (ask directions at the Visitors Center). Here you can see
a short audio-visual show explaining the work of the marine lab. With
this as background you'll have a greater understanding of the exhibits in
the halls, which detail the various projects the staff and students are
working on. The Visitors Center exhibits include seven marine aquaria
demonstrating marine environments ranging from the upland marshes
to offshore reefs. UTMSI has two boats: the 80-foot *Longhorn* used for
offshore research throughout the Gulf and the Caribbean and the 57-
foot *Katy* used for inshore work. When not at sea, they're berthed at the
boat basin on the channel.

SHOPPING

THE COTTAGE
104 E. Cotter
749-6087

Many of the paintings and pottery for sale in this gift shop are produced by the co-owners, Kathy Sayre and Toni Hair, but there are also
works of other Texas artists. The tiny shop, set up in a cottage next to
the Tarpon Inn (see Offbeat), is filled with fine watercolors, pastels,
prints, ceramics, stained glass, shell art, and ironwood carvings.

OUTDOORS & SIDE TRIPS

The Beaches

The Gulf side of Mustang Island is one long beach, and you can drive
on much of it. The width varies, but at Port Aransas, at low tide, it is
wide enough to almost lay out a football field between the water's edge
and the dune line. Aside from the facilities provided their guests by the
motels and condos, the only other beach facilities on the north end of

the island are in Port Aransas Park (749-6117) near the jetty. This Nueces County park has restrooms, showers, a fishing pier, food concessions, and some RV beach camping sites with electric and water hookups (permit required).

POINT PARK
First road to the left off ferry
This city park on the channel includes the city marina, public boat launching ramp, and a free fishing pier. It's also a good place to stop and watch the big ships slicing through the waters of the ship channel and the pelicans and other birds that spend their days near the ferry landing.

SAN JOSÉ ISLAND
Jetty boat at Woody's Boat Basin
749-5252
Approximately every hour from 6:30–5
Adults $7, children $4, group rates available
This is a private island, but the area near the jetty and the beaches is open to the public. No facilities, just miles and miles of white sand beach for swimming, fishing, picnicking, surfing, beachcombing, or just enjoying nature, unsullied and uncrowded. It takes only about 15 minutes to go over on the jetty boat, and your round-trip ticket is good for any return trip during the day. If you're going to be there a while, take drinking water along.

KIDS' STUFF

TEXAS TWISTER WATER SLIDE
Corner of Alister and Ave. G
749-5666
$3 half hour, $5 all day
If the beach gets dull, this is a good place to take the kids and let them wear themselves out, happily climbing up and sliding down.

SPORTS & ACTIVITIES

Birdwatching

See Tour & Guide Services, Whooping Crane Boat Tours. The laughing gulls, cormorants, terns, pelicans, and herons are all full-time residents of Port A and Mustang Island. All seem to have a fondness for the ferry and jetty area, but you can also see them on the beach away from the crowds. Migrating birds, including ducks, are usually most numerous in the spring.

Fishing

Port Aransas boasts that it's the place "where they bite every day." And if you want to try to prove or disprove that boast, you can do it in the surf, on the jetties or piers, in the bay, or offshore. Close-in catches may include redfish, flounder, speckled trout, skipjack, and drum. The J. P. Luby Pier at Point Park and the Ancel Brundrett Pier at the north end of Station Street, two city piers on the ship channel, are free. To fish off the Horace Caldwell Pier on the Gulf in the Nueces County Park costs fifty cents per person and a dollar per pole.

The deep-sea boats usually go out either about an hour's distance offshore to the oil rigs, which provide artificial reefs for the fish to gather around, or to the natural reefs that mark the drop-off of the continental shelf about two hours away. The deep-water catches often include tarpon, king, mackerel, ling, marlin, and red snapper. Both party boats and charters are available at Deep Sea Headquarters, 416 W. Cotter, 749-5597; Dolphin Docks, 300 W. Cotter, 749-4188; and Fisherman's Wharf, 900 Tarpon, 749-5760. All these boats are located on the ship channel near the ferry. Party boat rates start at $20–$25 for a four-hour trip. Charter boats for bay and offshore are also available at Woody's Sports Center, 114 W. Cotter, 749-5252. Charter rates start at about $325 for eight hours in a 25-footer.

There are a number of fishing tournaments during the summer. These include several for billfish and several for king mackerel, at least two for women anglers only, and the week-long Deep Sea Roundup (see Annual Events).

Hunting

The vast expanse of tidal flats and marshland makes Mustang Island another prime stopping place for migrating ducks and other game birds during the winter. For up-to-date information on hunting and guides, call the Chamber of Commerce.

ANNUAL EVENTS

DEEP-SEA ROUNDUP
Marina and other locations
One week early in July
This is the successor to the Tarpon Rodeo that started in 1932. When the tarpon ran out they switched to the Roundup. So if you go back to tarpon days, this is the oldest fishing tournament on the Texas coast. As such, it draws contestants from all over. Champions are crowned for the biggest catch on light tackle, heavy tackle, and several other categories. There are also activities ashore to round out the week. For information call the Chamber of Commerce.

HOTELS & MOTELS

Most of the available accommodations on Mustang Island are in condominiums. Port A has several small motels, only one of which is a chain operation.
Summer rates for a double:
  $: under $40
 $$: $40–$45
$$$: over $45

BEST WESTERN TEXAS REBEL
Sand Castle Drive off 11th St.
749-4105
$$$
W

This three-story motel is right on the beach. The 50 units consist of 26 regular motel rooms and 24 suites ($80 a night). There is a pool, and a small restaurant serves breakfast and lunch.

DOUBLE BARR COTTAGES
415 Ave. G, near Station
749-5582
$$; V, MC
W

The 12 old cottages have been refurbished. If you can do without all the extra motel-type amenities, this is one of the best bargains in town since each cottage has two bedrooms, a small kitchen, and bath. There are also two trailer houses with the same accommodations.

DRIFTWOOD MOTEL
300 Ave. G, near Alister
749-6427
$$$
W

This motel has grown so it now has 63 units in a new two-story building and 12 units in the old one story. Although the new may look better, one advantage of the old units is their kitchenettes. Heated pool and hot tub.

TROPIC ISLAND
303 Cut-Off Road, approximately two blocks from the ferry
749-6128
$$
W

This small complex includes 16 motel rooms, 22 small one- or two-bedroom apartments ($$–$$$), and 41 RV spaces with three-way hookups that go for eight dollars a night. Heated pool.

OTHER ACCOMMODATIONS

There are well over 30 condominium projects in Port A now—and more on the way. All are on the water and about half of them have units that are entered in the rental pool by the owners. Many of these require minimum stays of three nights, but they also offer weekly and monthly rates that are substantially below the daily rates. Most accept credit cards. Condos in which a two-bedroom is the smallest unit are noted. Daily rates in summer for a one-bedroom condo are:

$: under $80
$$: $80–$95
$$$: $96–$110
$$$$: over $110.

BEACHHEAD
1313 11th St.
749-6261
$$

Not a single building, but a complex of five clusters of buildings, nestled in the dunes behind the beach, with eight one- and two-bedroom apartments in each building. About 30 units are available in the rental pool. The exterior looks weather-beaten, but inside the apartments are bright. Each apartment has a balcony from which you can see at least a patch of the Gulf. The main building, which includes the office and recreation room, was originally a hunting and fishing lodge. Covered parking, two tennis courts, heated pool, and boardwalk to the beach.

CHANNELVIEW
631 Channelview Dr., east of the Coast Guard Station
749-6649
$$
W elevator

You can watch the ships in the channel from all the units, and those guests with a view to the east can also see the jetties and the Gulf. The 20 or so units for rent range from one to four bedrooms. Covered parking, lighted fishing pier (only private one in town), and pool. Boat slips available at marina next door.

CORAL CAY
1321 11th St.
749-5111
$$$$

Located on the beach, the more than 60 units in the rental pool go from efficiencies up to three bedrooms. Downstairs units have patios; upstairs have balconies, most of which offer a good view of the Gulf. Two pools and four tennis courts (two lighted).

THE DUNES
1000 Lantana
749-5155
$$$$
W

This is luxury living in a high rise on the beach. All the apartments have private balconies with a view of the Gulf. From the upper floors you can see across the channel to the far reaches of San José Island in one direction and to Padre Island and the Corpus Christi skyline in the other. There are about 50 one- to three-bedroom apartments available for rent, all spacious and tastefully decorated. Heated pool with covered lanai, two tennis courts, boardwalk to the beach. The building adjoins and overlooks the county beach park, which has a lighted fishing pier. Landscaping includes 900 pilings rescued from the old railroad trestle.

EXECUTIVE KEYS
Access Rd. 1A, off Park Rd. 53 (P.O. Box 1087, Port Aransas 78373)
749-6272
$$$; two bedroom
W

About 50 of the 70 units in the eight wooden two-story buildings are available for rent. These include efficiencies, two- and three-bedroom apartments, and two-story townhouses. All have a private balcony or patio, but even though the complex is on the beach, not all units have a Gulf view. Pool, picnic areas with grills, game and recreation room, and boardwalk to the beach.

GULF SHORES
Park Rd. 53, approximately seven and a half miles south of ferry landing (P.O. Box 1298, Port Aransas 78373)
749-6257
$$$; two bedroom
W

There are about 40 units in the rental pool, all two bedroom and all with balconies overlooking the beach and the Gulf. Its away-from-town location and relatively small size make it a good choice if you're looking for peace and quiet. Pool with wading area, two tennis courts.

ISLAND RETREAT
700 Island Retreat Court, off 11th St.
749-6222
$
W

These 106 rental units offer condo living at economy rates. This is another low-rise complex of two- and three-story buildings clustered together at the beach. The one- to three-bedroom apartments all have a patio or balcony, most with view of the Gulf. Pool and recreation area with a boardwalk to the beach.

SEA GULL
Park Rd. 53, approximately eight miles south of ferry landing (P.O. Box 1207, Port Aransas 78373)
749-4191
$$$
W

Only about a third of the 105 units in this 11-story building are in the rental pool. These range from one to three bedroom, and all are large, pleasantly decorated, and have balconies that look out on the Gulf. Its location, well away from Port A, means the beach is rarely crowded. Heated pool with large sun deck, tennis court.

SEA ISLE VILLAGE
1129 11th St.
749-6281
$
W

Built on the beach in 1965, this was the first condominium complex on Mustang Island. Now, more than twenty years later, the well-kept units in this low-rise complex are among the island bargains for condo renters. The 45 units in the rental pool include one-, two-, and three-bedroom apartments. All have a patio or balcony with a view of the Gulf. Pool and recreation area.

SUNDAY VILLAS
1900 11th St., near Ave. G
749-6408
$$; No cr.

This unusual complex consists of 16 circular, one-story, furnished houses built atop one-story platforms. In a way, they resemble a modern version of an African village of huts on stilts. Thirteen of the two- and three-bedroom houses are available for rent. Each has a large porch facing in toward the central pool, recreation area, and covered parking underneath. The complex is only about a block from the beach, but because there's private property between the complex and the beach, you must go by road to get there.

RESTAURANTS

Dinner for Two

MERI'S MALIBU
Park Rd. 53 and I St.
749-5533
Open seven days for lunch and dinner

$$$; MC, V
W
   The house specialties on the menu show imagination, and the chef
prepares them with flair. Beachcomber's Trove, for example, is made
with lobster chunks and shrimp sautéed in white wine with fresh
mushrooms in a garlic cheese sauce. Seafood, steaks, and veal are also
available. The dining room ambience is pleasantly subdued and condu-
cive to conversation. But if you want more of the beach resort flavor,
there's a pool and patio outside with less fanciful dishes available. Bar.

American

OLD MOSS HALL
320 N. Alister
749-5816
Open seven days for all meals
$–$$; MC, V
W
   The daily luncheon specials, served Monday through Friday, are a
favorite with the locals. The menu includes seafood—sautéed, broiled,
or fried—steaks, barbecue, sandwiches, and there's an all-you-can-eat
fish fry every day. Beer and wine.

Delicatessen

SEABREEZE DELI
811 Tarpon, opposite the Tarpon Inn
749-5571
Open 9 a.m.–9 p.m., closed Sunday
$; No cr.
W
   Variety is the real spice of life in this tiny treasure—breakfasts with
everything including muffins made from scratch, thick sandwiches
made to order from the many tempting cold cuts and cheeses in the
display case, seafood quiche, Greek salad with feta cheese, soups, and
blue plate specials that change daily. Eat at one of the tables crammed
inside, at the even tinier sidewalk cafe, or take out. Beer—a wide choice
of imported and domestic—and wine.

Mexican

BUENOS DIAZ
224 E. Beach St. at Station
749-4772

Open seven days for all meals
$; MC, V
Hot, but not too hot, Tex-Mex dishes include a variety of taquitos.
American food, too. Take out. Beer.

Seafood

BLUE MARLIN
414 W. Cotter, near the ferry
749-4726
Lunch and dinner, closed Tuesday (and Wednesday in winter)
$$–$$$; Cr.
W
The menu covers the waterfront—and the farm. In the gourmet section you'll find lobster stuffed with crabmeat dressing and Steak Diane,
but there is also fried catfish, chicken-fried steak, and u-peel-m-shrimp.
The blue decor with brass trim gives a nautical feeling reinforced by the
view of the harbor and Point Park Marina from the window seats and
the outdoor patio. Bar.

SEAFOOD AND SPAGHETTI WORKS
709 Alister at Ave. G
749-5666
Dinner only, closed Mondays in winter
$$; Cr.
There is a silver lining under every oil spill. Jay and Sunny Kenigsberg
proved it. They started out with a geodesic-domed game room and fast
food place next to their water slide. When the Mexican oil spill hit a few
years ago it scared off the tourists, and the Kenigsbergs saw ruin on the
horizon. What to do? Ah!—open a good restaurant. Sunny could cook,
and neither of them was tainted by restaurant experience. So they
slowly developed a restaurant they themselves would patronize. The
result is an oasis of creative fish cookery with all the familiar regulars
prepared as they should be, plus surprises like shrimp sweetened with
brandy, amaretto, and fresh oranges. Also available are steaks and, of
course, pasta, pizza, and other Italian dishes. And if you're a recipe
collector, ask about Sunny's cookbooks. Bar.

TARPON INN RESTAURANT
200½ E. Cotter, behind Tarpon Inn
749-6434
Dinner only, closed Monday, closed from after Labor Day through
February
$$–$$$; MC, V
W
The catch of the day is usually an excellent choice here because almost
all the seafood comes fresh from local waters. And you can have it

broiled or fried. Steaks are also on the menu. Beer and wine. Breakfast and lunch are served right next door in the Silver King Bar and Grill where you can eat outdoors on the deck. You can also get pre- or after-dinner drinks there since, as the name says, there's a full bar (W+).

THE WATERFRONT
730 Tarpon, at the Wharf
749-4294
Dinner only, closed Tuesday and Wednesday in winter
$$–$$$; MC, V
Blackened redfish is one of the specialties in this casual seafood house. The heart of the menu is freshly caught local fish. When fried in slivered almond butter, it's listed as the Crunchy Catch. Or you can get the catch of the day broiled in white wine and butter sauce. Steaks also available. Bar.

OFFBEAT

THE TARPON INN
200 E. Cotter
749-5555
$$$
This is the third generation of this inn. The original, built in 1886, was destroyed by a fire, and its replacement went in the 1919 hurricane. But the present building is a true survivor, lasting through hurricanes and annual tourist invasions since 1925. The 26 rooms in this barracks-like, two-story building may range from wearing-out to worn-out, but putting up with the inconveniences is worth it if you like to live a little bit of history and sample life in the 1920s or 1930s. And somehow, as you sit on the wide upstairs veranda, cooled by a gentle breeze off the Gulf and watching the world go by, the slow pace of life in that bygone era seems appealing. Perhaps more than for its endurance, the inn is known for the collection of tarpon scales that decorate its otherwise unpretentious lobby-office. Each scale is marked with the fisherman's name and home-town and the date the tarpon was caught. The prize signature in this collection—not exposed like the others but kept under glass—is that of President Franklin D. Roosevelt, dated May 8, 1937. The tarpon, once so numerous in area waters it was hard to keep it off the hooks, is now rarely seen. But its namesake, the Tarpon Inn, lives on.

★★★
MUSTANG ISLAND

PORT ARANSAS TO CORPUS CHRISTI
Mustang is one of the few barrier islands with a good road that you can drive from one end to the other. As you head south from Port Aran-

sas, the beachfront condominium projects get sparser. But the developers are busy, and each year seems to see the open spaces shrink as another high rise goes up.

MUSTANG ISLAND STATE PARK
Park Rd. 53, approximately 14 miles south of Port Aransas
1-749-5246
Open seven days 8–10 for day use, open at all times for camping
Autos $2
W+ but not all areas

This 3,704-acre park is almost equidistant from Port Aransas and Corpus Christi—about 14 miles either way. It slices a cross section of the island between Corpus Christi Bay on the east and the Gulf on the west. There are 48 multi-use camping sites with hookups ($6 a night), and primitive camping ($3) is permitted on the beach. Other facilities include 100 shaded picnic tables in the day-use area, restrooms, showers, an RV dump station, and a self-guided nature trail. Fishing from the jetties at the north end of the park is generally excellent. Surf fishing is also permitted. With open beaches for miles on both sides, this beach is rarely crowded, so it remains pretty much in its natural state. For information or camping reservations, write Box 326, Port Aransas 78373.

★ CORPUS CHRISTI ★

NUECES COUNTY SEAT ★ **231,999** ★ **(512)**

The tourist bureau used to call this the "Sparkling City by the Sea" in tribute to the shimmering reflections of the sun and city lights on Corpus Christi Bay. Not too long ago, however, the bureau decided that slogan did not reflect the image of the growing sophistication of this tourist mecca, so now they call it the "Texas Riviera."

The change is fitting. The sparkle is still there, but the sleepy coastal resort city is now a memory. Corpus, as it is called by most people, is in the midst of a boom. Not a runaway boom like Houston—the city fathers have taken steps to keep it under control—but a boom that has brought an increasing number of fine restaurants, inviting clubs, world-class hotels, and facilities for the arts that are far and away better than what one would expect in a city this size.

As a result, both residents and visitors have discovered that there is more to the good life than just sun, sand, and the sea. Agreed, these are all still prime ingredients, but they've also found that fun can be had after the sun goes down.

Sophistication hasn't spoiled Corpus, it simply has made it more attractive. Corpus continues to offer the casual living of a country town

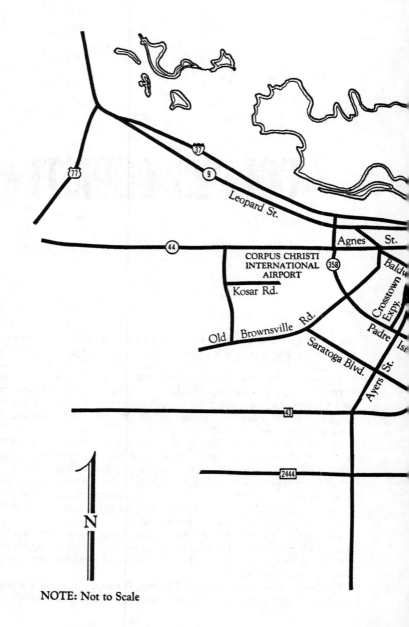

NOTE: Not to Scale

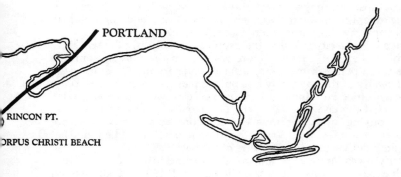

PORTLAND

RINCON PT.

ORPUS CHRISTI BEACH

CORPUS CHRISTI BAY

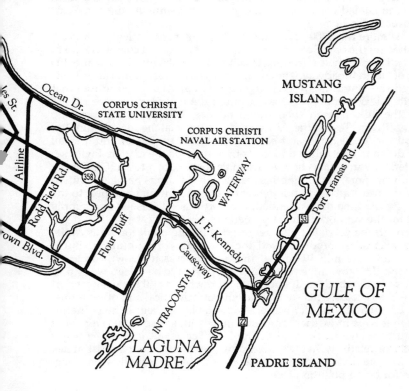

MUSTANG ISLAND

Ocean Dr.

les St.

CORPUS CHRISTI STATE UNIVERSITY

CORPUS CHRISTI NAVAL AIR STATION

Airline

Rodd Field Rd.

358

Flour Bluff

WATERWAY

Port Aransas Rd.

53

own Blvd.

J. F. Kennedy

Causeway

INTRACOASTAL

GULF OF MEXICO

22

LAGUNA MADRE

PADRE ISLAND

while providing all the quality living and cultural attractions that can make city life so enjoyable. Casualness has always been a way of life here. Perhaps because formal attire was too annoying in a subtropical climate before the joys of air-conditioning. Or perhaps casualness is just typical of those who enjoy outdoor life by the sea. Whatever the reason, with the exception of the more expensive restaurants and "first nights" at the symphony, Corpus is still not a dress-up town.

Corpus is also a city in which the people obviously love the sea. Why else would they put a large picture window in their art museum so visitors could pause from looking at man-made art and look out at the natural beauty of the bay? Why else build a marina close enough to the downtown office buildings so boat owners can walk down and relax with a sail at the end of a day? Why else would the city go to the expense of buying up all the undeveloped shoreline property to ensure that no more condos, homes, or other obstructions could be built that would limit both access to and views of the bay?

The city owes its unusual and religious name to that bay and to a Spanish explorer, Alonso Álvarez de Piñeda. In 1519 Piñeda discovered what he reported as "a beautiful bay." Since the discovery occurred on the religious feast day honoring the body of Christ (*Corpus Christi* in Latin), he named the bay after that feast day. Eventually the name carried over to the city.

It was more than 300 years later that a permanent settlement was established on the bay. Colonel Henry L. Kinney brought colonists here in 1839 and established a frontier trading post near what is now the 400 block of North Broadway. The colony grew, but it wasn't until after Texas entered the Union that the colony attracted any attention to fuel that growth. Mexico and Texas had disputed the boundary between them since the Texans won their independence. Mexico said it was the Nueces River; Texas, the Rio Grande. After statehood, Washington backed the Texas claim and sent General Zachary Taylor and a small army down to wait while diplomats tried to settle the matter. Taylor set up a tent city in what is now Artesian Park near downtown. Diplomacy failed, war came, Taylor and his men left; but Corpus had been put on the map, and supplies continued to be shipped through the port to the army. By the time the war ended, the port was established as a supply point for the support of military operations in the West.

Through the years the port became a shipping point for Texas cattle, crops, and other products; and the town grew up around it. But it wasn't until the mid 1920s that the real impetus to growth occurred when the U.S. government decided Corpus should be a deep-water port and sent in the dredges that turned it into what is still the deepest port on the Texas coast. This soon attracted petrochemical and other industries. Fortunately, the city was already established before the refineries and other large industrial complexes moved in, so the plants were built on the ship channel instead of the bay. The result is that the major plants are relatively hidden from downtown and other tourist areas. And, in spite of this industrial base, the city has repeatedly won recognition for being pollution-free.

The city itself sits like a quarter moon hugging the bay, and the city limits include more water than land area. From the air it looks long and thin, as if everyone was trying to build as close to the water as possible. On the north is Corpus Christi Beach, a small resort area. Immediately behind and south of this beach, on both sides of the Harbor Bridge, is the bustling port. South of the bridge, along the bay, is downtown with a concentration of major hotels as well as the cultural center at Bayfront Plaza and the business district. (Much of the business district is actually on a bluff behind the hotel area and is often locally referred to as "uptown.") To the west of downtown is the industrial area. The major residential, shopping, and small business section of the city is south of both downtown and the industrial area. And farthest south are Padre Island and the Gulf.

Ah! Padre Island. There are beaches all along the Texas coast, but it isn't until you reach the beaches of Padre that everything starts to look as it would in a travel poster. Only the north (near Corpus) and south ends of the 113-mile island are developed. Between them is more than 80 miles of the Padre Island National Seashore, which many consider the most beautiful stretch of natural beach in the country.

Named for Padre Nicholás Ballí, who received it as part of a Spanish land grant about 1800, this long barrier island was once a graveyard for ships driven onto its shore by storms in the Gulf. The most famous of these shipwrecks occurred in 1553 when a 20-ship Spanish fleet loaded with gold and silver stolen from the Aztecs was struck by a hurricane, and many of the galleons broke up on the island. But don't rush out to dig for the Aztec treasure. Laws prohibit private salvage operations on the island. In fact, it's against the law to even carry a metal detector.

Cooled by Gulf breezes, the average summer temperature is in the 80s and 90s. Those same Gulf breezes bring warm air from the south in the winter and keep the average temperature in the 50s and 60s. Unfortunately, those breezes also bring moisture, so the humidity is usually high except during the fall.

A GET-ACQUAINTED DRIVING TOUR

First, you need to realize that Corpus is basically a long, narrow city, built back from the bays—it's approximately 20 miles from downtown to Padre Island—so driving distances can get stretched out. Next, you need to be familiar with the numbers of the major highways in the city because many of the direction signs at critical turn-offs give those numbers rather than the street names. For example, South Padre Island Drive, a main street, is frequently listed on the signs as Texas 358. (It's also often cited as S.P.I.D.)

Now that you know those tidbits of information, the first stop and the starting point for this get-acquainted tour is the Convention and Visitors Bureau at 1201 N. Shoreline at Power Street (see Tour & Guide Services). You might want to park on Power Street facing away from the shore, since that's the way this tour begins. After you've gone inside and gathered up all information, brochures, and maps you think you might need for your visit, then drive west on Power to N. Chaparral and turn right. A short way down, on your left in the old Irishtown district, is Heritage Plaza, a restoration project that includes the Sidbury House (see Historic Places) and several other Victorian homes. A little farther on, on your right, is Bayfront Arts and Science Park and Bayfront Plaza, which contains the Harbor Playhouse, the Convention Center (home of the Corpus Christi Symphony), the Corpus Christi Museum, and the Art Museum of South Texas.

Continue on to the end of Chaparral and park at the observation point on the ship channel, under the bridge. From here you can see up and down the ship channel and a little of the port, which is the deepest on the Gulf of Mexico and the ninth largest in the nation in terms of cargo handled. On the opposite shore is another, larger observation point with a different view of these sights, plus a good view of downtown Corpus. You can reach that observation point by crossing the bridge and doubling back to it.

Parking is often hard to find in this area, so if you can't find a spot at the observation point, try in the bayfront park or plaza. Even if you don't want to visit the museums now, it's still worth walking around before going on with your tour.

When you're ready to continue, drive through the plaza back to Shoreline. Then drive up Shoreline past the tourist bureau and make a right to follow the signs to Texas 181 to Sinton and Rockport. This will take you over the Harbor Bridge. As you approach the top rise of the bridge, you can see the north shore facilities of the port on your left and Corpus Christi Beach—still called North Beach by many locals—along the bay on your right. In the 1930s this area was famous for its gambling casinos, amusement parks, and hotels. But then it fell on hard times, and it wasn't until the city and the Army Corps of Engineers rebuilt the badly eroded beach in 1978 that the area came back to life. Take the first exit. The resort area here is bordered by the beach and Texas 181. There are motels, condos, restaurants, and a couple of small parks over here, but the main attraction is the more than a mile of beach. You can drive around and see the entire area in a short time.

If you want to see more of the port, try the observation platform under the bridge, or from there, go under the highway and pick up Navigation Boulevard, which runs behind the port for about four miles to the lift bridge. (From here you can either retrace your route back to Texas 181 to resume the tour, or continue on Navigation across the ship channel to I-37, then take it back downtown to Shoreline and pick up the tour route there.)

Go back across the Harbor Bridge (Texas 181). At the top of the rise going this way you can see the south shore of the port on your right and Bayfront Plaza and downtown on your left. Get off at the Shoreline exit, just over the bridge. Follow the signs back to Shoreline Drive and turn right.

On your right are the bayfront skyscrapers as well as some smaller motels and restaurants. And on your left for the next couple of miles will be the seawall. More than two and a half miles long, this 14-foot-high seawall was designed by sculptor Gutzon Borglum and was built just before World War II (1939–1941), while he was still putting the finishing touches to his most famous project, Mount Rushmore. What is unique about the seawall is the steps down into the water. The steps are wide enough to sit—or doze—on, and many people working in the nearby buildings find it the ideal place to have a brown-bag lunch, feed the gulls and other shorebirds, or just relax and watch the ripples in the water as the boats glide by. The sidewalk atop the seawall is up to 20 feet wide, making it a favorite track for joggers, roller skaters, and bicyclists, as well as strollers.

A number of the palm trees along here, and throughout the city, were killed by the 1983 freeze. Fortunately, some survived, and others were replaced, so Shoreline is still a palm-lined boulevard.

A short way down, in the center island, is a statue of two marlin hurling themselves into the air. Called "Wind in the Sails," it is by noted sculptor Kent Oldenburg. Just past this is the yacht basin with its three man-made peninsulas, the T-Heads and L-Head, jutting out into the bay. In addition to being the marina for the boats of the local power and sail enthusiasts, the yacht basin is also the home of some luxury yachts, including the *Celika S*, which was originally built for R. E. Olds, the man who gave his name to the Oldsmobile division of General Motors. According to local tour guides, the *Celika S* was once owned by Al Capone. Sightseeing boats, fishing party and charter boats, and the local shrimp fleet—where you can buy fresh fish and shrimp right off the boats—are also berthed here. Or if you prefer your meals already prepared, the city's two floating restaurants—Captain Boomer's and The Wayward Lady—are permanently docked here, plus the land bound Lighthouse Bar and Grill (see Restaurants).

As you leave the skyscrapers behind, Shoreline Drive going south bends away from the the water just about at City Hall. As you drive along here, on your left, you'll see Exposition Hall and next to it the dome-roofed Memorial Coliseum. Everything from arts and crafts shows to school graduations, wrestling matches, and private parties are held here. (If you want to know what's happening while you're in town, call 884-8227 or check with the tourist bureau.) The helicopters in the park on your left have been mounted like statues to recognize the importance of the army's helicopter maintenance facility located on the grounds of the nearby Naval Air Station (NAS). During the Vietnam War, there was a steady stream of "choppers" shipped here from that country for major work and then shipped back across the Pacific and into combat again. Today this facility continues to do major repairs on helicopters shipped in from army bases all over the world.

At McGee Beach, the division of Shoreline ends, and it becomes a two-way called Ocean Drive, which continues along the bay all the way to the NAS, just north of the causeway to Padre Island. After you pass Spohn Hospital on your right, Cole Park will be on your left. The amphitheater in the park is the scene of concerts under the stars on Sunday evenings in the summer. There is also a municipal fishing pier.

For the next few miles, Ocean Drive becomes a residential area of manicured lawns and expensive homes. The architectural styles are eclectic with a tiled-roof, Spanish-style home next to a colonial or a Southwestern adobe neighboring a Tudor. If you like to look at mansions, watch for Hewit Drive on your right as you leave Cole Park. Turn in here, and you'll see some particularly large and beautiful homes as you follow it on its loop around and back to Ocean Drive.

Continuing on, note the elaborate 51-bell carillon in front of the First Baptist Church in the 3100 block of Ocean. Hymns are played on it at noon and in the evening, and it is also used to give carillon concerts.

Don't expect to see much of the bay along here. The condos and homes block much of the view, but there are several interspersed vest pocket parks that give you a glimpse of it now and then.

Stay on Ocean Drive across the little causeway to Corpus Christi State University (see Colleges & Universities). Go past the campus to East University Drive, then turn in and drive through the grounds circling back to Ocean. Turn left to head west, back the way you came. (If you continue east on Ocean you'll be turned around at the gate to the Naval Air Station.) At the fork, take Ennis Joslin Road, which will lead you along the little bay known as Cayo Del Oso to Texas 358, South Padre Island Drive.

If you want to go to Padre Island and Malaquite Beach, all you have to do is turn left and follow the signs (Texas 358 to Park Road 22). But that's more of a side trip (see Outdoors & Side Trips), not part of this tour to get you acquainted with the city, so turn right back toward downtown instead.

Soon after S.P.I.D. becomes a controlled access highway and you pass Sunrise Mall on your right, exit and turn right on Staples. Once you've turned, the Padre Staples Mall will be on your left. Stay on this street all the way back downtown. There's not much sightseeing along this route, but it will give you a view of another residential and shopping area of the city. Staples meets Alameda, another major east-west street, at Six Points. About a mile past here, on your right at 426 S. Staples, is the Museum of Oriental Cultures. A block farther on is Agnes or Texas 44. Turn right and follow it as it winds down to Laguna where another right will bring you to the seawall—and the end of your tour.

TOUR & GUIDE SERVICES

This is a city tuned in to visitors, so a number of people are available to tell you about and show you the sights.

CORPUS CHRISTI AREA CONVENTION AND TOURIST BUREAU
1201 N. Shoreline, one block north of where I-37 ends at Shoreline
882-5603
Monday through Friday 8:30–5, Saturday 8:30–noon
Free
W

One of the nice things here is they don't even have to be open to provide help. The usual flashing-light map is combined with a computer located in a little enclosure in the front of the building. This is open 24 hours a day to respond to your button pushing with a computer printout of information on accommodations, restaurants, shopping, and points of interest. Each one-page printout, called a VICIGRAM (Visitors Information Center), gives both directions and information on the places you select. There are also phones that require you to push only one button to make a direct connection with the hotel or motel of your choice. Inside, during office hours, you can get a ton of brochures and answers to your questions on Corpus and the surrounding areas. Detailed city and state maps are for sale. On weekends, when this office is closed, brochures and information are available at the Corpus Christi Museum (see Museums).

FLAGSHIP AND GULF CLIPPER SIGHTSEEING CRUISES
People's St. T-Head at Shoreline Blvd.
643-7128 or 884-1693
Morning, afternoon, and evening cruises
Adults $5 for day cruise, $5.75 for evening cruise; children $3 day and $3.50 evening; Friday and Saturday moonlight cruise 9:30–11:30 p.m., adults $9, children $5
W

These cruises give you a wonderful, often spectacular, view of the bayfront skyline as well as a close-up look at the operations of the port. The *Flagship* is a scaled-down version of an old Mississippi showboat, with the typical front-loading gangplank and paddle wheel in the rear. Although small compared to the original paddle wheelers, it still carries up to 400 passengers on an hour to an hour-and-a-half narrated tour of the harbor and the bay. The weekend early evening cruises and the Saturday moonlight cruise feature a live band. The *Gulf Clipper* is a smaller sightseeing vessel that makes a morning run Monday to Friday.

FUNTIME TOURS
601 N. Water, in lobby of La Quinta Royale
854-3257
Office open Monday through Friday 9–5
Tours $8 and $15

They usually offer two narrated bus tours: a city tour that takes about two hours and costs $8 and a four- to five-hour tour that loops through Padre Island and Aransas and costs $15.

GRAY LINE TOURS
416-A N. Chaparral, Suite 105
882-2011
Make tour reservations at most motels, hotels, or travel agencies
Tours from $8 to $45

The two-hour city tour runs Monday through Saturday starting at 9 a.m. The loop tour around the bay through Padre Island and Aransas Pass starts at 1 p.m. Monday through Friday and usually lasts about four hours. The most expensive tour is the four-hour Nite Life Party, which includes dinner, but is run by appointment only and requires a minimum of 30 people. Children are half price on all tours except the Nite Life, which is a "no-no" for them.

MARLIN BEACH TOURS
852-8492
Custom tours of Padre Island National Seashore
$140 for vehicle plus $20 per person
If you want to spend a day on the beach away from civilization, this company will take you there. The fee includes a four-wheel-drive vehicle holding up to four passengers, a picnic lunch, and a driver-guide who will furnish the expertise to take you almost anywhere you want to go on the more than 50 miles of undeveloped beach between the park at Malaquite Beach, near the north end of the island, and the Mansfield Channel cut. If you want to fish, the guide supplies everything for $15 extra each. Tours normally last six to eight hours.

SPARKLING CITY EXCURSIONS
P.O. Box 6094, Corpus Christi 78411
881-9591
Tours from $8 to $25
This company specializes in personalized tours in vans for small groups. Its offerings include a standard two-hour city tour ($8), a six-hour tour that loops the bay ($15), a beachcombing tour ($12), and a border town shopping tour ($25). Or you can design your own tour to the local museums, the Aransas National Wildlife Refuge, or anywhere else within a day-tour range.

POINTS OF INTEREST

ART COMMUNITY CENTER
Downtown
902 Park, in South Bluff Park near Tancahua
884-6406
Tuesday through Friday 10–4, Saturday though Monday 1–5
Free
W
This community gallery offers shows and exhibits of local and area artists working in all media. Some of the works are for sale. Classes and workshops are available.

BAYFRONT ARTS AND SCIENCES PARK AND BAYFRONT PLAZA
Downtown
North end of Shoreline Blvd.
Open at all times
W variable

Art, drama, natural history, and music are all concentrated for your convenience on these few acres near the Harbor Bridge. The Art Museum of South Texas, with its strikingly simple design, stands at the water's edge (see Museums). Facing it across the park lawn is the Corpus Christi Museum, where the animal and plant life of the coastal regions is superbly displayed (see Museums). In the adjoining Plaza are the Harbor Playhouse and the Convention Center, the latter with a banquet hall that will comfortably seat 2,000 and an auditorium that is the home of the Corpus Christi Symphony, seating 2,500. Even though all these attractions can make this a busy place on a summer weekend, there is still enough park space to relax and enjoy the sunshine.

CORPUS CHRISTI MARINA AND YACHT BASIN
Downtown
Along the seawall between Starr and Kinney
Open at all times
W variable

Corpus is one of the few cities where you can walk out of your office building at the end of the day and be in your sailboat on the bay in minutes. The downtown marina is built around three small, man-made peninsulas that take their names from their alphabetical shapes and the streets that lead to them: the People Street T-Head, the Lawrence Street T-Head, and the Cooper Street L-Head. In addition to the pleasure craft docked here, there are also two floating restaurants, a restaurant in a lighthouse, excursion boats, charter and party fishing boats, and commercial shrimp boats. Even if you never intend to go out on the bay, it's fun to walk around here, watching the real and sometime sailors at work or play and listening to the breeze humming and slapping out a tune as it wafts through the riggings and masts of the sailboats.

HARBOR BRIDGE
U.S. 181 between downtown and Corpus Christi Beach
Open at all times

This bridge over the ship channel at the port has a cantilever span of 620 feet, which is the longest such span on any bridge in Texas. It is 243 feet high and clears the water by 140 feet, which, surprisingly, is not enough clearance for some large ships that must lower their radar equipment before passing under. When you top the middle rise of the bridge going north, you have a view that includes all of Corpus Christi Beach and across the bay to Portland and beyond. Coming south there's an excellent view of the downtown skyline and the bay shore. When it opened in 1959, the Harbor Bridge replaced an old two-lane drawbridge that caused numerous traffic tie-ups as it went up as many as 20 times a day to let ships through. Although there was a lot of controversy about building the new bridge—some preferred a tunnel—most residents greeted its completion with cheers. But, according to some locals, there were a number of folks commuting between Portland and Corpus who were not so happy, since their most popular alibi for being late had to be scrapped along with the old drawbridge! If you're fearless, in good shape, and have time to take in this bird's-eye view, there are narrow pedestrian walkways you can take to the center of the bridge, which is also a favorite spot for adventurous photographers.

NAVAL AIR STATION & ARMY DEPOT
South
Gates at the east end of Ocean Dr. and at the end of Texas 358 after it turns off South Padre Island Dr.
Bus tour available, usually Thursday at 1 p.m., call Public Affairs Office, 939-2674, for exact time and starting place
Free
W

The station is closed to the public except for official tours. This is the headquarters of the Naval Air Training Command. All multi-engine pilots receive their advanced training here after graduating from primary flight school at Pensacola, Florida. From here they may go on to jet training stations including those at nearby Kingsville and Beeville. The other major tenant on the station is the army's helicopter repair depot, the largest in the nation. Damaged army and other service helicopters are shipped here from all over the world for repair and overhaul. Also at the station are the training facilities for naval air navigators and a Coast Guard search and rescue unit.

PORT OF CORPUS CHRISTI
Downtown
Office at 222 Power St.
882-5633

A protected bay leading to a 400-foot-wide and 45-foot-deep ship channel (the deepest on the Texas coast) has helped make this the ninth largest saltwater port in the nation in terms of cargo handled. The cargoes are mainly cotton, oil, grain, and chemicals; and they come and go in ships from almost every country in the free world. If you're interested in seeing port operations, there are several ways to do that. You can get a view of the docks near the entrance to the port through the telescope in the observation pavilion in Channelview Park on the north shore of the channel. (Cross the Harbor Bridge to Corpus Christi Beach and then double back under the bridge to the pavilion.) For a better view, take the harbor tour on one of the sightseeing boats (see Tour & Guide Services). Or you can drive along Navigation Boulevard behind the north shore of the port and get occasional glimpses between the buildings (see Get-Acquainted Driving Tour). Finally, for the fearless and the hearty only, there is the pedestrian walkway on the west lane of the Harbor Bridge, which offers a clear view of the entire port.

BIRD'S-EYE VIEW

Two places where you can get an excellent sky-high view of the shoreline and the bay are the restaurants and lounges atop the Hershey and the Sheraton Marina hotels (see Hotels & Motels).

HISTORIC PLACES

CENTENNIAL HOUSE
Downtown
411 N. Upper Broadway
992-6003
Wednesday 3–5 and by appointment for groups
Adults $1, students 50¢, children 25¢
W

Forbes Britton was in Zachary Taylor's army when it came through Corpus Christi during the Mexican War. Shortly after Britton retired from the army in 1849, he built this house, which still stands as the oldest existing structure in Corpus today. Britton later became a state senator. During the Civil War his house served as a hospital for both the Confederate and the Union forces. The two-story home was restored by the Corpus Christi American Heritage Society in 1965. Note the address—Broadway is on two levels, and this is on the upper level.

OLD IRISHTOWN–HERITAGE PARK RESTORATION PROJECT
Downtown
1600 block of N. Chaparral near Bayfront Plaza

The Junior League and several other local organizations are pitching in to restore the old Victorian homes in this historic district called Old Irishtown. These include the Lichenstein home, the Gugenheim home, and the Sidbury House, which were built around the turn of the century and moved to this location in the 1920s. Julius Lichenstein, a local department store owner, built his home on the corner of Chaparral and Brewster in 1905. It is now the Creative Arts Center for children. The Gugenheim home, at 1601, now houses the Camp Fire Council of the Corpus Christi Area; however, the front three rooms have been restored and furnished with period antiques and are open for visitors Monday through Friday from 9–5. (Large groups are requested to make advance reservations by calling 887-1601.) The Sidbury House is the only one of these three that accommodates public tours.

SIDBURY HOUSE
1609 N. Chaparral
883-9352

Tuesday through Thursday 9:30–12:30
Free
Call in advance for large groups
   This fine example of Victorian architecture was built on Broadway in
1893 by Charlotte Sidbury as a rental house. It was moved to Old Irishtown in 1926. The Junior League started the painstaking project of restoring the building in 1975. Every detail included in the restoration was
authenticated. Even the wallpaper in the living room was hand-printed
in Europe from the original blocks used during the Victorian era. Three
years and $180,000 later, it was opened to the public. Only the down-
stairs is open; the league offices are upstairs. Tours are conducted by
docents wearing turn-of-the century costumes.

MUSEUMS

ART MUSEUM OF SOUTH TEXAS
Downtown
1902 N. Shoreline in Bayfront Arts and Sciences Park
884-3844
Tuesday, Wednesday, and Friday 10–5; Thursday 12–8; Saturday and
Sunday 12–5; closed Monday and major holidays
Free (donations appreciated)
W+
   Starkly austere in design, this building is worth seeing just for itself.
It stands out, white and crisp, against the foreground of green park
lawn and the sparkling bay waters behind it. The building is of reinforced concrete formed and cast in place. All openings are enclosed
with bronze-tinted glass, which will not distort the color of the works of
art on display inside. At the same time, the windows provide gorgeous
views of the natural beauty of the bay. (There is also a good view of
Corpus Christi Beach to the north from the outside stairs on the north
side of the building.) The interior is just as striking, with much of the
first floor a sweep of white, virtually uninterrupted space and a large,
mezzanine-style second level that enhances the feeling of openness.
The museum has only a small, but growing, permanent collection, so
most exhibits are on loan from other institutions or private collections
and cover a wide variety of periods and media. Guided tours are available, with at least one week's notice, for groups of 12 or more. Gift shop.

CORPUS CHRISTI MUSEUM
Downtown
1900 N. Chaparral in Bayfront Arts and Sciences Park
883-2862
Tuesday through Saturday 10–5, Sunday 2–5, closed Monday
Free
W+
   Established by area teachers more than 20 years ago for their stu-
dents, this museum has grown to where is it now recognized as one of

the best in the state. Science and the natural history of the coastal region are the focal points here, but exhibits and educational programs go far beyond those limits. There are dioramas of wildlife native to the coast, Indian artifacts, a re-creation of a typical street in Corpus in 1930, a small aquarium, an antique gallery, and an art gallery featuring the work of local artists. For children (and the curious adult), "touch tables" enable them to experience the feel as well as the sight of exhibits. And the staff has a sense of humor, well illustrated in its exhibit of such rarities as the head of the Headless Horseman and a snow footprint of the Abominable Snowman, which melted and is now preserved as water. Programs include documentary films (and comedy classics) and weekend afternoon performances on what is known as the Front Porch—a stage that resembles an old-fashioned front porch and is used by local amateurs and professionals for everything from acrobatics to student dance and piano recitals. The best thing of all is that this museum is diverse enough to have something for everyone, while small enough to look at everything in a few hours without getting tired out.

KING HIGH SCHOOL PLANETARIUM
Central
5225 Golihar
992-0497
Open Tuesday evenings during the school year
Adults $1, senior citizens and students 50¢
W

Astronomy programs at various times during the year. The Corpus Christi Astronomical Society also meets here on clear weekend nights. Anyone interested in stargazing through the group's telescope is welcome. Call for society meeting information.

MUSEUM OF ORIENTAL CULTURES
Downtown
426 S. Staples, at Marguerite
Tuesday through Saturday 10–4, Sunday 2–5; closed Monday
Adults $1, students 50¢, children 25¢
W

The mission of this unusual museum is to increase awareness, understanding, and appreciation of the peoples and cultures of the Orient. That's a big task, and considering its size, the museum does the job remarkably well. Originally known as the Japanese Art Museum, the permanent exhibits still concentrate on that country; however, more and more space is being allotted to rotating exhibits from other Asian countries including China, India, the Philippines, and Korea. Among the exhibits are twenty scale-model dioramas depicting various aspects of Japanese daily life, history, religion, and art. The museum's collection of Hakata dolls is reportedly the largest in the United States, and there is also a collection of Noh and Kabuki masks and a bigger-than-life statue of Buddha that is more than 200 years old. Paintings, brass and bronzeware, ceramics, cloisonné, lacquerware, and woodcarvings are also on display. Guided tours are available for groups making reservations in advance.

GALLERIES

CORPUS CHRISTI ART GALLERY
Central
3209 S. Alameda in Alameda Shopping Center
854-1057
W

The emphasis is on western art here, but that covers a lot of territory. According to this gallery's definition, western art is not restricted to cowboy art but includes original art and sculpture on any subject west of the Mississippi. Wildlife and landscape are the principal subjects, and treatment ranges from realistic to light impressionist. During the year the gallery carries the works of about half the artists in the National Academy of Western Art.

OLIVER'S VILLAGE GALLERY
Central
3847 S. Alameda in the Village Shopping Center
855-0911
W

This small gallery specializes in sporting art, including duck stamps and prints and hand-carved decoys. But other items cover a wide spectrum including stone lithographs and bronze and stone sculpture.

MUSIC & THEATER

In addition to the listings below, both Del Mar College and Corpus Christi State University frequently have dramatic and musical programs open to the public (see Colleges & Universities).

CORPUS CHRISTI STATE UNIVERSITY THEATRE
South
Corpus Christi State University Center for the Arts
6300 Ocean Dr.
991-6931
W+

The season usually includes three full-length plays, a musical, a Readers' Theatre production, and several one-act plays. Season tickets run about $15. Tickets to individual performances cost $3–$4. Also summer productions.

CORPUS CHRISTI SYMPHONY
Downtown
Bayfront Plaza Auditorium
1901 N. Shoreline
882-2717
W+

Usually seven or eight concerts are held during the October through April season. Tickets run $6–$15. Season tickets are available. The Corpus Christi Ballet also occasionally performs in this auditorium.

HARBOR PLAYHOUSE
Downtown
No. 1 Bayfront Park
882-3356
W+

Comedies, dramas, and musicals are presented during the winter season, principally by a local theater group, and a melodrama series is held each summer. Tickets cost $4–$7. The playhouse is also used for recitals and other musical events.

COLLEGES & UNIVERSITIES

CORPUS CHRISTI STATE UNIVERSITY
South
6300 Ocean Dr.
Public Information Office, 991-6810 ext 335
W variable

This is an upper-level university for juniors, seniors, and graduate students studying in its four colleges: arts and humanities, science and technology, education, and business administration. Over 3,700 students are enrolled. The National Spill Control School is also located on the campus. Here students learn techniques for controlling and handling spills of all types of hazardous materials, including oil. CCSU is located on a 250-acre island between the end of the Ocean Drive residential area and the Naval Air Station. It is not only physically an island, but for both students and visitors, it is also an island of culture in the south end of the city. For visitors it offers traveling and local art exhibits in the Weil Gallery in the Center for the Arts, concerts by music majors and the school jazz band, a university theater, plus film, visiting artist and lecture series, and a limited number of continuing education courses. Visitors also may obtain a card to use the university's 225,000-volume library ($20 annual fee).

DEL MAR COLLEGE
Center
Baldwin and Ayers
881-6200
W variable

A two-year community college, Del Mar has an enrollment of approximately 10,000 in its full-time courses and an additional 13,000 enrolled in continuing education. Vocational, technical, and junior college programs are the mainstays of the college with offerings in such diverse fields as registered nurse education, respiratory therapy, police science, restaurant management, and marine-science-electronics. The college is located on two campuses: the east campus, primarily academic, is at Baldwin and Ayers and the west campus, primarily vocational-technical, is at Morgan and Old Brownsville Road. With more than a hundred course offerings each year, continuing education also covers a wide field, including arts and crafts, data processing, homemaking, music, and self-improvement. Most courses run 4 to 10 weeks, and fees generally run from $10 to $40 (for information call 881-6328). Visitors may also enjoy the college art gallery, on the second floor of the history building on the east campus, and a free cultural program series. On the musical side are frequent concerts by the Del Mar Jazz Band and free recitals by students and faculty of the music department as well as by visiting artists.

SHOPPING

There are two covered malls, several strip shopping centers, and a number of interesting specialty shops, mostly concentrated in the central and south sections of the city. Just a few examples of what's available follow.

BAUBLES & BEADS
Central
4873 S. Alameda in Cullen Mall
991-6181
W

This resale boutique is part of a chain of what might be called selective thrift shops. They buy and sell only name brands or currently stylish designer clothes. Items are priced at about 25 percent of the original, but even then some things sell for up to $500.

THE BRITISH SIDEBOARD GOURMET SHOPPE
Central
3154 Reid Dr. in the Gardens on the Plaza, one block south of S. Alameda near Glazebrook
851-0053
W

Kay Jones felt that the culinary talents of the fine kitchen staff of her

British Sideboard Restaurant (see Restaurants) weren't being fully utilized, so she started a catering service and this gourmet shop. Hot and cold specialties, including seafood salads, pâtés, terrines, pastas, breads, and pastries—everything for a gourmet feast or picnic—are all prepared in the kitchen across the courtyard. It's mostly take out, but there are some tables for coffee and pastries or the luncheon special or if you don't think you'll be able to make it home before breaking into your order.

THE MERCADO
Downtown
421 N. Chaparral
854-0093
W

Many of the quality shops in the downtown area have disappeared, but this one still holds its own and for good reason. The owner makes about 40 buying trips a year to Central and South America and, more recently, to Europe to stock his store with such desirable items as Brazilian and Colombian gems sold loose by carat weight, pre-Columbian pottery, hand-loomed rugs and wall hangings, embroidered dresses, and real Panama hats. Parking space is a little hard to find near the shop, but the Mercado is within easy walking distance of most downtown hotels.

THE PADRE ISLANDER
Padre Island
South Padre Island Dr. at Commodore
933-7011
W

This one-stop, warehouse-size tourist shop carries everything for the beach, as well as shells, tourist trivia, and all-cotton T-shirts.

PADRE STAPLES MALL
South
South Padre Island Dr. at S. Staples
991-3755
W

A recent remodeling has turned this from an unimaginative barn of a mall into a more pleasant place to shop. There are about 70 stores, anchored by Penney's and Dillard's.

PAGE ONE BOOKSHOP
Central
4248 S. Alameda near Robert Dr., in Town and Country Shopping Center
992-1741
W

An especially large selection of children's books draws members to their own book club for children. And photos of members adorn the walls. In addition to the usual bookstore stock, they also have a good selection of Texana, cookbooks, and reference books.

PILAR
Central
3814 S. Alameda at Doddridge, in Lamar Park Center
853-7171
W

A women's shop brimming with owner-selected merchandise mostly from Latin America: embroidered dresses, wcven tops, nubby woolens and cottons, jewelry, and tapestries. Some are made for export, but a surprising number are authentic village wear.

SÍ SÍ
Downtown
309 N. Water on the patio of Water St. Market
881-8477

This gift and accessory shop offers a wide selection of Mexican and Central American women's clothes, terra cotta sculpture, straw bags, some Mexican furniture, children's toys, and home accent pieces.

SUNRISE MALL
South
South Padre Island Dr. at Airline
993-2900
W

This two-level shopping center is the largest in the city, with trees and waterfalls and all the other interior landscaping typical of a modern mall. The 100 stores include a supermarket and the usual groupings of chain retail and fast food shops. Anchor stores are Joske's, Sears, and Frost Brothers; the latter closes daily at 5:30 no matter when its more plebeian neighbors do.

OUTDOORS

BAYFRONT SURREY RIDES
Downtown
Shoreline Dr. across from City Hall
887-8715
Open seven days 8:30 to dusk
$8 hour, deposit required

Drive yourself on a tour of the seawall in one of the these pedal-powered surreys with the fringe on top. Each holds two adults and a couple of small children.

COLE PARK
Downtown
2000 block of Ocean Dr.

All the park basics are here—playground, picnic tables, and restrooms, plus an amphitheater where they give concerts on summer Sundays at 8:30 p.m., a lighted fishing pier, and a small beach. This is a popular spot for windsurfers. If you want to try that sport, you can usually rent the sailboards at or near the park.

CORPUS CHRISTI BEACH
North of downtown across Harbor Bridge

The old-timers call it "North Beach" and speak of its 1930s heyday when it was the home of gambling casinos and amusement parks. But then it lost its glamour and turned into an eyesore. The city and the Army Corps of Engineers restored it in the late 1970s at a cost of $3.7 million. Now hotels, motels, and condos line most of the one-and-a-half-mile beachfront, and there's a park on the north end.

MAGEE BEACH
Downtown
Shoreline across from Memorial Coliseum

The sand on this 250-yard-long, man-made beach has burned a lot of feet since it was built in 1940, and this spot is still popular. Lifeguards are on duty from Memorial Day to Labor Day. There's a pier, concession stand, and freshwater showers. For fishing or a different view of downtown, walk out on the quarter-mile-long, lighted breakwater that protects the yacht basin.

SIDE TRIPS

CORPUS CHRISTI BAY LOOP DRIVE

If you don't get hung up at the Port Aransas free ferry, you can make the 75 miles of this complete circle around Corpus Christi Bay in about two hours of easy driving. Or plan some stop-overs and turn it into an all-day excursion. Since it is a loop, you can do it in either direction, but we'll begin by going north. Take U.S. 181 across the Harbor Bridge, past Corpus Christi Beach and Portland to Texas 361. Follow 361 to Aransas Pass (see Aransas Pass). Continue on the same road across Redfish Bay on the causeway, ending at the ferry to Port Aransas (see Port Aransas). In that fishing town you'll pick up Park Road 53 and go south the full extent of Mustang Island. Park Road 53 runs into Park Road 22 on Padre

Island. Turn right (west) and go across the JFK Causeway. This park road runs into Texas 358 (South Padre Island Drive). The next turn is at Ennis Joslin Road, shortly after you cross tiny Oso Bay. Turn right and go to the end at Ocean Drive. A left here will put you on Ocean, which becomes Shoreline and winds up back downtown.

KING RANCH
Kingsville
Approximately 40 miles southwest of Corpus Christi
Take Texas 44 to U.S. 77 to Kingsville, then Texas 141 to the ranch gates west of the city
1-592-6411
Open seven days 9–5
Free
    The King Ranch owns and operates almost 10 million acres in seven countries around the world. And it all started just outside Kingsville where Captain King set up his first camp. Today this is the site of the ranch's international headquarters and the Santa Gertrudis Division, named after the breed of cattle developed here. Stop at the gate house, and the guard will give you a brochure and map. Or you can rent a cassette, which will point out the sights on the 12-mile-loop road open to visitors. In truth, there's not much to see, but if you've never been on a working ranch, it might be worth the trip.

LAKE CORPUS CHRISTI STATE RECREATION AREA
Near Mathis
Approximately 30 miles northwest of Corpus Christi
Take I-37 to Texas 359 at Mathis, then south six miles to Park Rd. 25 to the park headquarters
1-547-2635
Open seven days 8–10 for day use, at all times for camping
Autos $2
W but not all areas
    Tired of saltwater? Then try this freshwater recreation area, which is less than an hour's drive from Corpus. The 350-acre park on the southern end of the 27-mile-long lake has camp sites, RV hookups, restrooms, showers, picnic areas, a boat launching area (rental boats are available), and snack bar and grocery. Sports include swimming (although the water isn't very clear), waterskiing, and fishing for catfish, sunfish, bass, and crappie.

MUSTANG ISLAND STATE PARK
    See Mustang Island.

NUECES COUNTY PARKS
Padre Island
Park Rd. 22
949-8121
Open at all times
Admission fee for camping

Nueces County Park Number 2 is a small, pleasant park with pavilion and restrooms. Usually referred to as the Young Adult Recreation Park, its location on Packery Channel—on the north end of Padre Island just off the JFK Causeway—where the waves are uniform makes it a favorite site for young surfers. Park Number 1, called Padre Ballí Park, is about two miles farther along on Park Road 22, just north of the Nueces–Kleberg County line. This one is on the Gulf, and in addition to a long stretch of beach, it has a free fishing pier extending more than 1,200 feet into the Gulf, campsites with hookups (fee), a bathhouse, and picnic areas. Since it is the closest Gulf beach to the city, it is extremely popular and often crowded, but it's worth a try if you don't feel like driving all the way down to the national seashore park at Malaquite Beach.

PADRE ISLAND NATIONAL SEASHORE AND MALAQUITE BEACH
Approximately 25 miles south of the JFK Causeway on Park Rd. 22
937-2621
Open at all times
Admission fee for camping
W variable

Padre Island, stretching 113 miles from Corpus Christi on the north almost to the Mexican border on the south, is the longest in the string of barrier islands protecting the Texas coast. The island ranges in width from a few hundred yards to about three miles and is separated from the mainland by Laguna Madre, a shallow body of water with a maximum width of ten miles.

Fortunately, a little more than 80 miles in the center of this island has been designated a national seashore, administered by the Department of the Interior. Originally called The White Islands (Las Islas Blancas) when discovered in 1519, the unspoiled, natural beach still lives up to that descriptive name. Development is restricted to the two ends to minimize harm to the fragile ecological balance of the island.

Malaquite Beach is the only developed area within the national seashore itself. The pavilion includes an observation tower, a visitors center with an interpretive display of the island's ecology, bathhouse, restrooms, showers, picnic tables, and a snack bar and concessions. Camping is permitted; there are no hookups, but there is a fee. There are also nature trails, and the rangers and naturalists conduct a number of programs for visitors during the summer. These include beach discovery walks, instructions on net fishing and crabbing, and evening slide shows. Swimming, surf fishing, shell collecting, and birdwatching are popular activities. More than 350 species of birds are either year-round residents or seasonal visitors.

The paved road continues for a few miles past Malaquite, and a regular car can go even a few miles past this on the beach. But from then on, you need a four-wheel-drive vehicle (with water and other safety supplies). With one of these and a competent guide, you can venture south and explore for more than 50 miles to the Mansfield cut. One place that rents four-wheel-drive vehicles is Foy's Beach Rental at 10001 S. Padre Island Drive (937-4001). For your own safety, you are required to check in at the ranger station before going out into the four-wheel-drive area.

For general information contact the National Park Service's Padre Island Headquarters on the mainland at 9405 S. Padre Island Drive, Corpus Christi 78412 (937-2621), open Monday through Friday from 8:00–4:30. The telephone number at Malaquite Beach is 949-8068, and for beach, weather, and driving conditions, call 949-8175.

KIDS' STUFF

WET & WILD
6685 S. Padre Island Dr.
Open seven days, 10 a.m. to 8 or 10 p.m., weather permitting
$2.50 to $6

A water slide with game room and snack bar.

SPORTS & ACTIVITIES

Bicycling

See Outdoors, Bayfront Surrey Rides.

Birdwatching

See Rockport-Fulton, Aransas National Wildlife Refuge. See also Mustang Island, Mustang Island State Park. See Side Trips, Padre Island National Seashore.

Fishing

Fishing the inshore waters around Corpus can yield redfish, trout, sheepshead, skipjack, drum, flounder, whiting, mackerel, ling, and pompano. The easiest way is from the many piers and jetties. These include:

BOB HALL PIER
Padre Island
Nueces County Park No. 1
  Lighted, concrete pier open 24 hours, concession, fee.

COLE PARK PIER
Ocean Dr.
  Lighted, open 24 hours, free.

CORPUS CHRISTI BAY MARINA BREAKWATER
Downtown
  Lighted, open 24 hours, concession, free.

NUECES BAY PIER
Corpus Christi Beach (Hull St. exit)
  Lighted, wooden, open 24 hours, fee.

OSO BAY PIER
6124 Ocean Dr.
  Lighted, open 24 hours on weekends, fee.

SEAWALL AND T- AND L-HEADS
Downtown
  Open 24 hours, free.

WATERWORKS MARINA PIER
Under north end of JFK Causeway Bridge
  Lighted, fee.

Surf fishing is good from the beaches on Padre or Mustang islands. For wade fishing, Laguna Madre and Cayo del Oso (near the Naval Air Station) are both rated excellent. The bottom in these waters is solid, the water is clear, and the depth of the water for miles seldom measures over three or four feet.

Party boats for bay fishing operate from Peoples Street T-Head. These usually run four-hour trips morning, afternoon, and night. The usual fare is $10 per adult and $5 for children. Tackle is furnished for $3 a person. Among the party boats available are: Captain Clark, 884-4369, and Star Trek, 883-5031.

There are also charter boats available at the T-head for private fishing parties.

If you want to go deep-sea fishing, the closest place to find a party or charter boat is Port Aransas, which is really Corpus Christi's outlet to the Gulf (see Port Aransas). Freshwater fishing is available just 40 miles north at Lake Corpus Christi State Recreation Area (see Side Trips).

Golf

GABE LOZANO, JR. GOLF CENTER
Central
4401 Old Brownsville Rd. between Navigation and Airport

883-3696
Open seven days
$4 weekdays, $6 weekends
Public 18-hole course. There is also an executive 9-hole course (fees: $1.50 weekdays, $2.25 weekends).

OSO BEACH GOLF COURSE
South
5600 S. Alameda at Glenmore
991-5351
Open seven days
$4.25 weekdays, $5.25 weekends
Municipal 18-hole course.

Jogging

Several places in Corpus are ideal for joggers. In the north is Corpus Christi Beach where you can get a runner's guide from Best Western Sandy Shores (see Hotels & Motels) that marks out four routes ranging from one to 12 miles in length. Or you can just jog the beach. The seawall and Ocean Drive continue south all the way out to the Naval Air Station. Traffic can be a problem along the Ocean Drive part of the route, but there is a marked jogging (and bicycle) lane. And all the way south, of course, there are the miles and miles of beach on Mustang and Padre islands.

Racquetball

RACQUETBALL PLUS
Central
1017 Barry Dr.
855-4175
This is a private club, but visitors are welcome to use the facilities, including whirlpool and sauna, for $5 a day.

Roller Skating

Want to breeze along the seawall on wheels? Skate rentals are available at Sea Skate on the seawall by the downtown marina and Bayfront Skating, 531 S. Shoreline (behind Memorial Coliseum), for about $3 an hour. Deposit required.

Sailing

If you want to see mad confusion, visit the downtown marina and yacht basin late on almost any Wednesday afternoon. What you'll see is dozens of sailboats dodging each other as they make ready to take off in the weekly Midget Ocean Racing Fleet (MORF) race. Corpus Christi Bay is almost perfect for this type of sailing, since it has shallow and protected waters and good breezes. The MORF also sponsors weekend regattas. The best view of the races is from the T-Heads and seawall. If you prefer to be indoors, join the crowd at the Lighthouse Bar and Grill on the Lawrence Street T-Head or the top floor lounges of the Sheraton Marina or Hershey hotels.

If you want to actually sail, captained and bareboat (no crew) charters are available from Charter Boat Associates (881-8503, P.O. Box 995, Corpus Christi 78403). The yachts range from 23- to 40-footers. For captained charters, rates run from a low of $140 a day up to about $1,700 a week. Bareboat charters start at a low of $90 a day to about $1,200 a week.

Want to learn to sail? The same group also operates the Corpus Christi International Sailing School. A one-week course costs $750. Weekend courses range from $110 to $250 depending on the yacht used and whether you live aboard.

Stock Car Racing

RIVERSIDE SPEEDWAY
West
8000 Greenwood (past Saratoga Blvd.)
852-2436 (call for race dates)
Adults $5
W

A 3.8-mile dirt oval track. Races normally start at 8:00 p.m. Children under 12 are admitted free with an adult.

SPEEDWAY PARK
West
241 Flato Rd., near Agnes
289-2861 (call for race dates)
Closed October through March
Adult $6, children under 12 $1
W

This is a racing complex containing a quarter-mile, asphalt stock car track, a motorcycle motocross track, and an area for truck mud drag races. Even if more than one track is in operation at the same time, one admission is all you pay. Races are held every Saturday night from April through September. Live entertainment is presented in the open-air beer garden Wednesday through Saturday.

Swimming

See Outdoors & Side Trips, Corpus Christi Beach, Cole Park, Magee Beach, Nueces County Parks, and Padre Island National Seashore and Malaquite Beach.

Tennis

H. E. B. TENNIS CENTER
Central
1520 Shely near Ayers in H. E. Butt Park
888-5681
Monday through Friday 9 a.m.–10 p.m., Saturday 9 a.m. until dark, Sunday 1 p.m. to dark
Days, $1.50 for 1½ hours; nights, $2 for 1½ hours
Twenty-four Laykold courts and a pro shop. Call for reservations.

SOUTH BLUFF CENTER
Downtown
502 King, near park
883-6942
8:30 a.m. to 10 p.m., closed Monday
Days, $1.25 for 1½ hours; nights, $1.75 for 1½ hours
Ten Laykold courts and a pro shop. Call for reservations.

ANNUAL EVENTS

April

BUCCANEER DAYS
Downtown at Bayfront, South Bluff Park, and various other locations throughout the city
882-3242
Ten or eleven days near end of the month
Most events free
W variable
This festival, which has been growing and growing since the 1930s, is kicked off traditionally with the capture of the city by the pirate queens (actually contestants in the Buc Days beauty contest) who make the mayor "walk the plank." Activities include a re-creation of the 1519 discovery of Corpus Christi Bay, a junior parade, an illuminated night parade that ranks among the best in the state, fireworks, a carnival, art show, music festival, and sporting events on both land and sea. And, of course, lots of food and drink.

July

TEXAS JAZZ FESTIVAL
Various locations throughout the city
992-4540
Three days early in the month
Many activities are free
W variable

Jazz comes up the Gulf and takes over the city attracting musicians from all over the country. Festivities include jazz cruises aboard the *Flagship* from Peoples Street T-Head, a jazz mass at Holy Cross Catholic Church (1109 N. Staples), fund-raising concerts, workshops, and jam sessions. And it all comes to a head with a Sunday afternoon and evening of free jazz, jazz, jazz.

September

BAYFEST
Downtown
Shoreline near Bayfront Plaza
Last weekend in month or first in October
Free
W variable

For this three-day event, colorful tents, filled with arts and crafts and what-have-you, spring up along the seawall. There's continuous music, dancing, and even plays on outdoor stages, an "Anything-That-Will-Float-But-A-Boat" Race, fireworks, a boat parade, a marathon, and a regatta. For the children there are magic shows, a puppet show, and contests. And naturally, there are booths selling all kinds of food and beer—lots and lots of beer.

December

CHRISTMAS TREE FOREST
Downtown
Art Museum of South Texas
1902 N. Shoreline
884-3844
Free (donations accepted)
W

A forest of close to a hundred spectacularly decorated Christmas trees all but takes over the Art Museum for most of the month before Christmas. As befits an exhibit in a seaside city, the trees are decorated with everything from seashells to fishing lures—a delight for both young and old.

HOTELS & MOTELS

Accommodations range from bed and breakfast homes and modest motels to luxury hotels and condos scattered throughout the city. Whether you are looking for a place downtown, on the beach, near the airport, or wherever, something can be found to fit your needs. The listings that follow are grouped by type and location.

Rates for a double room or a one-bedroom condo apartment in season:

   $: under $50
   $$: $50–$65
   $$$: $66–$75
$$$$: over $75

Corpus Christi Beach

Take U.S. 181/Texas 35 north across Harbor Bridge toward Portland.

BEST WESTERN SANDY SHORES INN AND RESORT
3200 Surfside, on beach north of Harbor Bridge
883-7456 or 1-800-528-1234
$–$$$$
W+ two rooms
A beach resort with 250 rooms built in two sections: a two story around a large outdoor pool and recreation area and a seven story on the beach. There is a coffee shop, restaurant and bar, indoor pool and spa, gift shop, and all the recreation and services you'd expect in a resort hotel.

FRIENDSHIP SEA SHELL INN
202 Kleberg Place
888-5391 or 1-800-453-4511 (Friendship Inns)
$$
There are 27 units in this small, two-story motel on the beach. Seventeen of them have large kitchenettes. The motel is built on pilings, so there is some shaded parking underneath. All rooms face Corpus Christi Bay. Pool.

VILLA DEL SOL CONDOMINIUM HOTEL
3938 Surfside
883-9748 or in Texas 1-800-242-3291
$$$–$$$$
W
About 300 of the 411 units in this four-story condominium on the beach are in the hotel rental pool. Each is a fully-equipped small apartment with a kitchenette, bath, bedroom, living area with sleeper sofa, and bunks in the hall, so it can sleep a family. All units have balconies; some overlook the beach, and from some there's a good view of the

downtown Corpus bayfront and skyline. Many hotel-type services are available. Two pools, three spas, children's playground, a beach and boat rental shop, and covered parking.

Bayfront-Downtown

HERSHEY CORPUS CHRISTI HOTEL
900 N. Shoreline
887-1600 or 1-800-533-3131
$$$–$$$$
W+ 15 rooms

One of the newer additions to the bayfront skyline, this 19-story, first-class hotel has 474 guest rooms and 24 suites. Each room has a private balcony with a view of the bay. Rates run higher for a suite on the 18th floor, called the Main Line Club, where there is a concierge as well as a VIP lounge. Situated behind the lobby is a two-story sports area that includes an indoor-outdoor pool, racketball courts, a health club, and a sun deck. Seating is tiered over two floors in the rooftop restaurant and lounge, so everyone enjoys a view of the city and the bay. There is also another restaurant and lounge and a nightclub. Free valet parking.

HOLIDAY INN–EMERALD BEACH
1102 S. Shoreline
883-5731 or 1-800-238-8000
$$$–$$$$
W+ one room

This is the only bayfront motel-hotel right on the water. The road separates all the others from the bay. As its name indicates, this Holiday Inn is located on a small beach not much bigger than an emerald, and even that beach sometimes disappears after a storm. Inside, however, is a heated pool, wading pool, sauna, whirlpool, and playground, all under a dome called the Holidome. There are 368 rooms, a restaurant featuring weekday, all-you-can-eat luncheon buffets and a Friday night seafood buffet. If later on you want to burn off those calories, try Lucy's, a disco bar.

LA QUINTA ROYALE
601 N. Water
888-4461 or in Texas 1-800-292-5200, outside Texas 1-800-531-5900
$$
W+ two rooms

When you sit in the lounge in the atrium lobby and look up 10 stories to the skylights in the cathedral ceiling, you know this isn't a run-of-the-mill member of the La Quinta chain. Each of the Royale's 200 rooms and suites has a balcony, but since the hotel is located a block from the water, not all have a bay view. Restaurant, pool, and free parking for guests in garage.

THE MARRIOTT
707 N. Shoreline
882-1700 or 1-800-228-9290
$$$$
W + three rooms
Another newcomer adding its high rise to the bayfront skyline. All 350 guest rooms and suites in this first-class hotel have a balcony with a bay view. Two restaurants, two bars, and a nightclub provide wining and dining, while recreation facilities include an indoor-outdoor heated pool, sun deck, tennis court, exercise room, and saunas. Free parking for guests in garage.

RAMADA INN–BAYFRONT
601 N. Shoreline
883-7271 or 1-800-272-6232
$
W
The combination of a location on the bayfront, high standards characteristic of this chain, and reasonable rates puts this motel in the bargain category. There are 120 rooms in this older, three-story complex, with 15 set aside for nonsmokers. Many of the rooms have a bay view. Restaurant, lounge, and pool.

SHERATON MARINA
300 N. Shoreline
883-5111 or 1-800-325-3535
$$–$$$
W
A lot of remodeling and redecorating has been going on to make this older resident of the bayfront competitive with the newer hotels being built around it. All 175 rooms in this high rise have been spruced up, but nothing had to be done to their main attraction—the view of the marina and bayfront. An even better view is available in the top floor restaurant and lounge that becomes a supper club in the evening with dancing and entertainment. It is also popular for its Sunday brunch buffet. There is another restaurant and another lounge downstairs, plus a sauna, outdoor pool, and two tennis courts. Occasionally the Sheraton offers a dinner theater with a touring show and a buffet dinner.

Central & Airport

EMBASSY SUITES HOTEL (GRENADA ROYALE HOMETEL)
4337 S. Padre Island Dr. (near Weber St. exit)
853-7899 or 1-800-EMBASSY
$$–$$$
W + two rooms

The dual name is because two chains have merged, and by the time you read this, this hotel will have wound up with one name or the other. But even if the name changes, the concept of offering small suites instead of a regular hotel room won't change. Nor will the other amenities, which include a free full breakfast in the morning and two hours of free cocktails in the evening. The 154 kitchenette suites are on three floors grouped around an enclosed Spanish-style courtyard, which also contains an indoor pool and sauna. It is located about six miles from downtown on the road to North Padre Island, near the shopping malls.

HILTON INN
6255 I-37 at Corn Products Rd.
289-0600 or 1-800-442-7260
$$–$$$
W + two rooms
Located right next to I-37, this motel is between the airport and downtown, which means it caters mostly to corporate guests. The 500 rooms and suites are all up to the usual Hilton standards. Three pools, saunas, whirlpool, tennis courts, a nine-hole putting green, two restaurants, and three clubs are among the amenities.

HOLIDAY INN–AIRPORT
5549 Leopard St. (Texas 9) at Texas 358 and 44
289-5100 or 1-800-238-8000
$$
W + two rooms
It's about three miles to the airport and three miles to downtown, which makes this a prime stop-over for business travelers. After a hot day of traveling, just looking at the waterfall in the lobby as you check in can be refreshing. And if you really want to cool off, you can sit at a table by the waterfall and order a drink or a snack. The small indoor pool is heated, and there are saunas and a whirlpool. Some of the 247 rooms and six suites are set aside for nonsmokers. There are two restaurants and a large and popular lounge.

SEA RANCH MOTEL
4401 Ocean Dr.
853-7366
$–$$
W
This 30-unit motel is located about four miles south of downtown across the road from the bay on one of the prettiest residential streets in Corpus, and its rustic-looking, ranch style blends in nicely. Family-oriented, there are refrigerators in most of the rooms, and some have kitchenettes. Pool, playground, tennis court, and coffee bar.

North Padre Island

HOLIDAY INN–NORTH PADRE ISLAND
Take Padre Island Dr. (Texas 358) across JFK Causeway, go
approximately three miles to Park Rd. 53, turn east, proceed to hotel
on Windward Dr.
949-8041 or 1-800-238-8000
$$$–$$$$
W+ two rooms
In an area where condos reign supreme, this is the only major beach-
front hotel. Built in 1973, it recently had some extensive face-lifting.
This included installing safes in all 148 rooms for guests who want to
leave valuables behind when they go out—a great anxiety-reliever, es-
pecially when lightly dressed for the pool or beach. Features include a
mile-long boardwalk, pool with snack bar, lounge, and a Gulf-view res-
taurant that turns into a supper club with entertainment at night.

PUERTO DEL PADRE HOTEL AND CONDOMINIUM SUITES
14300 S. Padre Island Dr., one mile south of JFK Causeway bridge
949-8141
$$–$$$$
W
As its name states, this is another combination hotel and condo, built
on a canal that leads to Laguna Madre and the Intracoastal Waterway. Its
design is unusual in that the approximately 100 small efficiencies and
suites are all entered from a covered atrium, and some are on corridors
leading to balconies on the second and third stories around the large,
heated indoor swimming pool. There is also covered parking, an outdoor pool, spa, a small restaurant (closed September through November), and a marina. Guest privileges are available at the country club,
which is just a few blocks away.

OTHER ACCOMMODATIONS

Apartments

CHRISTY ESTATES APARTMENTS
Central
3942 Holly Rd. at Weber
854-1091
$$
W
There are about 95 one-, two-, and three-bedroom apartments out of
the 250 in this two-story complex that can be rented by the day. The
furnishings are simple, but everything necessary is provided; and most

of the apartments offer a lot of room. Centrally located in a residential and small business district, they are within walking distance of stores and restaurants, but you will have to drive to the beach or bayfront. Rates drop sharply after a three-night stay, so these are a bargain for longer visits, especially for a family. Covered parking. Pool.

Bed & Breakfast

SAND DOLLAR HOSPITALITY
3605 Mendenhall
853-1222 or (evenings) 853-8953
$
W variable
   This is a reservation agency offering rooms with breakfast in about 16 private homes. These are not like old rooming houses but are mostly newer homes owned by people who enjoy having guests. Most of the homes are on the south side of the city, in the direction of Padre Island; but some are downtown, and many are near the water. Some have several rooms available and can accommodate families or small groups. Rates range from $20–$40 a night, with weekly rates available. Contact them early, since they do require you fill out a reservation request to help match you with a compatible host. And, since you are going into a private home, they do require a reference—usually just the name of your employer will do.

Condominiums

   All those listed are on North Padre Island.

GULFSTREAM
14810 Windward Rd. off Park Rd. 53
949-8061
$$$$
W
   All the apartments in this six-story building on the beach have the same floor plan: one bedroom, two baths, a living room that converts into a bedroom, small living-dining room, kitchen, and a small balcony overlooking the Gulf. Facilities include a heated swimming pool, Jacuzzi, and game room. Guest memberships are available for golf and other activities at the nearby country club. There are about 80 apartments in the rental pool. The minimum reservation is for two days.

ISLAND HOUSE
15340 Leeward Dr. off Whitecap Blvd. (Access Rd. 3A)
949-8166
$$$$
W

The apartments are large and bright in this three-story building on the beach. There are about 65 one-, two-, and three-bedroom apartments available. All have balconies and a view of the Gulf. Furnishings are simple, mostly beach-style rattan. Heated pool and wading pool. Two-day minimum reservation.

PUENTE VISTA
14300 Aloha, take first right off JFK Causeway bridge to Suntan, then right to Aloha
949-7081
$$$–$$$$
W

There are about 20 two- and three-bedroom townhouse apartments available in this development situated on a man-made peninsula that juts into Laguna Madre just after the causeway bridge. All are tastefully furnished and have both a deck and a patio overlooking the water. Facilities include a boat dock for each unit, a pool, steam rooms, and saunas. Guest privileges are available at the nearby country club. Two-day minimum reservation.

In addition to the above, there are a number of agencies on Padre Island handling condo and beach house rentals with summer rates running from $50 to $150 a day.

Century 21
14517 S. Padre Island Dr.
949-8110

Island Properties International
14617 S. Padre Island Dr.
949-8505

Padre Island Rental Clearinghouse
14602 S. Padre Island Dr.
949-7033 or in Texas 1-800-242-0117 and outside Texas 1-800-531-1030

RESTAURANTS

The restaurant listings in the telephone book go on and on, but unfortunately, there is only a relatively small number of restaurants in Corpus that rise above the routine—either with culinary delights, by making eating a fun experience, or just by putting out good food at reasonable prices. Some of these are in the better hotels (see Hotels & Motels), others are long-time local favorites that have built and maintained their following over the years, and a few are relative newcomers making their mark with imagination in the kitchen and attention to the details of pleasing diners. It's sad to say that in this city by the sea, you have to dig to find a good seafood chef who knows other ways to cook besides frying and that most restaurants give in to the temptation of convenience and use frozen fish rather than the fresh that is so readily available.

Following is a selection of restaurants that do rise above the ordinary in one way or another.

Putting on the Ritz

THE BRITISH SIDEBOARD
Central
3154 Reid Dr., in Gardens on the Plaza, one block west of S. Alameda near Glazebrook
852-4838
Lunch and dinner, closed Saturday lunch
Reservations recommended, jackets requested at dinner
$$$$; AE, MC, V
W +

Elegant dining on hand-rubbed antique tables with fine linens, china, silver, crystal, and fresh flowers—all enhance the pleasure of well-chosen entrées. Kay Jones makes no bones about saying she wants her restaurant to be the best on the coast, and she spares no effort to reach that goal. The menu changes frequently to take advantage of the best that's available while emphasizing the staples of European cuisine, including *chateaubriand* for two, roast rack of lamb, and *escalopes of veal marsala*. There are also American favorites such as red snapper, quail, and selected Mexican dishes. Bar.

Dinner for Two

THE WAYWARD LADY
Downtown
On the Cooper St. L-Head
887-9716
Open seven days for lunch and dinner
Reservations suggested
$$–$$$$; Cr.

This replica of a nineteenth-century riverboat stands four decks high, and there are restaurants on every deck. If you are looking for a romantic setting, the restaurants to visit are on the second and third decks. There is a dining room forward and another in the stern on the second deck. Each has a cozy plushness, resembling a Hollywood version of a Mississippi riverboat salon, and a view of the city skyline or the bay. Seafood dominates the menu—a blackboard lists the catch of the day—but there are other entrées, including steaks. For more elegant, and

expensive, dining, the restaurant on the third deck offers gourmet entrées. The first deck is for informal, stand-up eating with an oyster bar
and grill at each end, while the top deck restaurant is outside, open to
the Gulf breezes. If you are not sure where to go, check the menu board
posted outside at the entrance. Bar.

COOPER'S ALLEY
See Clubs & Bars.

LIGHTHOUSE BAR AND GRILL
Downtown
Lawrence St. T-Head
883-3982
Open seven days for lunch and dinner
$$; Cr.
W
Casual dining with a menu that ranges from u-peel-em shrimp and
oysters on the half shell to steak sandwiches and the catch of the day.
But the real catch of the day—or night—is the view of the bay and the
Harbor Bridge, which also makes this a favorite spot for watching the
midget sailboat races every Wednesday evening (see Sports & Activi-
ties). Bar.

American

HOME PLATE
Central
1133 Airline, near McArdle
991-2300
**Open seven days: Monday through Thursday 7 a.m.–8 p.m., Friday
and Saturday 7 a.m.–9 p.m., Sunday 7 a.m.–4 p.m.**
$–$$; MC, V
W
For the big breakfast eater there's a buffet from 7:00–10:30 a.m. that
offers all you can eat of the usual morning fare, including biscuits and
gravy and grits, plus homemade blueberry muffins. Lunch and dinner
menus highlight hearty portions of such popular home-style dishes as
meatloaf, pot roast, and chicken-fried steak.

Chinese

MAO TAI
Central
4601 S. Padre Island Dr. between Weber and Everhart

852-7624
Open seven days for lunch and dinner
$$; Cr.
W

Even though they can't seem to make up their minds what Chinese style of cooking to follow—sometimes it's Cantonese but more recently Hunan and spicy Szechuan—the kitchen consistently prepares tasty food. The secret, apparently, is in their ability to create delightful combinations and serve them at their peak, so each fine ingredient retains its own individual flavor. Bar.

Italian

FRANK'S SPAGHETTI HOUSE
Central (near downtown)
2724 Leopard at Palm
882-0075
Monday through Friday 11 a.m.–9:45 p.m., Saturday 5–10 p.m., closed Sundays and holidays
$$; AE, MC, V
W

The typical wine bottles, checkered tablecloths, cloth napkins, and crowded tables in the rooms of an old house give this restaurant a little of the feeling of a neighborhood *trattoria* where the customer is still valued as a friend. Equally important, the old Italian-style of cooking with care carries over to most dishes the kitchen produces. Bar.

LUCIANO'S
Central (near downtown)
1618 S. Staples, one block north of Six Points
884-1832
Lunch Monday through Friday, dinner seven days
$$; AE, MC, V
W

Over the years, the menu has grown to 30 entrées and 80 specialty items, but the Luciano family has kept the faith with their customers by continuing to serve many of the tried-and-true recipes they started with in the forerunner of this restaurant back in 1949. There's a variety of pasta dishes, homemade Italian sausage, authentic Italian desserts, and *espresso* and *cappuccino* good enough to be served on the Via Veneto. To put you in the mood there's Italian music, a long wine list, and a 30-foot mural of old-world Venice that was painted in Italy. Bar.

Mexican

JOSIE'S
Central (near downtown)
1000 Santa Fe, near Buford, in Gaslight Square
884-5951
Lunch and dinner, closed Sunday
$$; MC, V
W

According to the local Tex-Mex food enthusiasts, Josie's soft tacos live up to her claim that they are among the best (she says "the best") anywhere. Otherwise, the menu is typically Mexican with enchiladas, tamales, chalupas, and the rest with the spicy levels running from gringo-mild to volcanic. Beer.

OLD MEXICO
Central (near downtown)
3329 Leopard at Nueces Bay Blvd.
883-6461
Lunch and dinner, closed Sunday and Monday
$$; AE, MC, V
W

"Puffy tacos" are just about the only item that's different here from ones on the standard Tex-Mex menu. These are the creation of the Lopez brothers who have run this restaurant for more than 30 years. The place is large and largely unadorned, the service is simple and fast, and the food remains a cut above the ordinary. Beer and wine.

Seafood

BAJA COAST
Central
5253 S. Staples, near S. Padre Island Dr.
992-FISH
Open seven days, dinner only
$$; Cr.
W

The cooks are part of the show here. The dining area is tiered, so you can watch them at work on the stoves behind a long counter, grilling the seafood over coals made from mesquite wood and stir-frying the vegetables. In addition to local fish, fish is also flown in from both the east and west coasts. A supplement to the menu tells you which catch is the freshest. And if you want to take some home with you—or select your own dinner—a fish market is just inside the entrance. Oyster bar and regular bar, too.

BLACK DIAMOND OYSTER BAR
Central
5712 Gollihar at Airline
992-2382
Lunch and dinner, closed Sunday
No reservations
$–$$; No cr.
W

The atmosphere is hole-in-the-wall with mismatched furniture and beat up floors, and the only way the seafood is prepared is fried. Still, customers line up to get in, so come early if you have any other plans for the night. Perhaps it's because the seafood is fresh and the servings are plentiful, but whatever the reasons, this is an original and has become an institution in Corpus. Beer and wine. A prettier version with a full bar is farther south at 7202 S. Padre Island Drive at Rodd Field Road (992-2432), which is open seven days.

CAPTAIN BOOMER'S
Downtown
People's St. T-Head
882-8341
Open seven days for lunch and dinner
$$; Cr.

The older of the two floating restaurants, Captain Boomer's offers Gulf fish that's fresh, live lobster from Maine, and a view of the skyline that is hard to beat. Steaks and chicken are also on the menu. Oyster bar and regular bar.

CATFISH CHARLIE'S
Central
5830 McArdle at Airline, in Crossroads Village Shopping Center
993-0363
Open seven days for lunch and dinner
Reservations accepted on weekends only
$–$$; MC, V

A casual Cajun fish-fry is what you walk into when you enter this barn-like restaurant. As the name says, the mainstay is all-you-can-eat freshwater catfish served with hush puppies (lightly zipped up with jalapeño), cole slaw, beans, and country-fried potatoes. They also serve Louisiana-style seafood gumbo, fried shrimp, frog legs, fried oysters, and red beans and rice with ham. For meat eaters there's chicken-fried steak and fried chicken. Beer.

JB'S CRAB POT
South
10649 S. Padre Island Dr. at Nagle
937-1581

Open seven days for lunch and dinner
$$; Cr.
W
   The menu is printed inside a four-page newspaper called the *Crabpot Gazette*. The furniture, china, glassware, and almost everything else comes from swap shops and antique stores making the decor a collection of mismatches. In other words, it's all in the spirit of fun. But J. B. Baker isn't fooling when he says the fish is "just as fresh as we can get it." The variety ranges from crabmeat (naturally) to shark, and they cook it whichever way is best for bringing out the flavor. J. B. takes pride in his secret technique of preparing a flounder for stuffing by extracting the bones without filleting the fish or removing anything but the head. Chicken and steaks are available for landlubbers. Bar. Upstairs is Mom's Oar House, a lounge with live entertainment, mostly guitarists.

SNOOPY'S PIER
South
10875 S. Padre Island Dr., under the south end of the JFK Causeway bridge
949-8815
Open seven days for lunch and dinner
$–$$; No cr.
W
   Snoopy's was once a fisherman's hangout, and with bare floors and checked oilcloth tablecloths on picnic tables, it still looks it. It's also a little hard to find—coming from Corpus go over the bridge and exit to the right. The dirt road along the water is bumpy and prone to turn to mud after a rain. But they serve only locally caught seafood and know how to broil or fry it to bring out its best. The shrimp and rice dish alone is worth the trip. Bar.

UNCLE CHESTER'S OLDE CRAB HOUSE
South
6810 Saratoga near Airline
991-8730
Open seven days, dinner only except for lunch on Sunday
$$; Cr.
W call ahead
   The menu doesn't hold any surprises—the usual shrimp, crabs, catfish, flounder, and catch of the day—but the preparation is better than average. Even the fried seafood retains its flavor and is not overwhelmed by the frying process. There is also a variety of steaks to choose from. Although a large restaurant, it still imparts a cozy feeling, since it is divided up into sections with a number of semi-private booths. Bar.

WATER STREET OYSTER BAR
Downtown
309 N. Water at Williams
881-9448
Open seven days for lunch and dinner
$$; AE, MC, V
W+

This popular spot was once a transmission shop, and remains of the yellow driving lane lines still mark the bare concrete floor. Now it is a downtown mecca for seafood lovers, serving mostly fresh Gulf catches grilled over mesquite. Be sure to look at the house specials on the huge blackboard over the open grill kitchen. Among the favorites is blackened redfish. They use the same searing technique to blacken steaks, too. This is also one of the few restaurants around that knows how to select and cook shark. Stand-up oyster bar and large patio. Bar.

WATERWORKS
South
13245 S. Padre Island Dr., under north end of JFK Causeway bridge
937-0072
Open seven days for lunch and dinner
$$

There are binoculars chained by each table so you can get a better view of Laguna Madre and the Intracoastal Waterway. The restaurant itself is small, but the windows and the blue and white decor make it seem bigger. In addition to seafood—broiled, fried, or grilled—you can also order a tasty burger or a steak. Check the blackboard specials. There's a porch where you can dine when it's not too breezy and watch the sunset. Beer and wine.

THE YARDARM
Central
4310 Ocean Dr., near Robert
855-8157
Dinner only, closed Monday and Tuesday, usually closed November through February
$$; Cr.

The only bad thing about this restaurant is that it's closed too often. There are rumors it may stay open in the winter, but only time will tell. Meanwhile, this weathered Cape Cod house on the bay side of Ocean Drive continues to draw the crowds for its outstanding and imaginative seafood entrées as well as such meat cookery as its famed *grenadine of beef with béarnaise*. All dinners include homemade soup or chowder, a salad served family-style in a large bowl, and potato. Bar.

CLUBS & BARS

The attraction of the increasing numbers of plush or trendy clubs opening in the major hotels (see Hotels & Motels) has weeded out some of the independents. But there are still plenty of places around town with devoted patrons who refuse to abandon them for the competition. Here are a few that have weathered the storm and look like they will continue to survive no matter what pops up in town.

CANTINA SANTA FE
Central
1011 Santa Fe
884-1756
Cover Friday and Saturday; AE, MC, V
W

Sometimes it's acoustic music, sometimes folk or jazz that fills the evening air in this unpretentious club. Dart games are inside, and ping-pong tables are in the outside beer garden. Mexican and American food is available before the nightly entertainment starts.

COOPER'S ALLEY
Downtown
15 Gaslight Square, 3rd between Buford and Hancock
888-4141
Closed Sunday night
Cover for men only; Cr.
W call ahead

During the day this is a popular restaurant serving a full range of seafood, steaks, chicken, and homemade desserts. But late at night, about the time the kitchen closes, it is transformed into a club featuring rock both on records and in live performances. Don't look for much to happen before 10 o'clock, but after that it can fill up fast, especially on weekends.

DALLAS
Central
24 Parksdale Plaza, Golihar and S. Staples
852-8088
Cover on Friday and Saturday; AE, MC, V
W

Recorded country and western and some pop tunes for dancers, table-hoppers, and aisle prowlers.

OFFBEAT

FRENCH THE BEACHCOMBER'S BOARDWALK
N. Padre Island
14330 South Padre Island Dr., approximately one mile south of JFK
Causeway bridge

949-8150
W variable
   The boardwalk leads you to a beachwear and shell shop, an import
shop, an oyster bar and seafood restaurant, and—the real offbeat—a
shark exhibit. Viewing the shark costs a dollar for adults, but if you
don't understand what you're going to see before you pay that buck, you
might think you've been ripped off. There *is* a 12-foot, 730-pound tiger
shark, just don't expect to see it swimming around. It's frozen and displayed, much like the day's catch in a retail fish store, in a large, glass-
walled freezer case. The recorded narration tells all about the shark and
the other Gulf fish exhibited in the case, and if you pay attention, you
will learn more about this man-eating fish and its companions here than
you would at most aquariums or museums. It's all owned and operated
by Gene L. French, a long-time island resident who built a business
from beachcombing and treasure hunting. One thing that distinguishes
his shell shop from others in the area is a corner display of items found
on the beach by French and others over the years—everything from an
old camera to a Chinese opium pipe.

CORPUS CHRISTI TO PORT MANSFIELD
   When you head south from Corpus you enter the big ranch country
in Kleberg and Kenedy counties, where most of the land along the
shore of Laguna Madre is privately owned. The closest you can get to
the coast is on U.S. 77 through Kingsville, which parallels the water for
about 25 miles inland.
   From Corpus take Texas 44 west to the junction with U.S. 77 near
Robstown, then south on 77 to Kingsville—a total of about 35 miles.

★★

KINGSVILLE

KLEBERG COUNTY SEAT	★	28,808	★	(512)

   In the early 1850s Richard King quit working as a riverboat captain,
bought an abandoned 75,000-acre Spanish land grant called the Santa
Gertrudis, and started what was to be one of the largest and best-
known ranches in the world. The King Ranch holdings now include
close to 10 million acres in seven countries, and more than 800,000 acres
of that is in the area encompassing several counties from Kingsville
south to Raymondville. The Kings later intermarried with the Klebergs,
and the descendants of these two families still own this huge private
corporation.
   The King Ranch was one of three ingredients that came together to
form the city of Kingsville. The second was the successful sinking of
wells, which provided a permanent source of water, and the third was
the arrival of the St. Louis, Brownsville, and Mexico Railroad in 1904.
   Kingsville is also the home of Texas A&I University and the U.S. Naval
Air Station where pilots are given advanced flight training.

JOHN E. CONNOR MUSEUM
W. Santa Gertrudis and Armstrong, on campus of Texas A&I
University (take Texas 141 from U.S. 77 and follow Texas A&I signs)
595-2819
Monday through Friday 10–5, Sunday 2:30–5
Free
W

This small museum concentrates on the history and heritage of the area, from fossils to current economic development. One of the largest collections of cattle brands and branding irons in the state is on display here.

KING RANCH HEADQUARTERS
Approximately two and a half miles west on Texas 141
592-6411
Open seven days 8–4
Free
W

Starting with Longhorns, the ranch soon began raising such pure-bred cattle as Brahma and Hereford. The next step was developing its own breed—the Santa Gertrudis. Named after the original Spanish land grant on which the ranch was started, this is the first breed of cattle originated in the Western Hemisphere. When oil was discovered on ranch land in 1945, the King Ranch corporation moved into other enterprises. But the world-wide headquarters of ranch operations is here. It is also the home of a stable that in the past produced several Kentucky Derby winners but now concentrates on breeding and training championship quarter horses. Only a 12-mile loop on ranch roads is open to the public for self-guided tours. Pick up a map or rent a guide-cassette at the gatehouse. The drive includes views of feeding pens, show pens, and pastures containing cattle and quarter horses. Deer are abundant on the ranch and often cross the loop road, vaulting the fences.

LEO KAUFFER PARK
Loyola Beach
Take U.S. 77 south nine miles, then left (east) on FM Rd. 668
approximately 11 miles
1-297-5738
Open seven days 8–9
W variable

This county park is located on Baffin Bay, which opens into the Intra-coastal Waterway and Laguna Madre inside the boundaries of the Padre Island National Seashore. Although the water here is shallow and salty, there's a beach for swimming, a lighted fishing pier, boat ramp, playground, restrooms and over 100 sites for both RV and tent camping (some with hookups), but no showers or dump station. RV sites run $5 a night, and other camping facilities are $2–$4. Reservations accepted. For information, Route 1, Box 77D, Rivera 78379.

KINGS INN
Loyola Beach
Take U.S. 77 south nine miles, then left (east) on FM Rd. 628 about
nine miles to Baffin Bay
1-297-5265
Open seven days for lunch and dinner, closed Easter and Christmas
Reservations recommended
$$–$$$; Cr.
W

This unpretentious, washed-out blue building perched at the water's
edge is yet another proof that a restaurant in the middle of nowhere will
draw patrons as long as it feeds them well. It's almost 20 miles from
Kingsville, but if you don't have reservations, especially on weekends,
be prepared to wait. There's no written menu, you're told what's available and how it's cooked. Most repeat customers swear by the crab pat-
ties, but all varieties of seafood—as fresh as long-time owners, Faye
and Randy Ware, can get it—are served. Most of it's fried and brought
out family-style, by the pound. So if you have a party of three or more,
do as you would in a Chinese restaurant—each diner order a different
entrée, then share. Each order is more than enough for all but the most
hearty eaters; plus each table gets a plate of tomatoes and a plate of
french fries, so three or four orders can easily stoke up six travelers
with enough to get them back to Kingsville or Corpus.

TO PORT MANSFIELD
Take Texas 77 south 58 miles, from Kingsville to Raymondville, then
left (east) on Texas 186 for about 23 miles to where it ends at Port Mansfield. A word of caution: from Kingsville south this is open ranch country with long distances between service stations, so before you start,
make certain you have plenty of gas and won't need a rest stop anytime
soon.

★ PORT MANSFIELD ★

★★
WILLACY COUNTY ★ **731** ★ **(512)**

This is another one of those fishing holes that anglers don't even want to share with their best friends. But the secret is out. Port Mansfield has been touted by several sports magazines as one of the best fishing spots on the coast, perhaps in the nation. You can cast a line in Laguna Madre or in ten miles be through the cut that separates North and South Padre Island into the Gulf. If it swims in Gulf waters, you can probably catch it here: redfish, sand and speckled trout, sheepshead, flounder, croaker, drum, skipjack, tarpon, marlin, kingfish, mackerel, ling, pompano, bonito, red snapper, and more.

It wasn't always so. Oh, the fish were here, but the only way to reach these grounds was by boat from far up or down the coast. Shrimpers and other commercial fishermen worked the area, but getting here was too much trouble for most sport anglers. Then in the late 1940s, the officials of Willacy County worked out the financing, got 2,500 acres of the King Ranch, built a port, and dug a channel across Laguna Madre to what's now called the Mansfield Cut through Padre Island to the Gulf, opening up this great fishing area to the world.

One of the unique features of this immense project is that the agreement with the King Ranch states that only the Willacy County Navigation District can own the land. If any is put up for sale, the King Ranch has the right of first refusal on it. The result is that all the property here is on 30 to 50 year leases to the residents. This may scare off some potential residents, but there's little chance of this situation turning out like the British lease of Hong Kong, which is running out and the city is being returned to China. The leases here are automatically renewable, and leasehold rights can be sold just as if the property were owned outright.

Today the town is still restricted to the 2,500 acres, now bordered by the Tom East Ranch (once part of the King) and the El Sauz Ranch. That limitation on its size may be one reason the waters around here have remained pollution-free. And fortunately, everything points to the waters remaining so. First, because the city sits behind the undeveloped Padre Island National Seashore. Next, because there are no rivers anywhere nearby that might carry pollution down from upstream cities or industry. And finally, because of the unique land ownership situation. The Willacy County Navigation District is opposed to anything that might pollute the fishing grounds and restricts leaseholders from selling to industry; therefore, unless the neighboring ranchers sell some of their property, there's little chance that industry will come in to spoil the area.

Port Mansfield is unique in another way. It's the only city in the county that voted "wet" under the Texas local option law to allow the sale of mixed drinks.

And regardless of whether you're interested in fishing, this is also the place to come if you want quiet, quiet. Most days the only sounds are an occasional boat or car motor, birds singing, neighbors greeting each other, and fisherfolk telling fish stories—mostly true. If you want even more solitude, you can take a boat from here over to the undeveloped stretches of Padre Island (see Outdoors & Side Trips).

For additional information, contact the Port Mansfield Chamber of Commerce (944-2354), P.O. Box O, Port Mansfield 78598.

OUTDOORS & SIDE TRIPS

PADRE ISLAND NATIONAL SEASHORE

Several charter boats will take you to unspoiled Padre Island near the Mansfield Cut for beachcombing, shell hunting, fishing, or camping. The trip costs about $40 per person. The boat owners will supply the camping gear for about $80–$100; this price includes the drop-off and pick-up. Also available are sightseeing trips to the Laguna Madre. Contact Captain Keith Moncus, 944-2624 or New Horizons Charter, 944-2230.

RAYMONDVILLE HISTORICAL CENTER
427 S. 7th (Business 77) at Harris (four blocks south of Texas 186)
1-689-3171
Usually open Wednesday and Friday afternoons 2–5 p.m. or by appointment, call
Free
W

Some of the artifacts recovered from Spanish ships wrecked on Padre in the mid 1500s are on display here. Most of the exhibits, however, relate to local farm and ranch history dating back to the time when the region was part of a huge Spanish land grant. Included are dioramas, photos, murals, and furniture and memorabilia from the nearby Kenedy Ranch.

SPORTS & ACTIVITIES

Boating

Boating enthusiasts will love it here. Small craft can go for miles in either direction on the Laguna Madre and the Intracoastal Waterway, while large vessels can go through the Mansfield Cut out into the Gulf.

Fishing

The International Game Fish Association has rated Port Mansfield as one of the ten best bill fishing spots in the world. According to local experts, the currents are responsible. Gulf currents come in to about 40 miles offshore here, which is closer than to most of the other fishing centers on the coast. At one point, called Devil's Elbow, five different currents converge bringing big fish in as close as 8 to 10 miles offshore.

If you don't want to go out that far, there are a lot of places close inshore where the fish bite. In addition to boat fishing in Laguna Madre or the Gulf, there's surf fishing on Padre Island, jetty fishing at the Mansfield Cut, and pier fishing in town. The one lighted public pier is at Fred Stone County Park, a small park squeezed against the northern boundary of the town, but many of the rental beach houses have small private piers. Another fishing arrangement you won't find many other places is barge fishing. The barges are really floating platforms with bunkhouses, some air conditioned, holding 6 to 12 fishermen on them. The owner-guides move the barges, when necessary, to follow the fish runs. They ferry their clients out to the anchored barges each night, where they can fish and sleep and fish and sleep all night, depending on how the fish are biting and how long it takes the client to catch his or her limit. Average cost is $30 a person.

A guide for boat or wade fishing in Laguna Madre's Redfish Bay will run about $175 a day for two or three people and $25 extra for each additional person up to six. Offshore fishing in the Gulf runs from $400 to $600 a day, depending on the size of the group and the kind of fish they want to go after. Since fishing is the main business here, a number of excellent guides are available. Among the better known ones are:

Capt. Corky Cobb
Corky's Charter
Bay and barge fishing
944-2225

Capt. Bob Fuston
Red Bandana Charters
Bay and Gulf fishing
944-2519

For information on these or other guides, barges, and charter boats, contact the Port Mansfield Guides' Association (944-2528) at P.O. Box 148, Port Mansfield 78598.

Another unusual fishing operation in the area is the Gulf Winds Fishing Service (944-2340). If you really want to be away from it all, Guy Bailey offers the opportunity at his small fishing camp equipped with all the basic necessities (and not much more) about 20 miles north of Port Mansfield on one of the spoil islands that was thrown up when the Intracoastal Waterway was dredged. His camp sleeps six, has a lighted pier, and costs about $150 a night for the whole place if you feed yourself. You can take your own boat, or Guy will ferry you there. If you want to add a gourmet touch to your hermitage, Guy will cook for you for about $14 extra a head. And gourmet it will be, since he was once a chef at the Houston Country Club, which may be the reason a number of wealthy fisherfolk and celebrities have taken to this rustic isolation.

Hunting

The hunting here is mostly for duck and geese and usually from air boats. For information and guides contact the Port Mansfield Guides' Association (see Fishing).

Again, Port Mansfield offers the unusual: hunting deer and nilgai with bow and arrow inside the city limits. Not many deer stroll in here, but nilgai often do. What's a nilgai? It's a species of antelope weighing in at around 200 pounds. A dozen of them were imported from India by the King Ranch in 1929. Now the progeny of that handful number in the thousands and have become a big problem for the ranchers, since they compete with the range cattle for food. There's a season for deer, but you can hunt nilgai all year. Unless you have a hunting lease on a neighboring ranch, however, you do have to wait until the animals leave private property and enter into the city. And then remember, you can hunt with bow and arrow only.

ANNUAL EVENTS

PORT MANSFIELD FISHING TOURNAMENT
Usually third or fourth week in July, Wednesday through Sunday
944-2354
The Chamber of Commerce describes this event as family fun. It costs $40 to enter the bay-surf division and $75 for the offshore, but for that you also get a gimme-cap, T-shirt, and three meals. Even though there are no big money prizes, it still attracts 500 to 600 entrants each year. Trophies and prizes are awarded for just about every category of fish you could catch in Laguna Madre or offshore, from barracuda to white marlin. There's also a children's fishing tournament held at the pier (entry fee: $5).

MOTELS

RED FISH MOTEL AND CAFE
Texas 186 and Water St.
944-2391
Double: $32–$42
W
This simple, concrete block motel on the water with 35 rooms, some with kitchenettes, offers a swimming pool and a lighted fishing pier. The manager also answers the Chamber of Commerce phone. Cafe open from 5:30 a.m. to 10 p.m.

OTHER ACCOMMODATIONS

Since this is a small community, there are only a few beach houses and condos that can be rented by the day or longer. All are furnished and most have cable TV. Some have a private fishing pier or access to a nearby pier. High season rates for a beach house, from Memorial Day to October, range from about $40 a day for a one bedroom to $80 for a four bedroom. Three-bedroom condos go for $100 to $175 a day. Rates drop considerably in winter. For information, contact Glaze Realty (944-2355), 701 Bayshore 78598 or Port Mansfield Realty (944-2289), 207 Bayshore 78598.

RESTAURANTS

WINDJAMMER INN RESTAURANT AND LOUNGE
South Harbor Drive
944-9394

Lunch and dinner in summer, dinner only in winter
$$; MC, V
W
   Seated inside on the deck overlooking the harbor, you can dine on the usual variety of seafood and steaks. The cocktail lounge stays open until 2 a.m. The "inn" part of the name consists of four rooms for rent.

TO HARLINGEN
   Return to U.S. 77 at Raymondville and continue south to Harlingen.

★★

HARLINGEN

CAMERON COUNTY	★	43,543	★	(512)

   This is one of the major cities in the Lower Rio Grande Valley, which is the region along the eastern end of the Rio Grande River. Anchored by Harlingen, South Padre Island, and Brownsville on the east, this area extends west about 140 miles to Falcon Lake. Although Harlingen is not on the coast, you have to pass through it to reach South Padre, and there are several sights worth an enroute stopover.

TEXAS DEPARTMENT OF HIGHWAYS AND PUBLIC
TRANSPORTATION VISITOR CENTER
Intersection of U.S. 77 and U.S. 83
428-4477
Open seven days 8–5
Free
W+
   Even if you aren't interested in the maps, brochures, and wealth of free information on both Texas and the Rio Grande Valley that the courteous bilingual travel counselors dispense here, this is still a good place for a rest stop. The building is cool and quiet, a slide show presents points of interest in Harlingen and the Valley, the restrooms are clean, and a patio out back has a small reflecting pool that is relaxing just to sit by. This is one of 12 information centers the state has established near its borders.

CONFEDERATE AIR FORCE HEADQUARTERS
Rebel Field, Harlingen Industrial Air Park at Valley International
Airport
From U.S. 77 north take FM Rd. 508 east approximately four miles to airport entrance, or from U.S. 77 south take Loop 499 east approximately five miles to airport
425-1057
Museum open Monday through Saturday 9–5, Sunday 1–5, closed Christmas
Adults $3, children $1.50
W

You didn't know the Confederates have an Air Force? Shame on you. I bet you also don't believe Texas still has a navy either. Well, you may have to hunt a bit for the Texas Navy, but the proof of the existence of the Confederate Air Force (CAF) is sitting at Rebel Field waiting for you. Usually a third or more of the 142 flyable World War II aircraft in the CAF is parked here. The others are either on tour at air shows, working in movies (17 so far), or scattered throughout the 72 world-wide squadron chapters. With this number of aircraft, the CAF is the 13th largest air force in the world and the largest private one. The organization is totally self-supporting with more than 7,500 members dedicated both to preserving the mystique of the war fought in the skies during World War II and maintaining and flying the aircraft from that period.

The CAF headquarters and museum are located at Harlingen. The entrance building of the museum displays uniforms, weapons, and other memorabilia from both sides in World War II. But the heart of the show is outside in the display hangars and on the airport apron, where the restored planes are found: Japanese Zeros, German Heinkels and Messerschmitts, and U.S combat aircraft ranging from the P-39 Aircobra to the B-29 Superfortress. All are clearly marked with gobs of information and are flyable. For the World War II historian, the plane buff, and children (young and old), this is a don't-miss show.

The CAF Officers Club, right next to the museum, is open to the public. In addition to food and drink, a 30-minute film about the CAF's Ghost Squadron is shown. The film is free, and if it's not running when you arrive, just ask and they'll show it.

Twice a year, usually in March and October, the CAF puts on an air show here to which as many as 200 World War II aircraft, both squadron planes and those privately owned, fly from all over the country to re-enact air battles and perform acrobatics and precision flying.

Harlingen's airport is expanding, and the roads and parking are in a state of flux. So if you can't find the CAF Headquarters, stop in at the terminal and ask for directions. For information, Box CAF, Harlingen 78551.

MARINE MILITARY ACADEMY
320 Iwo Jima Blvd., across from terminal building at Valley International Airport (see directions for CAF Headquarters) 423-6006
Open seven days, contact Public Affairs Office for group tours

If you ever wanted to see a Marine Corps precision drill or parade but couldn't get to the real thing, this academy offers a good substitute. Students at this private military prep school wear uniforms similar to those of the U.S. Marines and follow the customs and traditions of the corps as well. During the school year, visitors are welcome to watch the daily noon dress parade in which the cadets march from the main parade field to the dining hall (they call it the mess deck). On special occasions, parades also are held at the school's Iwo Jima War Memorial, some featuring fly-overs by World War II planes from the nearby Confederate Air Force. The Iwo Jima statue is the original working model used to cast the famous bronze memorial that stands in Arlington National Cemetery. (The Marine placing the flag pole into the ground was Corporal Harlon H. Block, who was from Weslaco in the Valley and was killed later in that battle.)

RIO GRANDE VALLEY HISTORICAL MUSEUM
Boxwood and Raintree streets, Harlingen Industrial Air Park near Valley International Airport (see directions for CAF Headquarters)
423-3979
Tuesday through Friday 9–noon, 2–5; Sunday 2–5
Free (donations accepted)
W variable
This is really three museums in one. The main building features the cultural and natural history of the Lower Rio Grande Valley. Two outbuildings, moved to this site, house the restored Paso Real Stagecoach Inn (where three meals and a bed cost 35¢ a night) and Harlingen's first hospital built in 1923 and now restored as a medical museum. The complex is a little hard to find since it's behind a street filled with warehouses. Look across the street from the student quarters of the Texas State Technical Institute or ask the students for directions.

LAGUNA ATASCOSA NATIONAL WILDLIFE REFUGE
Approximately 25 miles east of Harlingen
From U.S. 77, take FM Rd. 106 right approximately 25 miles until it dead-ends, then north (left) about 2 miles to park headquarters
748-3607
Open seven days dawn to dusk
Free
W variable
This 45,190-acre bushland and coastal marsh refuge lies on the Laguna Madre, behind Padre Island. It is the southernmost refuge on what's called the Great Central Flyway along which waterfowl and other birds migrate annually from Canada to the Gulf. There are both walking and driving trails. Visitors should register at the visitors center where information, maps, and bird and animal lists may be obtained. Limited fishing and bow hunting. For information, P.O. Box 2683, Harlingen 78550.

TO PORT ISABEL & SOUTH PADRE ISLAND
From Harlingen, take U.S. 77 south approximately 12 miles to Texas 100, then turn east (left). It's about 25 miles to Port Isabel and the causeway to South Padre Island.

★ SOUTH PADRE ISLAND ★ & PORT ISABEL

★★★

SOUTH PADRE ISLAND

CAMERON COUNTY	★	791	★	(512)

★★★

PORT ISABEL

CAMERON COUNTY	★	3,769	★	(512)

As you leave the mainland city of Port Isabel, South Padre appears like an island in the sun, luxurious and dreamlike, at the end of Texas' longest bridge, the Queen Isabella Causeway. Here the sun-bleached essence of the modern summer resort—long, white beaches and towering white condominiums—seems to be captured all year round.

South Padre is the southern tip of the longest barrier island in the world. The island is a narrow strip of land—in reality a giant sandbar—

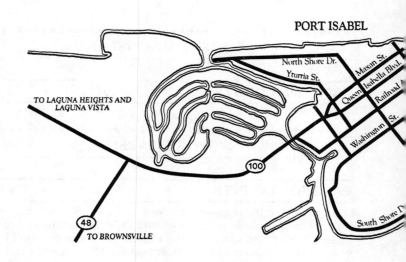

LAGUNA MADRE

PORT ISABEL

North Shore Dr.
Yturria St.
Maxan St.
Isabella Blvd.
Queen
Railroad A
Washington St.

TO LAGUNA HEIGHTS AND
LAGUNA VISTA

100

48
TO BROWNSVILLE

South Shore D

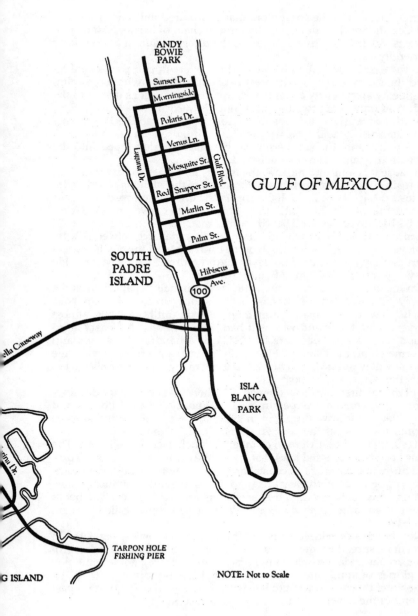

ANDY
BOWIE
PARK

Sunset Dr.

Morningside

Polaris Dr.

Venus Ln.

Mesquite St.

Red Snapper St.

Marlin St.

Palm St.

Hibiscus Ave.

Laguna Dr.

Gulf Blvd.

GULF OF MEXICO

SOUTH
PADRE
ISLAND

100

Isabella Causeway

ISLA
BLANCA
PARK

TARPON HOLE
FISHING PIER

G ISLAND

NOTE: Not to Scale

running parallel to the coast more than a hundred miles north to Corpus Christi. South Padre is one link in the chain of barrier islands that protects most of the Texas coast from the direct assault of a sometimes unfriendly sea.

To the east is the Gulf of Mexico, where white-tipped waves spill toward the sandy shore. To the west is Laguna Madre, where the calm, fish-filled waters reflect a sun that doesn't so much set as melt into the land. And only about twenty miles south is Mexico.

South Padre Island extends north about 34 miles to the Port Mansfield Channel. Its width varies from a few hundred yards up to about half a mile. Only the southernmost five miles are developed into the city with the same name as the island.

Because it is long and narrow, the island city is easy to get around in. The main street running right up the center of the island is called Padre Boulevard (also Park Road 100). This is the only paved road that goes beyond the city limits, continuing north another seven miles. (After that it's back to nature with beach, dunes, marshes, birds and other wild creatures but no creature comforts.) Running parallel between Padre Boulevard and the Gulf for much of the central part of the city is a street appropriately named Gulf Boulevard. And on the Laguna Madre side is—you guessed it—Laguna Boulevard.

On the mainland, Port Isabel, which was originally established as the supply port for General Zachary Taylor's army in the Mexican War, slowly grew to be a small fishing town. But up until the 1950s, almost everything on the island was as it had been for eons. A Coast Guard station was established there in 1891, and a handful of hermits and fishermen built their shacks. Eventually, some people from Brownsville and the Valley put up beach houses, but not many, since the only way to reach the island was by boat.

In 1954 the first causeway opened. But there was no rush for development. Sure, some developers moved in, and more beach houses and even a few motels went up; but in general, the island continued to be ignored for most of the next 20 years. Then, in the early 1970s, two things happened that were to change the whole face of the island. The Texas Legislature passed laws that forced the insurance industry to provide hurricane coverage to coastal areas, and the new four-lane causeway was opened. With easy access to the island and insurance protection on construction loans, the developers arrived in force. The boom has been so rapid that now South Padre is sometimes called "Miami Beach West."

Not that this development is bad. In fact, as long as it is regulated to prevent its spread up the island, it is beneficial. South Padre today provides accommodations and other amenities, so more people can enjoy the glories of sun, sand, and surf without having to rough it. At the same time, those who want to live with nature need only go north past the end of the paved road to find the joys of solitude.

Accommodations run the full gamut from camping at the county parks to luxury hotels and chi-chi condos, and the restaurants do the same ranging from fast food to posh dining.

Whatever its duration, a visit to the island is bound to be wonderfully full, even if you choose, as many do, to spend the entire time lazing in the sun, listening to the call of the gulls and the fond and steady slap of the waves. On the other hand, if you want to do more, your choices are numerous.

High on the list, of course, is fishing. It is an island, and so fishing is a way of life for both residents and visitors. You can bay fish from boat or pier or up to your hips in waders, or you can put a line in the Gulf from the beach, the jetty, or the deck of a deep-sea charter.

If you just want to enjoy the water, there's swimming in the Gulf (the shores of the bay and Laguna Madre are mostly too marshy for this pleasure), waterskiing, surfing, and sailboarding.

The miles of white sandy beach offer other activities. Shell collecting and beachcombing are best on the relatively undisturbed beach north of the paved road, especially after a high tide. And if you want to treasure hunt, there are no laws here, as there are on the island above the Mansfield Cut, against using metal detectors. The sand also packs beautifully for the construction of sand castles—or condominiums.

A couple of cautions: in addition to sea, sun, and surf, there are also rattlesnakes and jelly fish. Rattlers live in the sand dunes north of the city, so don't stray from the beaches unless you're wearing boots. And in the spring and fall, jelly fish and Portuguese man-of-war often dot the Gulf surf and pile up in iridescent, and still dangerous, heaps on the beach.

Cautions noted; in addition to the joys of nature, there are man-made attractions including the biggest water slide on the Texas coast, animal shows at Ocean Safari Park, a paddle-wheel tour boat, go-carts, and a marine life museum. And life doesn't stop at dark. There are a number of places to dance and enjoy music and other live entertainment.

Overall, South Padre is a getaway island with all the conveniences.

Temperatures in the summer range from the high 70s to the low 90s, in winter from the low 50s to the high 60s.

TOUR & GUIDE SERVICES

SOUTH PADRE ISLAND TOURIST BUREAU
600-A Padre Blvd., just north of causeway
943-6433 or in Texas 1-800-292-7508
Monday through Friday 9–4:30, Saturday and Sunday 10–3
Free
W

The wall racks are filled with brochures on South Padre, Port Isabel,

and the Lower Rio Grande Valley. Newspapers covering island entertainment and activities are also available, some free. And the coun-
selors will gladly answer your questions, give directions, or recommend where to go and what to do.

THE COAST LINE: SOUTH PADRE TRAM
Padre Island Dr. (main station at Retama St.)
Seven days in season, usually 11–9
Free
Pulled by a truck converted to look like the Little Engine That Could,
this open-air sightseeing tram makes frequent, but slow, trips between
Isla Blanca Park on the south and Andy Bowie Park on the north end of
the city. You can flag it down anywhere along the route, but scheduled
stops are made at a number of places including City Hall, Bahia Mar,
Ben's Go-Carts, Ocean Star and Paradise Cove shopping centers, the
tourist bureau, and Ocean Safari. The driver will also let you off anywhere you ask. It's slow, but it's free. Schedules vary with the season.
For information call the tourist bureau (943-6433).

GRAY LINE TOURS
South Padre Travel Agency
2600 Padre Blvd., next to Post Office
943-2144
Open seven days 8–5
Tours from $10 to $35
The three-hour tour of Port Isabel and South Padre costs $10. Other
tours available include trips to the Confederate Air Force Museum in
Harlingen and the citrus groves in the Valley, the Gladys Porter Zoo and
Boca Chica Beach in Brownsville, and sightseeing and shopping in
Matamoros, Mexico. There's a free hotel pick-up service for tours.

ISABELLA QUEEN
6201 Padre Blvd., approximately four and a half miles north of
causeway
943-7893
Call for cruise schedule, closed Monday
Adults $8.50, children $4.25 for sightseeing cruise
W
The basic two-hour sightseeing cruise on this two-deck, paddle-
wheel steamboat runs Monday through Saturday. The lower deck is enclosed and the upper is open. It takes you around Laguna Madre and
down into the Brownsville Channel near the jetties. There's also an
early dinner cruise at 5 p.m. daily except Monday, a Captain's Brunch
cruise at 11:30 a.m. every Sunday, and a sunset (or moonlight—depending on the time of year) dinner cruise starting at 8 p.m. when
there's enough demand for it. Bar.

236

SEAPLANE TOURS
6201 Padre Blvd., at *Isabella Queen* dock, approximately four and a
half miles north of causeway
943-7893
Open seven days from 10–5 when the pilot's in town
Adults $15–$20, children $10–$15
A great view from 500 feet, but iffy. The plane and pilot live in Dallas
and are only in South Padre on a rather erratic schedule. If the listed
number doesn't answer, check the tourist bureau. There's a short flight
that goes about 18 miles and costs $15 for adults ($35 minimum), and a
long one that goes 34 miles and costs $20 ($45 minimum).

POINTS OF INTEREST

THE *LADY BEA*
Port Isabel
Beulah Lee Park, Texas 100 near the causeway
Free
A shrimp boat moored to her dry land foundation, *Lady Bea* is a
monument to the local shrimping industry and the first installment of
what the Laguna Madre Museum Foundation hopes will soon be a combined maritime and local history museum. There's a ramp up to the
deck. You can see into the wheelhouse, and windows have been cut in
the cabin walls so you can also see the small galley and tight crew
quarters.

PADRE BALLÍ STATUE
End of Queen Isabella Causeway on South Padre Island
Padre José Nicolás Ballí was a missionary priest, the first American
born Spaniard ordained on this continent. In 1765 his mother gave him
the land grant she'd received from the king of Spain, which included
the island that now bears his title. The statue stands at the South Padre
end of the causeway, arms wide as if welcoming people to his island.

PAN AMERICAN UNIVERSITY MARINE BIOLOGY LAB
Isla Blanca County Park
943-2644
Monday through Friday 1:30–4:30, Sunday 1:30–4:30
Free
W+
This stucco building is located just north of the jetty in the county
park at the southernmost tip of the island. Although it's a university
research and teaching center engaged in coastal studies, a large area is
open to the public. Local marine life is shown in both static displays and
several large aquarium tanks. Most of the varieties of shells that can be

found on Padre are on exhibit, and the lab's experts will identify any shells brought to them.

QUEEN ISABELLA CAUSEWAY
Between Port Isabel and South Padre Island
Open at all times
Measuring 2.6 miles, this causeway is in the record books as Texas' longest bridge. At the center, the span is 73 feet above mean high tide, permitting seagoing ships to pass underneath. About 15,000 cars cross it on the average day.

SHRIMP FLEET
Port Isabel docks
When combined with the large number of shrimp boats at nearby Port Brownsville, this is one of the largest shrimp fleets on the coast. The boats can be seen at the docks all along the waters around Port Isabel and from the jetty as they go to and from the Gulf.

BIRD'S-EYE VIEW

PORT ISABEL LIGHTHOUSE
Port Isabel
Texas 100 and Tarnava at the causeway
943-1172
Open seven days 10–11:30, 1–5
Adults $1, children 25¢
This is the only lighthouse on the Texas coast that's open to the public, and it sits in the middle of one of the state's smallest parks. Completed in 1853, this guardian of the coast cast its light up to 16 miles out into the Gulf for more than half a century, until 1905. During that time it survived occupation by both sides in the Civil War, several hurricanes, and a six-year shutdown while a legal battle took place over ownership of the lighthouse land. It seems the government had neglected a minor technicality when it built the lighthouse—acquiring the land it was situated on. From the top, on a clear day, you can almost see forever. At least you'll have an unobstructed view of Port Isabel, the Queen Isabella Causeway across Laguna Madre, Padre Island, and well out into the Gulf. But this bird's-eye view doesn't come easy. To reach the very top, you have to climb more than 70 winding steps, including three short ladders. Once there you'll be in a glass enclosure that is comfortable on cool days and summer mornings but turns into an oven in the summer sun. If you're in shape to make the climb, you might want to stop at the fenced platform just below this enclosure. It's cooler, and you can see just as far.

GALLERIES

ART GALLERIES
Bahia Mar Resort, 6300 Padre Blvd.
943-2282

Located in a separate building at the north end of the resort, this small gallery and gift shop has paintings, crafts, and needle art. Most of the paintings are sea scenes by local artists. A branch is at the Ocean Palm Shopping Plaza farther south on the boulevard.

LA POSADA
Port Isabel
Queen Isabel Inn, 300 Garcia, near the causeway
943-5571
W downstairs only

Dating from the turn of the century, the Queen Isabel is one of the oldest surviving hotel buildings in the area, but it's not a hotel anymore. It's now rental apartments, and the old lobby houses this gallery, which concentrates on the work of South Texas artists. In addition to paintings, the gallery also features fish prints made from the Japanese art form called Gyotaku, wood art crafted by the ancient skill called marquetry in which various colored woods are inlaid into a picture or design, and woven wall hangings and other fabric art.

SHOPPING

BOOKCOMBER
2312 Padre Blvd. at Ling
943-4906
W

Best-sellers, Texana, children's books, magazines, games, and gifts in a bright and comfortable store that makes browsing a pleasure.

THE BOUTIQUE
103 E. Redsnapper near Padre Blvd.
943-5123

This upstairs shop is tightly packed with easy living, carefree cottons for women. It also carries swimwear from Israel, hats, shoes, belts, and other accessories.

RARE ART ESTATE SALES
708 Padre Blvd. in Franke Plaza shopping center
943-5510

It looks like a combination museum, art gallery, and antique shop with oriental and Persian rugs, bronzes, paintings, sculpture, period furniture, crystal and old glass, and estate jewelry. In addition to regular sales, there are periodic auctions. The owners, Allen and Sara Goald, also open their store several evenings a week for informal wine and coffee chats about art history with anyone who wants to drop in.

TEXAS SHELL FACTORY
Laguna Heights
Texas 100 approximately three miles west of Port Isabel
943-1709
W
This is the retail outlet of a wholesale dealer, so if it's made out of seashells you'll probably find it here. The emphasis is on novelty items of the type that make forgettable souvenirs. But if you want untarnished samples of nature's art, there are shelves and open boxes filled with all kinds of shells and preserved marine life. Conch shells, sand dollars, coral, barnacles, starfish—you name it, they probably have it.

OUTDOORS & SIDE TRIPS

ANDY BOWIE PARK (CAMERON COUNTY PARK)
Padre Blvd. approximately four miles north of causeway
Open at all times
Free
Primitive camping is allowed on this Gulf beach park. And it is primitive, since there are no facilities except an open pavilion. Driving on the beach is permitted, which makes this a popular spot for the younger, car-oriented crowd. Plans are in the works to improve this park. For information contact the county parks office at 943-5493.

ISLA BLANCA PARK (CAMERON COUNTY PARK)
South of the causeway at southern end of the island (Box 2106, South Padre Island 78597)
943-5493
Open at all times, office open seven days 8 a.m.–10 p.m.
W variable
The largest camping area on South Padre Island is located here. In addition to more than 300 RV spaces with hookups ($10 a night, long-term rates available), there are 18 basically furnished, screened cabins sleeping four ($18 a night), 134 tent camping sites ($10 a night), and a 25-unit motel with one- to three-bedroom apartments ($36 to $108 a night). For day use, there are 22 cabanas by the beach ($7.50 a day). Up to six persons can use each five-by-ten-foot cabana with its picnic table and shower. The park office's computerized system keeps track of all these accommodations, and they accept reservations up to 15 days in advance. The park also has a beach, swimming pool, marina, picnic tables, restrooms, showers, dump station, grocery store, starlight amphitheater, and two restaurants. The park ends at the granite-block

north jetty of the Brownsville Channel, and the waters north of the jetty are reportedly the best spot on the island, some say the best on the whole Texas coast, for a long ride on a surfboard.

BROWNSVILLE AND MATAMOROS, MEXICO
See Tours & Guide Services and Brownsville.

CONFEDERATE AIR FORCE MUSEUM
See Tours & Guide Services and Harlingen.

KIDS' STUFF

BEN'S GO-CARTS
Padre Blvd. at Andy Bowie Park, approximately four miles north of causeway
943-5421
Open seven days 9 a.m.–dusk
Go-Carts $3 for six minutes, dune motorcycles $15 an hour ($20 deposit)

This isn't all kids' stuff. Kids can ride the go-carts, since they're confined to a track, but you have to be an adult to rent the single-seat, three-wheeled dune motorcycles. These you can take out to the sand flats north of Ben's and roar around to your heart's content. Just don't try riding them over the dunes—that's against the law, and the fine will be a lot more than the rental cost. Two-seater dune cycles are also available for $20 an hour.

JEREMIAH'S LANDING
Padre Blvd. at Gulfpoint, just south of the causeway
943-2131
Open weekdays 11–12, until 2 a.m. on weekend nights in high season, usually closed November through February
Water slide $5 per hour, mini-golf $3

Jeremiah's lives up to its billing as a "family amusement center." For the young, and the young at heart, there's the 240-foot, three-flume water slide (the biggest on the coast); an 18-hole mini-golf course, with three holes in the middle of the water slide hill; video game rooms; a T-shirt souvenir shop; and a snack bar. And, for those of age, there's a covered but open-air bar (beer and wine) on an upstairs deck overlooking all this madness. From June through September, Jeremiah's offers live entertainment nightly starting about 8 p.m. One of the best deals in town may be the snack bar's Sunday night special: starting at 6 p.m. it's all the shrimp you can eat for about $3.

OCEAN SAFARI PARK
Southern tip of the island on Laguna Madre in Isla Blanca Park
943-3271
Open seven days in high season 10 to dusk, closed Wednesday in fall
and winter (schedule subject to change, call)
Adults $7, children 4–12 $5, senior citizens $6
W variable

What type animal act would you like to see? An unusual big cat act
with lions, tigers, a puma, panther, leopard—and a German Shepherd
dog? A show with rattlesnakes, a cobra, and a python? A bird act with
colorful macaws? Or would you prefer to see streamlined dolphins zip-
ping through the water at incredible speeds and jumping 20 feet into the
air? No matter what your favorite, you can see them all at Ocean Safari.
The acts are scheduled so you have time to move from one show location to another. Overall, it takes about two hours to see the whole show.
It's all outdoors, and there's little or no overhead cover, so wear a hat to
ward off the sun. There are also bumper boats, a petting zoo, and for
the big people, a beer garden.

TROPIC ISLE GOLF
Padre Blvd. at Campeche, two miles north of the causeway
943-6621
Open seven days 12–11
$3

Eighteen holes of mini-golf plus a game room and T-shirt shop.

SPORTS & ACTIVITIES

Birdwatching

If you have a four-wheel-drive vehicle, try the Gulf beaches and bay-
side marsh between the developed area and the Mansfield Cut. Also
Laguna Atascosa National Wildlife Refuge (see Harlingen).

Boating

Small craft can use the protected waters of the Laguna Madre and the
Brownsville Ship Channel, while larger craft are just minutes away from
the waters of the Gulf. Among the places that charter the larger sailboats
are: Island Charters, Port Isabel, 943-4778 and Yellow Rose Charters,
Port Isabel, 943-4507. For smaller craft try:

ISLAND SAILBOAT RENTALS
212 W. Dolphin (on Laguna Madre)
943-5061
Open seven days, weather permitting, usually closed January and February (unless the weather is good for sailing)
    Most of the boats for rent are 14-footers that go for $10–$12 an hour, but they also offer sailboards for windsurfing for $7 an hour or a 16-foot Hobie Cat for $20 an hour. Lessons run $15 to $30 an hour, depending on the size of the boat, and it usually takes at least two hours of lessons before they'll let you go out on your own.

Fishing

    South Padre offers anglers the full range of opportunities. You can pay big bucks to go out on a high-powered charter boat after trophy fish in the Gulf or on a party-boat for a half-day in the bay, wade fish along the flats of Laguna Madre (loads of crabs for the grabbing there, too) or in the surf, or just throw a line off a jetty or a pier. Offshore catches include red snapper, grouper, kingfish, marlin, and sailfish. Inshore fishermen can expect to hit redfish, speckled trout, sheepshead, drum, flounder, ling, pompano, mackerel, and tarpon. Tarpon is making a comeback in this area after years of declining catches.
    Bay fishing party boats usually make a four-hour trip each morning and afternoon. Rates average $8–$10 a person (about $2 extra if they furnish tackle). For information, contact Colly's Fishing Service (943-2623) at the Sea Ranch Marina or Jim's Pier (943-2865) at 209 W. Whiting. Both of these also operate charter boats. The list of charter boat companies goes on and on. The following are just a few of the charter services available.

AUSTIN FISHING SERVICE ★ 943-6282

CAPTAINS JOE & TOM BRYANT ★ 943-1791

CAPTAIN DICK DENNIS ★ 943-1972

CAPTAIN JIM FUZY ★ 943-6216 (also boat rides)

CAPTAIN MURPHY'S CHARTER SERVICE ★ 943-2764

CAPTAIN BRYAN RAY ★ 943-6301

CAPTAIN DALE STOCKTON ★ 943-1621

CAPTAIN DEWITT THOMAS ★ 943-3332

For others, check the Yellow Pages, the tourist bureau, or Fisherman's Wharf (943-2412) at 211 W. Swordfish, on the bay. Several charter captains operate out of there. Charter rates for a half-day of bay fishing run about $150 for two people ($10 each additional). For offshore fishing the rates average about $300 for four people ($20 each additional).

If you want to go out in the bay on your own, Fisherman's Wharf also rents 14-foot johnboats for about $35 a half-day. This is also one place to go to charter a boat just for a ride. A two-hour ride will cost about $60 for up to six passengers.

For pier fishing, the place to go is the state fishing pier.

QUEEN ISABELLA STATE FISHING PIER
South of causeway near Isla Blanca Park
943-9807
Open 24 hours seven days
$1 for each fishing device
Sightseers free
W

Another old causeway put to good use. When they built the new causeway, they cut out the middle of the old one to let the boats pass. Then the state converted almost a mile of the South Padre end of the old one into this lighted pier. A concession stand sells tackle, bait, and snacks and rents out poles. Catches here include whiting, sand and speckled trout, and croakers. It's a good idea to bring a folding chair or something to sit on. Restrooms available. The other end of the old causeway, on the Port Isabel side, is called the Tarpon Hole Fishing Pier. It's privately owned, but hours, fees, and concessions are just about the same as on the state pier.

Golf

The nearest courses open to the public are the Brownsville Country Club (1-542-3500) and Riverview Golf Course (1-542-9861) in Brownsville (see Brownsville) and the Tony Butler Municipal Course (1-423-9913) in Harlingen.

Sand Sailing

This is sailing without the probability of getting dunked. You sit in a bucket seat attached to a low-slung frame on three small wheels with a small sail overhead, and the wind propels you over the sand flats. You might have to keep your eye out or ask around to find these, since the people who rent them don't have a permanent site. One place to check is near Ben's Go-Carts (see Kids' Stuff) just below the open sand flats on the bay. They rent for about $15 single or $20 double (plus deposit).

Waterskiing

SOUTH PADRE ISLAND SKI SCHOOL
B-201 Sand Castle Motel, 200 Kingfish Street
943-6386
   Ski lessons or ski rides are available. Rates are by the hour running from $40 an hour for one skier up to $30 each for an hour for three or more. The school has nothing to do with the motel, that's just where the owner-operator, Captain Bill Bride, lives.

ANNUAL EVENTS

March

SPRING BREAK
Various locations on the island
943-6433
Usually middle two weeks of the month
Most events free
W variable
   When you get right down to it, this is a big, boisterous beach bash for the tens and tens of thousands of college students from all over the country who informally convene here when their schools close down for spring break. Concerts, sports events, wild contests and competitions, give-aways, and whatever else the local Chamber of Commerce—aided by sponsors who cater to the young crowd—thinks will keep the kids happy, so they will come back again (and will leave the town in one piece when they leave).

July

FOURTH OF JULY CELEBRATION
Various locations on the island
943-3112
July 4th weekend
Most events free
W variable
   Both the city and the big hotels have fireworks demonstrations for several days leading up to and on the Fourth. Other activities include concerts, sand sculpture and other contests and sports competitions, and a street dance in Port Isabel.

August

TEXAS INTERNATIONAL FISHING TOURNAMENT
Various locations on the island and Port Isabel
943-5571
Usually early in month
Entry fee
With its 50th tournament just ahead of it, this is the second oldest fishing competition on the coast, bowing only to the Deep Sea Roundup at Port Aransas. Trophies and awards are given for both bay and offshore fishing. Categories include silver tarpon, marlin, sailfish, tuna, Grand Champion Bay Fisherman, and Texas Grand Champion. For marlin and sailfish, contestants may choose to "tag and release" their catch. Each type marlin is worth a set number of points, and an instant photo of the catch, signed by members of the fishing party and the crew, must be turned in to qualify for the score. Entry fees range from $15 for children under 10 to $70 for the adults. There are also social events most nights during the tourney. The entry fee includes these events, or for the non-anglers, a $45 fee pays for entry to all of them.

HOTELS & MOTELS

High season usually lasts from the beginning of March through Labor Day. High season rates for a double:
   $: under $50
   $$: $50–$69
   $$$: $70–$90
$$$$: over $90

BEST WESTERN BAHIA MAR RESORT
6300 Padre Blvd., approximately three and a half miles north of causeway
943-1343 or in Texas 1-800-292-7502, outside Texas 1-800-531-7404
$$$–$$$$
W
This combination hotel-condo resort on the Gulf has 196 units in the high-rise hotel and 87 one- to three-bedroom apartments in the townhouse-style, wooden condo buildings (higher rates for condos). In addition to the beach, there are two pools (one heated), two lighted tennis courts (fee), a putting green, Jacuzzi, a barber and beauty shop, a restaurant that ranks with the best on the island, and a lounge.

HOLIDAY INN BEACH RESORT
100 Padre Blvd., just south of causeway near Jeremiah's Landing
943-5401 or in Texas 1-800-292-7506, outside Texas 1-800-531-7405
$$$
W

Each of the 148 rooms in this six-story building has a private balcony with a Gulf view. The LaFitte Club has live entertainment every night during the high season. Beach, plus heated pool, wading pool, whirlpool, and restaurant.

SOUTH PADRE HILTON RESORT
500 Padre Blvd., just north of causeway
943-6511 or 1-800-292-7704
$$$$
W

The largest resort complex on the island, this is another hotel-condo arrangement with 128 hotel rooms and 150 two- and three-bedroom apartments, all with private balconies overlooking the Gulf. Five swimming pools, seven Jacuzzis, and eight tennis courts (fee) offer plenty of alternatives to the beach. There's a restaurant, and the Quarterdeck lounge has some of the best live entertainment around.

SURF MOTEL
2612 Gulf Blvd. near Amberjack, approximately one and a half miles north of causeway
943-2831
$
W

One of the first motels built on the island, the Surf is now one of the endangered species here: a small, moderately priced, no-frills motel on the beach. The fifteen simply furnished units on two floors include several with kitchenettes. The only outside amenity is a beachfront patio for sunbathing that has a grill for cook-outs.

THE TIKI
Padre Blvd. approximately three and a half miles north of causeway, just south of Andy Bowie Park
943-2694
$$–$$$$
W

This is an apartment hotel with 144 one- to three-bedroom units. There are two pools, saunas, a lounge, and the Tiki restaurant, which sports both Polynesian decor and menu.

YACHT CLUB HOTEL
Port Isabel
700 Yturria about two blocks north of Texas 100
943-1301
$
W

If you don't mind being a little away from the beach (a few minutes drive over the causeway) and are looking for quiet and seclusion, this older hotel is worth considering. As its name implies, it was originally established as a club for the local well-to-do. But their timing was bad.

They built it in 1926, just before the Depression hit. The club folded, and the building was turned into a hotel, which also went downhill quickly. In the 1970s, it was cleaned up and reopened. Most of the 24 rooms are comfortable but small. The four corner suites don't cost much more and give more turning around room, and the second floor rooms compensate for their size by opening onto a wide veranda that offers a restful view of Port Isabel's harbor. There's a small heated swimming pool, and you get a continental breakfast. The major attraction is the superb hotel restaurant, which unfortunately, is only open for dinner (see Restaurants).

OTHER ACCOMMODATIONS

There are more condominium units on Padre Island than hotel and motel rooms. Of course, not all of the condos are available for rent, but the renter's choice is still wider here than just about anywhere else on the Texas coast.

High season rental rates for a two-bedroom apartment start at about $90 a day and range up to $200. (Weekly rates are usually available.) The difference, of course, depends on the location and the extras. At the high end of the scale you should expect to get a prime location on the beach and trimmings that include a heated or indoor pool or both, sun deck, Jacuzzi, sauna, tennis courts, assigned or covered parking or both, decorator-designed apartment interiors, private balconies with Gulf view, all the modern kitchen conveniences, and HBO. At the lower rate your condo will probably be away from the Gulf beach—perhaps on the generally less attractive bayfront or on a side street with a limited view. The rooms should be just as large, but lay-out and furnishings tend to be more motel-style than individualized, and about the only amenity that's a sure thing is a pool. But since the island is only about four blocks wide at its widest, even those condos that aren't on the beach are only a short distance away, and the luxury extras should be weighed against the extra cost.

Fortunately, finding a condo rental on Padre is not difficult because almost all the available rental units are handled by one or more of the following property managers or rental agencies. Some of them also handle beach house rentals. They'll send you a list and brochures on request. Their post office box number is given in parentheses after the name. All addresses are South Padre Island 78597.

HELEN ADAMS RENTALS ★ (3414) ★ 943-7281

ISLAND INVEST GROUP ★ (3587) ★ 943-7955

ISLAND SERVICES • (2092) ★ 943-7901 or in Texas 1-800-292-7522

PADRE ISLAND RENTALS ★ (3469) ★ 943-5512 or in Texas 1-800-292-7520, outside Texas 1-800-531-4540

PADRE RENTAL AND MAINTENANCE ★ (2452) ★ 943-5100 or in
Texas 1-800-292-7518

PIBCO PROPERTIES ★ (2250) ★ 943-5465 or in Texas 1-800-292-7517

RUSHING CORPORATION ★ (2482) ★ 943-7888 or in Texas
1-800-292-5428

SAND DOLLAR PROPERTIES ★ (2163) ★ 943-7857 or in Texas
1-800-527-0294, outside Texas 1-800-531-4541

TROPICAL CONDOMINIUM SERVICES ★ (2220) ★ 943-1323

USAVE RENTALS ★ 943-6485

RESTAURANTS

Just a few years back it was hard to find a good restaurant on the
island. But that has all changed. Now, in addition to the hotel restaurants, there are enough choices to keep a visitor happy even over a
lengthy stay.

Dinner for Two

THE YACHT CLUB
Port Isabel
700 Yturria, about two blocks north of Texas 100
943-1301
Dinner only, closed Wednesday
Reservations suggested
$$–$$$; Cr.
W

Even though it hasn't been a yacht club since the Depression, it still
retains the air of substance—nothing cheap but nothing ostentatious—
that one associates with old money. And the cuisine carries out this
promise, but at a more moderate cost than expected. The menu features
fresh seafood, with just a dash of steak dishes. A house specialty, when
available, is red snapper throats (a dish which will please the seafood
gourmet despite the unpleasant name). The wine list is small but admi-
rably selected, and the lime pie is light enough to be a fitting, but not
filling, finale to any meal. Bar.

Breakfast & Lunch

RO-VANS RESTAURANT AND BAKERY
5304 Padre Blvd., approximately two and a half miles north of the
causeway

943-6972
Open 6–6, closed Monday
$; No cr.
Bountiful breakfasts all day, reasonably priced plate lunch specials, and fresh-from-the-oven bakery goodies—but only ten tiny tables, so expect to wait for a seat.

TED'S
5717 Padre Blvd., approximately three miles north of the causeway
943-5327
Open seven days 7–3
$; No cr.
W
The most expensive breakfast dish is built around the house specialty of fajitas marinated for five days. Appropriately called "Our Specialty," it includes the fajitas, two eggs, hash browns or refried beans, and toast, biscuits, English muffin, or tortillas—a day-starting combination for about $5. The fajitas share the lunch menu with poorboy "Philly" sandwiches (grilled roast beef with sautéed onions and melted cheese), burgers, and other sandwich combinations and salads.

American

BLACKBEARD'S
103 E. Saturn, approximately two miles north of the causeway
943-2962
Open seven days for lunch and dinner
$–$$; AE, MC, V
Casual is the key here, so you can pop in right from the beach. An oyster bar, hamburgers worthy of the name, seafood and steak platters, sandwiches, and salads you can eat inside or out on the upstairs deck. Beach bum talk on into the night. Bar.

CALLIE'S KITCHEN
2412½ Padre Blvd. near Ling, approximately one and a half miles north of the causeway
943-5627
Open for all meals, closed Wednesday evening
$–$$; Cr.
W
That this is a family restaurant is evidenced by the personal touches amidst the nautical decor. Much of the wall space is covered with art by local artists and framed photos of friends and customers, many from the time when Callie's started out as a six-table restaurant. The menu includes a bit of everything: Tex-Mex, barbecue, seafood, hamburgers, and steaks. Also daily luncheon specials and all the fish you can eat on Fridays. Draft beer and wine.

Italian

CAPPUCCINO'S
Port Isabel
317 E. Railroad, one block south of Texas 100
943-4201
Lunch Monday through Friday, dinner nightly except Tuesday
$$–$$$; Cr.

Lasagna, cannelloni, *eggplant parmigiana*, and all the better-known Italian favorites, plus seafood with an Italian flavor make this truly a *ristorante Italiano*. And the old country feeling is enhanced by the building, which the is oldest in Port Isabel. Lounge upstairs.

Seafood

THE JETTIES RESTAURANT
At the jetties at south end of Isla Blanca Park
943-6461
Open seven days for lunch and dinner
$–$$; MC, V
W

The food—fresh seafood and Tex-Mex—would be rather ordinary if you ate it without the attraction of the view. Try for a window seat to take full advantage of the location of this restaurant right on the north jetty of the Brownsville Ship Channel. From here you can follow the shrimp boats and the yachts and, occasionally, large tankers easing through the waters of the Brazos Santiago Pass going to and from the Gulf. At the rare times when nothing's sailing by, you can watch folks fishing on the jetty, surfers and beach-goers at the park beach or look across the channel at Brazos Island, just about eight miles north of the Mexican border.

LOUIE'S BACKYARD
2205 Ling at Laguna on the bayfront
943-6406
Dinner only, closed Monday
Reservations suggested
$$$; Cr.
W downstairs

Sunset over Laguna Madre can be breathtaking, which is a good thing for Louie's, because this is another place where the view adds immeasurably to what too frequently turns out to be a mediocre meal. The menu is simple: you can have prime rib or the seafood buffet. The buffet costs $15 for adults, but there's a sliding scale for children with the final price left up to the waiter's observation of the amount they ate. Adjoining, in the same building, is Louie's Key Largo Club, where you can enjoy the view without dinner. Dancing in both the restaurant and the club.

SCAMPI'S
206 W. Aries at Laguna
943-1755
Dinner only, closed Tuesday
Reservations suggested
$$–$$$; Cr.
W downstairs
The dining here is more casual than at its sister restaurant, the Yacht Club in Port Isabel, but the kitchen does just as well. Everything from the fish chowder to the old Yacht Club specialty of red snapper throats seems to have had the chef's personal attention. Even the fried entrées are delicately prepared. Steaks, too. Dine inside or out on the patio. Lounge upstairs.

CLUBS & BARS

Much of the nightlife on the island centers on the lounges in the major hotels and the better-known restaurants (see Hotels & Motels and Restaurants).

BERMUDA'S
205 W. Palm Blvd., third street north of the causeway on the bayfront at Laguna
943-4308
Open seven days in high season
Thursday through Saturday nights
Cover $3; Cr.
W downstairs
The dance floor looks out on the bay, so you can watch the sunset or dance under the stars. If the weather's bad, there's an air-conditioned lounge upstairs. Usually a guitarist or other sunset entertainment until nine o'clock, then a DJ for dancing during the week and live music on weekends. On the food side, there's a Friday night seafood buffet and a Sunday fajita buffet backed by a live mariachi band.

SUPER SUB MOVIE PUB
3901 Padre Blvd.
943-9619
Shows Monday through Friday at 9 p.m., Saturday at midnight,
Sunday at noon
Admission $2
W
By now everyone knows that movie theaters don't make money on admissions anymore; the profit's in popcorn and other candy counter

sales. This is the candy counter–snack bar taken to the next logical step. Pay a couple of bucks to get in, sit down in a comfortable chair at a clean table, and watch a second-run movie while munching popcorn or a bulging sub sandwich and sipping a beer, wine, cocktail, or soft drink. Features change regularly.

OFFBEAT

Normally this category is reserved for unusual places, but in this case, it lists two people who have become local legends by refusing to be jammed into any ordinary category.

BILLY BOOMERANG
Usually found afternoons on the beach near the Hilton
He wears an Aussie bush hat and a necklace of shark's teeth, and most afternoons you can find him gathering a crowd by tossing his hand-hewn boomerangs out over the surf for up to a hundred yards, handily catching them on their return flight. His real name is John McMahon, and in his past life back in the sixties, he worked in a machine shop in New York. Now he makes, demonstrates, and sells his home-crafted boomerangs, plus shark jaws mounted on wall plaques and jewelry fashioned out of rare stones and sharks' teeth. The stones he buys, but the jaws and teeth come from sharks he catches in his off-season business as a shark fisherman.

ILA LOETSCHER, THE TURTLE LADY
5805 Gulf Blvd. near Parade Dr.
943-2544
Programs for visitors: Tuesday and Saturday at 10 a.m. and 11 a.m., May through August; Tuesday and Thursday 1 and 2 p.m., November through April
Reservations for other times or for special tours or associations
Free ($1 donations accepted to Sea Turtles, Inc.)
Turtles all dressed up for a show may look silly, but if that's what it takes to raise money and educate the public to save them from extinction, that's what Ila Loetscher and her volunteer helpers in Sea Turtles, Inc. will do. Their lofty purpose is to save the kemp's Ridley sea turtle from extinction as well as preserve seven other endangered species of marine turtles. The Turtle Lady's home is an unofficial sea turtle museum open to the public. You don't have to wait for the scheduled shows. Just drop by, and in all likelihood, there will be someone there to show you around and tell you of the turtles' plight.

TO BROWNSVILLE
From Texas 100 just west of Port Isabel, take FM Rd. 1792 to the Port of Brownsville where it continues as Texas 48 to downtown Brownsville, a distance of about 22 miles. (From Harlingen, simply continue south on U.S. 77-83.)

★ BROWNSVILLE ★ & MATAMOROS

★★

BROWNSVILLE

CAMERON COUNTY SEAT ★ 98,000 ★ (512)

★★

MATAMOROS, MEXICO ★ 300,000

Brownsville gives you two countries for the price of one—or for even less than the price of vacationing in just about any other city on the Texas coast. Perhaps it's because the competitive lure of low-cost shopping and dining across the border in Matamoros keeps the prices down on the Brownsville side. Or perhaps it is because the driving distance to these sister cities at the southernmost tip of Texas has kept them from being discovered by the tourist trade. Whatever the reason, Brownsville-Matamoros remains a bargain for those visitors willing to drive there.

Technically, Brownsville and Matamoros are not on the coast, but together they make up the largest metropolitan area within an easy

255

TO PORT ISABEL

...into Rd.

...rt Isabel Rd.

802

Coffee Port Rd.

Ebony Rd.

Vermillion Ave.

48

Central Ave.

...ica Blvd.

4

Billy Mitchell Blvd.

BROWNSVILLE
INTERNATIONAL
AIRPORT

...) Blvd.

...oln St.

30th St.

East. Ave.

Southmost Rd.

Calle Milpa Verde

...RANDE RIVER

...RAS

drive—only about a half hour—of the wide beaches of South Padre. Also, Brownsville, a deep-sea port, is linked to the Gulf by the 17-mile Brownsville Ship Channel and is the Texas terminus of the Intracoastal Waterway.

Although separated by a national boundary, Brownsville and Matamoros share a common Spanish culture. Matamoros was a full-blown city long before Brownsville existed, and its Latin customs and heritage lapped over to its younger sister. So strong is this feeling of a common bond that many of the residents on both sides think of the two cities as one. Each year more than 30 million border crossings are recorded at the two bridges joining them, and the vast majority aren't tourists but locals going to visit, shop, or work on the other side. Even the Chamber of Commerce ignores the border and operates on both sides of the Rio Grande. More evidence of this cultural relationship can be seen in Brownsville's downtown shopping district where, perhaps more than anywhere else in the city, you can feel the Mexican influence. The narrow streets are usually crowded with Mexicans who have come across the bridge to shop, and there are as many signs in Spanish as in English. The most frequently seen signs are those found on the money changing shops and stores, which give the daily exchange rate for buying and selling pesos and dollars.

Brownsville originated as a fort in 1846, a fort that ignited the fuse that led to the Mexican War. A major cause of that war was a dispute over establishing the Rio Grande or the Nueces River as the border between Mexico and the United States. General Zachary Taylor deliberately built this fort, then called Fort Taylor, on the Rio Grande across from Matamoros as a statement of the American claim. The Mexicans, who said the Nueces was the border, considered this an invasion and attacked the fort. Among the first casualties was Major Jacob Brown. The fort, and then the city, was named after him.

In 1848, after that war ended, Charles Stillman, one of the many New England merchants who had set up shop in Matamoros, bought the land around Fort Brown and laid out the townsite.

The sister cities survived revolutions, border skirmishes, the Civil War, hurricanes, and bandits who either ignored the border or used it to their advantage. In the early 1850s, the citizens of Matamoros repulsed a revolutionary uprising, earning the official designation of "Heroic Matamoros" for their city. Today many signs and all official documents continue this tribute to valor with the letter "H," for *heroica*, before the city's name. While Brownsville, then a vital cotton shipping center, was being battled over by both sides in the Civil War, Matamoros was involved in a war between the revolutionary forces of Juárez and those of the French emperor, Maximilian.

Today life is much quieter along the border. The subtropical climate, tempered by cool—and surprisingly dry—Gulf breezes, encourages a leisurely lifestyle. It also encourages year-round gardens of bougainvillea, hibiscus, oleander, and roses (to name just a few), all set against a background of stately palms, banana and citrus trees, bamboo, orchid trees, and the ubiquitous oak and mesquite. And scattered among these are the *resacas*, the lagoons left behind as, over the centuries, the wandering waters of the Rio Grande continuously carved out new paths.

The leisurely pace does not mean either city is a backwater. Both are growing. Brownsville's port is not only booming, it is bringing in new industries to both sides of the border, adding to the economic stability of a region once dependent almost entirely on agriculture. In addition, Brownsville is home to one of the largest shrimp fleets on the coast, and plants in both cities process shrimp from all over the world at a rate of over 100 million pounds a year.

But for the visitor, the major attractions are still the opportunity to experience another country and the bargains available to the shrewd shopper and discriminating diner.

GOING TO MEXICO

As long as you don't plan to travel much farther into Mexico or stay over 72 hours, all you need to cross over to Matamoros is proof that you're an American citizen—so you won't have any difficulty getting back—and the bridge toll. The Mexican immigration and customs officers rarely ask for any identification, and U.S. immigration officers on the way back ask to see documentation only if they aren't convinced of your citizenship by your appearance or your answers to such questions as where you were born.

Of course, if you take your own car, you will also need proof that it is yours (or that you have the right to drive it). This means a license receipt, title, or bill of sale. Just as important is auto insurance recognized by the Mexican authorities. Most American insurance is not. And since Mexican law is based on the Napoleonic Code (which usually means you are guilty until proven innocent), if you have an accident you may wind up in jail unless you can prove financial responsibility—with Mexican insurance. There are a number of insurance and travel agents in Brownsville who can give you fast and relatively inexpensive coverage. You can find them in the Yellow Pages or check the Brownsville Information Center or the Chamber of Commerce. Just don't drive from the U.S. without it.

If you don't want to go to all this trouble to take your car over, you can usually find a parking place at the Brownsville Civic Center on International Boulevard or across from the Chamber of Commerce on Elizabeth Street. Both are within a short walk of the Gateway International Bridge.

You don't need Mexican pesos in Matamoros. The dollar is more than welcome. Some shops and restaurants list prices in both dollars and pesos. If the merchandise or menu is marked in pesos, make sure that you have at least a fair idea of the current exchange rate. (The peso also is indicated by the "$" sign, but if the merchandise sticker price or menu is referring to the U.S. dollar, it will indicate that with "U.S. $.") If you're planning to do a lot of shopping in stores that may not give a good exchange rate on dollars, a pocket calculator can come in handy. If you do decide to buy pesos, however, save yourself potential headaches by buying them in a reputable money exchange or other shop. There are a number of places to change money on both sides of the Gateway Bridge. And then buy only as much as you think you'll need. Otherwise you'll definitely lose money on the exchange back to dollars.

There are two bridges between the cities. The main one is the Gateway International Bridge at the end of International Boulevard. At the time of publication, the toll to walk across this bridge was 10¢ going to Matamoros and 18¢ coming back. If you drive, the fee is 50¢ per car. Farther south along the river, about half a mile down Perl Boulevard (the southern extension of 12th Street), is the old railroad bridge. This bridge is privately owned and operated, and it's still a railroad bridge, so you may have to wait for a train to pass. The car toll here is the same, but the walking toll is 20¢.

If you don't want to walk, you can also take a bus (call the Brownsville Urban System, 541-8359, for schedules and fares) or a taxi. You can also catch a taxi on the other side.

A Mexican tourism office staffed by English-speaking personnel is located in the immigration and customs building on the Mexican side of the Gateway Bridge (phone 23630). You can get a Matamoros map there. A booth housing licensed guides is also just over the bridge. Before you get in a taxi or hire a guide, make sure that you and the driver or guide have settled on a fair price. Most of the taxi drivers and guides are honest, and genuinely friendly, but there's always one out to stick the *turista*.

An inexpensive way to get around Matamoros is in a maxi-cab. You'll find a herd of them gathered on the first street to the left (east) after you cross the Gateway Bridge. Maxi-cabs are small passenger vans that follow definite routes around the city, but they will stop almost anywhere to pick up or let off a passenger. They cost pennies to ride and go to the markets and other places of interest to foreign visitors. The destination of each maxi-cab is painted on its front, and with a map and an understanding of a few, simple Spanish words—or if you aren't too embarrassed to ask—you should have no trouble getting around. For example, if you want to go to the Juárez Market, look for a maxi-cab marked *Mercado*. To get back from anywhere in town, look for one marked *Puente* (bridge). A maxi-cab marked *Sexta* travels up and down Calle Sexta or 6th Street, a major north-south street in the city. Simple— and fun!

Both bridges come out on Avenida Alvaro Obregón, a major street with many shops and restaurants listed in this guide. Obregón starts at the Gateway Bridge, and the railroad bridge road intersects it about four blocks south.

Eating in Matamoros can be a pleasant experience if you don't let all the cautions kill the enjoyment. You can probably drink the water and eat just about anything (that wouldn't otherwise give you trouble) in any of the restaurants that cater to Americans. But, if it makes you feel any better, order bottled water—or indulge yourself with a good Mexican beer—and skip anything that isn't cooked, like a salad. Also, go light on the hot stuff if you're not used to it.

In general, you can legally bring back to the U.S. up to $400 in merchandise duty-free each 30 days. There are exceptions, so if you're planning to do a great amount of shopping, check with U.S. customs *before* you go over. Customs has a couple of free booklets that will explain exactly what you can and can't bring back. Liquor is one of the exceptions. Liquor is inexpensive in Matamoros, and the temptation is to bring back as much as one can carry. But the $400 limit doesn't apply here. The details change occasionally, but recently each Texas resident was permitted to bring back one liter of liquor or three gallons of wine every 30 days. Non-Texans could bring back more. But whatever you return with, you have to pay state tax on it. And anything over your allowance doesn't pass, no matter how eager you are to pay the tax.

The average winter temperature is in the 70s, and the average summer temperature is in the mid 80s.

A BROWNSVILLE GET-ACQUAINTED DRIVING TOUR

The logical place to start, after a visit to gather maps and information, is the Brownsville Information Center (see Tour & Guide Services). From here you can look east across the highway and see Sunrise Mall, one of the two enclosed malls in the city.

Go south on U.S. 77-83 to the Boca Chica Boulevard exit. Turn right on Boca Chica and then, almost immediately, left on Palm Boulevard. Take Palm about half a mile to the traffic light at Ringgold Street, then turn left. On your left, a short distance down Ringgold, you'll see the Camille Lightner Playhouse, the home of the local little theater group (see Music & Theater). The playhouse is in Dean Porter Park. Turn left at the first entrance into the park and follow the road around as it doubles back to Ringgold. This 12-acre park includes a children's playground, picnic areas, and a 50-meter swimming pool. As you exit the park, directly across the street will be the Gladys Porter Zoo. This is a jewel among zoological parks—listed among the 10 best in the country—so if you don't stop to visit it now, make sure you do before you leave Brownsville.

Take a right and retrace your route to Palm, then turn left. Continue down Palm for a little over a mile until you reach Amigoland Mall at Mexico Boulevard. Turn left on Mexico. This is the other major mall in the city. Follow Mexico to Perl Boulevard, just past the railroad overpass. If you were to continue on Mexico, you would wind up *in* Mexico. The old railroad bridge just ahead, called the B&M International Bridge, is open to car traffic and will take you to Matamoros. But, unless you have auto insurance valid in Mexico, that driving adventure should wait (see Going to Mexico). So, turn left on Perl. On your right, behind the levee, is the Rio Grande River and Mexico. Perl becomes one way (named 12th Street) against you just before downtown. Following the one-way signs in your direction will put you on 13th (the Gateway International Bridge will be on your right), which intersects with Elizabeth Street (U.S. 77-83) in two short blocks. Turn right on Elizabeth. This street was named in the late 1840s by Charles Stillman, the founder of the town, after his bride-to-be, Elizabeth Goodrich. Be especially careful when driving here. The street is narrow, and the bridge traffic—both car and foot—is always hectic (bordering on the chaotic).

Stay straight on Elizabeth past the bridge on your right, crossing International Boulevard. At the next cross street (Taylor), the Chamber of Commerce building (see Tour & Guide Services) will be on your left and the city's International Friendship Pavilion on your right. This circular building is often used for cultural exhibits and art and fashion shows featuring other countries in the Western Hemisphere. It also provides convention and meeting space.

Continue down palm-shaded Elizabeth, passing the Fort Brown Motor Hotel, until it ends. Turn right to loop back around the *resaca*. Keeping to the left at the fork will put you on Neale, a short street on which you'll find the Brownsville Art League and the Art Museum (see Galleries). The league's headquarters is in the old home on your left, and the museum is in the larger building just past that.

Continuing on will bring you quickly back on Taylor at the intersection with Elizabeth. The little engine on the corner opposite the Chamber of Commerce is a relic of the Rio Grande Railroad built in 1872 to connect Brownsville and Port Isabel. This was the first railroad south of Corpus Christi.

Keep going straight on Taylor. On your left is the Fort Brown Memorial Civic Center, a complex that provides facilities for convention, recreational, and social activities. The street ends at the parking lot of Texas Southmost College (see Colleges & Universities). Almost directly in front of you is the combined college and city library. Behind the library are other college buildings and, on the adjoining campus, the buildings of Pan American University at Brownsville (see Colleges & Universities). The old buildings you can see on your right are part of old Fort Brown (see Historic Places) and are now used by the college.

Turn left. At the next block is International Boulevard. Take another left, but get over into the right lane as soon as you can, because the next turn at U.S. 77-83 (Washington Street) is just two short blocks away. A right turn onto Washington puts you on a typical, narrow downtown shopping street.

Stay over to the right. On the corner of 13th Street is the Stillman House, built in 1850 by the founder of Brownsville (see Museums). Turn right on 13th, go two blocks and turn left onto Jefferson. On your left is the Immaculate Conception Cathedral, built in 1859. At 12th and Jefferson, diagonally across from the church, is the old courthouse, now a Masonic Lodge. Continue on Jefferson to 10th, then turn left.

The imposing building on the corner of 10th and Elizabeth is the U.S. Courthouse. Turn right on Levee and take it to Palm. A right and then an immediate left puts you on Elizabeth (U.S. 77-83), which becomes two-way at that point. Follow the U.S. 77-83 signs—you will soon veer to the right and be on Central Boulevard. Central will take you through an area of small businesses, restaurants, and Mom and Pop motels for about two miles to your starting point.

TOUR & GUIDE SERVICES

BROWNSVILLE INFORMATION CENTER
U.S. 77-83 at FM Rd. 802
541-8455
Monday through Friday 8:30–5, Saturday 9–1, closed Sunday
Free
W+
   The building's design is ancient Aztec, but the information available inside is up-to-the-minute. Manager Lorena Curry and her helpers really know the town and cheerfully dispense brochures, maps, and whatever else you need to know about accommodations, restaurants, shopping, and local sights. You can also book Gray Line tours here. Operated by the Chamber of Commerce.

BROWNSVILLE CHAMBER OF COMMERCE
1600 E. Elizabeth St., just south of the Gateway International Bridge
542-4341
Monday through Friday 8–5
Free
W
   More business- than tourist-oriented, but if you missed the Brownsville Information Center on the way into town or you're near the bridge to Mexico, you can stop here for brochures, maps, and helpful hints. This is a joint Chamber of Commerce representing businesses on both sides of the border, so they can tell you about Matamoros, too.

GRAY LINE TOURS
1301 Los Ebanos
542-8962
Matamoros tour $11
Book at most hotels-motels, travel agents, Brownsville Information Center, or Chamber of Commerce
   There is a morning tour at 9 o'clock and an afternoon tour at 2 o'clock every day but Sunday and Mexican holidays. Each tour lasts about three and a half hours and includes visits to Matamoros' Casa Mata Museum, the Main Plaza, a major residential area, and all the major shopping centers including both the old and the new Juárez market.

SANBORN'S
1922 E. Elizabeth
542-7222
Johnny Ginn's Travel Center
1945 N. Expressway at Holiday Inn
546-6644

If you plan to drive in Mexico, even just across the bridge into Matamoros, Sanborn's is a good place to stop first. This is a travel agency, but it is also a place to pick up car insurance that's good in Mexico (your U.S. insurance probably is not). A number of other agents sell Mexican insurance, but Sanborn's is probably the best known. Complete basic coverage for most cars costs about $6 a day. They'll also give you a map of Matamoros, and if you plan to go farther into Mexico, Sanborn's road condition bulletins and Mexico Travelogs, which describe almost every mile of every major highway in that country, come with the insurance (see Going to Mexico).

TEXAS DEPARTMENT OF HIGHWAYS AND PUBLIC TRANSPORTATION VISITOR CENTER
See Harlingen.

POINTS OF INTEREST

GLADYS PORTER ZOO
Ringgold and 6th
546-2177 (activities recording) or 546-7187
Gates open Monday through Friday 9–5:30, Saturday and Sunday
9–6:30, once inside visitors may remain until dark
Adults $3.50, children under 14 $1.50
W+

Here is proof that good things do come in small packages. Although the ingenious design and landscaping give the appearance of open spaces, the 1,800 mammals, birds, and reptiles from five continents in this zoo are actually squeezed into only 25½ acres. Still, it has been ranked by zoo professionals as one of the ten best in the country—right up there with the huge Bronx Zoo, San Diego Zoo, and the National Zoo in Washington, D.C. It also has earned an international reputation as a haven and breeding facility for endangered species such as the Jentink's Duiker, considered one of the rarest antelope in the world. The zoo is laid out so you can see all the exhibits in a leisurely stroll along a circular path. Even if you're in a hurry, it is so wonderfully compact you can see it all in about one and a half to two hours. The path will take you through four major areas of the world: Africa, Asia, Australia and Indonesia, and tropical America. In each you'll see the animals native to that area living in miniaturized naturalistic habitats on islands or in large open areas separated from visitors by concealed moats or visible waterways—no bars or cages. This open environment results in healthy, happy-looking animals instead of the neurotic pacers found in caged

zoos. The children's zoo includes both an animal nursery for viewing
and a petting zoo stocked mostly with barnyard animals. There is also a
walk-through aviary; an indoor herpetarium exhibiting snakes, turtles,
lizards, and smaller crocodilians; an aquarium; and a wealth of well-
labeled plants and flowers to make this a botanical garden as well.
Strollers and wheelchairs are available for rent. A tour train makes a
half-hour narrated tour Sundays between 1:30 and 3:30 (50¢). Concession stands, gift and souvenir shop. A visual delight, this is what a zoo
should be—and is a *must see*.

PORT OF BROWNSVILLE
**Intersection of Texas 48 and Farm Rd. 511, 10 miles northeast of
downtown**
831-4592
A 17-mile ship channel, opening into the Gulf of Mexico at South
Padre Island, makes this a deep-sea port. It is also the end of the line for
the Intracoastal Waterway. The port services not only the Rio Grande
Valley but also northeastern Mexico. More than 5 million tons of cargo
are handled here each year. The Shrimp Basin in the port area is home
to one of the largest shrimp fleets in the world.

U.S. COAST GUARD STATION
Port of Brownsville
**FM Rd. 1792 at Anchor Rd., approximately two and a half miles east
of FM Rd. 511**
831-4140
This is home port for the Coast Guard cutter *Durable*, which has the
whole Gulf of Mexico in its patrol area. When it is in port, visitors are
welcome to tour the 210-foot ship on weekends and holidays between 1
and 5 p.m. Drive through the station gate to the end of the dock for
visitor parking. Call to make sure the ship is in before making the trip.

HISTORIC PLACES

FORT BROWN
600 International, just east of Gateway International Bridge
542-3367
W
Now it is part of the campus of Texas Southmost College, but in the
102 years between its founding in 1846 and 1948 when it was closed, this
border post saw a lot of action. Its very construction was one of the
immediate causes of the Mexican War (see Mexican War Battlefields). It
was occupied by both sides in the Civil War and, as a border post,
helped defend the area against bandits well into the 1900s. The post
hospital ranks high on the list of the fort's more peaceful achievements,
because that was where Dr. W. C. Gorgas started his research into tropical diseases, reportedly against the orders of the Fort's commander,
which eventually led to his important contribution to the control of

yellow fever when he was surgeon general of the army. The hospital is one of the fort buildings still standing, but now it is used as the college administration building. Other fort buildings remaining include the post headquarters, guard house (now the fine arts center), the medical laboratory, and the morgue.

IMMACULATE CONCEPTION CATHEDRAL
Jefferson and 12th
546-3178
W

Built in 1859, this Gothic Revival church was to become a haven for Catholic priests fleeing the anticlerical revolutions in Mexico. The first bishop of the area and a number of former parish priests are buried in the graveyard by the entrance.

MEXICAN WAR BATTLEFIELDS
Marker commemorating the battles of Palo Alto and Resaca de la Palma
Intersection of FM Rd. 1847 and FM Rd. 511

When Texas entered the Union, it brought with it a long-standing dispute with Mexico over the border between the two countries. Mexico claimed the border was the Nueces River, which had been the southern boundary of the old province of Texas. The Texans claimed it was the Rio Grande. The dispute led to a breaking of relations between the U.S. and Mexico. Then President Polk sent Brigadier General Zachary Taylor with an army of about 4,000 to Corpus Christi and deployed naval ships along the Mexican coast. When efforts to reestablish relations failed, Polk ordered Taylor to the Rio Grande.

Taylor set up his main base at Port Isabel (then called Point Isabel), where he could count on supplies from the sea, and then moved farther inland to build a fort on the Rio Grande across from the city of Matamoros. For about two months the two sides merely exchanged threats. Then on April 25, 1846, a skirmish took place between an American cavalry patrol and Mexican troops at what is now called Galveston Ranch, about 20 miles west of the fort. The entire patrol was either killed or captured.

Worried about the safety of his lightly defended supply base at Point Isabel, Taylor took the majority of his army back there. He left a small force of infantry and artillery at the fort, under the command of Major Jacob Brown, with instructions that if they were in need of help they should signal by firing their heavy cannon at regular intervals.

On May 3, 1846, the Mexican army started to lay siege to the fort, but it wasn't until May 6 that Brown thought his position threatened and started firing his signal guns. That same day Brown was killed by Mexican cannon fire.

On May 7, Taylor left Point Isabel with about 2,300 men to relieve the garrison at the fort. The next morning, at Palo Alto, about 10 miles from the fort, the Americans clashed with a Mexican force of about 6,000.

Taylor's light horse artillery was a major factor in the battle. Dashing from position to position, the "Flying Artillery," under Major Samuel Ringgold, laid down deadly fire that overcame the three-to-one odds and forced the Mexicans to withdraw. Among the nine Americans killed in the battle was Major Ringgold. Over 300 Mexicans died.

When Taylor pressed on the next morning, the Mexicans were waiting a few miles down the road, dug in at a strong position in a dry streambed called Resaca de la Palma. The Americans attacked and, in a fierce and bloody battle, broke the Mexican line and caused a rout. In this second battle, 120 Americans were either killed or wounded, but the Mexican army lost over a thousand. Among the American infantry company commanders in this second battle was Second Lieutenant Ulysses S. Grant, who later noted that the Mexican soldiers were brave but poorly led.

While this battle was taking place, the word finally reached President Polk of the cavalry patrol that had been wiped out at Galveston Ranch two weeks before. On May 13, 1846, war was declared against Mexico.

Today these two battles, which started a major war with our neighbor, are marked by a poorly maintained cannon and marker on the northeast corner of the intersection of FM Road 511 and FM Road 1847.

PALMITO HILL BATTLEFIELD
Marker on Texas 4, approximately 14 miles east of downtown

While the Mexican War battles around Fort Brown were fought before that war was actually declared, the Civil War battle of Palmito Hill was fought about six weeks after that war was officially over. In this so-called "last battle" of the War Between the States, about 300 Confederate soldiers from Fort Brown drove off about 1,600 Federal troops trying to capture the cotton stored in the warehouses at Brownsville. A few days later, the Confederates acknowledged Lee's surrender and surrendered too. Coincidentally, this Civil War battle took place on May 13, 1865, the same date that war had been declared against Mexico just 19 years earlier.

MUSEUMS

CASA MATA MUSEUM
Matamoros
Guatemala one block north of Avenida Lauro Villar
Wednesday through Monday 9:30–5:30, closed Tuesday
Free

This small, thick-walled fort, built in the mid 1830s to help control the unruly American immigrants in the area, now serves as a city museum. Unless you read Spanish, the labels and descriptions on the exhibits will be hard to follow. But the collection of photographs of patriots of the Mexican (not Texan) Revolution and the costumes and military artifacts create an authentic atmosphere and tell a story that often needs no explanation.

STILLMAN HOUSE AND MUSEUM
E. Washington and 13th
542-3929
Monday through Friday 10–12 and 2–5, Sunday 3–5, closed Saturday
Adults $1, children free
W

This restored, well-preserved building is one of the oldest in the city. It was built in 1850 by Charles Stillman, a merchant from Connecticut who set up a business in Matamoros and became the founder of Brownsville. Locally made bricks were used for the walls, but the slate shingles on the roof were shipped in from New England. Many of the furnishings and memorabilia were donated by the Stillman family in Cornwell, New York, and date back to the mid 1800s. The oldest item is a 1790 grandfather clock in the central hallway. The museum part of the house consists of two rooms with exhibits of artifacts and documents relating the history of Brownsville and Matamoros. Street parking is a problem. If you don't mind walking a few blocks, parking is usually available at the Brownsville Civic Center or the Chamber of Commerce.

GALLERIES

BROWNSVILLE ART MUSEUM
230 Neale Dr., one block west of Chamber of Commerce
542-0941
Monday, Wednesday, Thursday, Friday 9:30–2:30, Tuesday 1–4, closed Saturday and Sunday except for special exhibits
Free
W

One gallery in this unpretentious building houses the Brownsville Art League's eclectic permanent collection, ranging from well-known artists of the Southwest to Hogarth prints. The other gallery is used for loan exhibitions, lectures, art films, and free classes. If the building isn't open during the hours it's supposed to be, reach inside the iron gate and push the bell on the left-hand wall. Or go next door to the league's headquarters in the Neale House, which is in the oldest frame house in the city, and someone will probably be available to show you around the museum. Also note the bandstand next to the league's home. It was moved to this site from its original location at Fort Brown, where it was used by the cavalry band stationed there. The league, which celebrated its 50th anniversary in 1985, usually sponsors a Rio Grande Valley Arts and Crafts Show in November and an International Arts Festival in March.

DON BREEDEN ART STUDIO AND GALLERY
1200 Central Blvd. (Artemis Square Shopping Center)
542-5481
Wildlife painting and drawings in various media are the specialty of artist-owner Don Breeden, who works in his studio over this small gallery.

MUSIC & THEATER

CAMILLE LIGHTNER PLAYHOUSE
Dean Porter Park across from Gladys Porter Zoo
542-8900
W
The local little theater group's season runs from September through May and usually offers about six productions that lean heavily toward musicals and comedies. Shows run for two weekends, and a new one is presented about every six weeks. General admission is $6 with reduced rates for senior citizens, students, and groups.

COLLEGES & UNIVERSITIES

PAN AMERICAN UNIVERSITY AT BROWNSVILLE
1614 Ridgley Road, located on same campus as Texas Southmost College
542-6882
W+ but not all areas
This branch of the parent university, at Edinburg, Texas, in the Rio Grande Valley, has the distinction of being the southernmost upper-level institution in the continental United States. Enrollment averages about 1,200, and the university offers 20 programs leading to bachelor and master's degrees. It also takes advantage of its border location with a degree and a certification program as a Spanish-English translator. For the long-term visitor, the school also offers a wide variety of non-credit seminars, presentations, and workshops, mostly in the fields of education, business, and Spanish—some of the latter include tours to Mexico.

TEXAS SOUTHMOST COLLEGE
1614 Ridgley Road
544-8200
W+ but not all areas

This campus is on what was once the center of Fort Brown, the U.S. Army post established by General Zachary Taylor in 1846 as a base for operations in the Mexican War. The college administrative offices are housed in the old hospital and the fine arts center in the old post jail (the cells are used for storage). A two-year community college, Texas Southmost has an enrollment of more than 6,000 and offers over 500 technical, vocational, and junior college courses. For the general public, the community services and continuing education department offers a number of noncredit courses in everything from flower arranging to conversational Spanish. Other school functions open to the public include guest speaker programs and seminars, a series of noon concerts in the fall, various music concerts and art shows throughout the year, and a weekend Folklife Festival in the spring. Visitors are also welcome to use the combined city-college library.

SHOPPING

AMIGOLAND MALL
301 Mexico at Palm
546-3788
W

This is the closest mall to the bridges to Matamoros, so it is especially popular with Mexican shoppers. Anchored by Ward's, Dillard's, and Penney's, it offers the usual collection of chain stores and fast food stalls, plus a movie theater and a cafeteria. An oriental rug store and a boutique that features items from the Orient distinguish this mall from most others.

BARBARA DE MATAMOROS
Matamoros
40 Avenida Alvaro Obregón, four blocks south of Gateway
International Bridge
25058
W

Looking for a full-scale brass monkey? A brass lion as big as a small cub? Or how about a colorful larger-than-life papier-mâché macaw on a perch? These are just a few of the Sergio Bustamente originals elegantly displayed, and elegantly priced, in this pink stucco shop. There are also unusual ceramics, jewelry, and other selected items from the interior of Mexico. Upstairs is a fashionable boutique featuring clothing of Barbara's own design.

GARCIA'S
Matamoros
82 Avenida Alvaro Obregón and Puerta, one block south of Gateway International Bridge
31566
Location is one of the keys to Garcia's success. It attracts the curious as they come over the bridge by being one of the first places they see, and it offers the convenience of last-minute shopping for those on the way back to Brownsville by being one of the last places they pass. It carries a large stock of liquor as well as leather goods, arts and crafts items, clothing, and the usual stock of curios and souvenirs. Upstairs is a restaurant and lounge (see Restaurants).

MARY'S
Matamoros
26 Avenida Alvaro Obregón, four blocks south of Gateway International Bridge
22431
St. Francis must be this shop's patron saint, because carved wooden statues of him are scattered throughout both of its display floors. In a lighter vein, there are gobs of colorful papier-mâché animals, clowns, and other funny-looking characters to brighten a child's room. Other offerings include liquor, chess sets, silver, gifts, and other fine curios, furniture, and clothing. And if you want to take a cooling respite from shopping, there's a quiet cocktail lounge in the middle of it all.

MERCADO JUÁREZ
Matamoros
Matamoros at Calle Nueve
W
There are two markets here, the old and the new, on both sides of the street. But don't look for a big, open-air market. Each is made up of many, many small shops under a low roof. The tunnel-like pathways through the markets are crammed with wares that seem to overflow from the shops. Here you can find the gaudy and the good. Piñatas, leather belts and saddles, sombreros, clothing, linens, and curios are just a few of the items available here. Much of it is run-of-the-mill, over-priced tourist bait, but there are also a few treasures for the sharp shopper. The key is to know what you want, how much it costs elsewhere, and how much you're willing to pay. And then bargain. But go in with your eyes open, being aware that the shopkeepers are the bargaining experts and will always, *always* make a profit. However, you can at least have fun at the game and lower the price a bit—perhaps a lot.

SUNRISE MALL
2370 N. Expressway and FM Rd. 802
541-5302
W
   Another medium-sized covered mall. The big stores here are Sears and K-Mart, and they are joined by a collection of chains such as Beall's, Waldenbooks, and Zales.

OUTDOORS & SIDE TRIPS

BRAZOS ISLAND STATE PARK
At end of Texas 4, approximately 22 miles east of Brownsville
   There are no facilities at this undeveloped park, but you can camp, fish, swim, surf, or just soak up the sunshine on the wide beach. A four-wheel-drive vehicle is strongly recommended if you drive on the beach. At the north end of Brazos Island is the stone jetty that, along with the jetty on the south tip of South Padre Island, forms the entrance to the Brownsville Ship Channel.

CONFEDERATE AIR FORCE HEADQUARTERS
See Harlingen.

LAGUNA ATASCOSA NATIONAL WILDLIFE REFUGE
See Harlingen.

SABAL PALM GROVE SANCTUARY
Take FM Rd. 1419 (Southmost Rd.) to Ernest Ortiz Rd.
Adults $3, students $2, children under 6 free
   The sabal palm, the only palm native to extreme South Texas, is now considered endangered in this area. This Audubon sanctuary preserves 32 acres of these scarce palms and the native plant and animal life associated with them. It is located just about as far south as you can go in Texas, on a bend of the Rio Grande about four miles directly south of the Brownsville International Airport. Visitors are welcome for wildlife and plant observation and photography, but vehicles, camping, picnicking, hunting, and fishing are prohibited. Group size is limited to 20 unless prior arrangements are made. The sanctuary is closed June through August and only open one to three days a week the rest of the year. For details on hours and other information, contact the Refuge Manager, Sabal Palm Grove Sanctuary, National Audubon Society, P.O. Box 8277, Brownsville 78520.

SOUTH PADRE ISLAND
See South Padre Island and Port Isabel.

KIDS' STUFF

CHILDREN'S ZOO AT GLADYS PORTER ZOO
See Points of Interest.

SPORTS & ACTIVITIES

Birdwatching

See Harlingen, Laguna Atascosa National Wildlife Refuge. See also South Padre Island.

Golf

BROWNSVILLE COUNTRY CLUB
1800 W. San Marcelo
542-3500
Green fees: Monday through Friday $7, weekends $10, fees are for all day
Thirteen of the 18 holes on this 5,718-yard course are water holes.

RANCHO VIEJO COUNTRY CLUB
U.S. 77-83 at Rancho Viejo Dr., approximately nine miles north of downtown
350-4000
Call for non-member green fees
There are two 18-hole courses here. Green fees are cheaper if you are a guest at the resort or play with a member.

RIVERVIEW GOLF COURSE
300 River Levee, south of Fort Brown
542-9861
Green fees: Monday through Friday $4, Saturday and Sunday $4.50
This 18-hole, 5,955-yard course is laid out on a peninsula in a bend of the Rio Grande.

Fishing

Freshwater and channel fishing is recommended in the old beds of the Rio Grande, in canals, in some *resacas*, and from the banks of the

Brownsville Ship Channel. For bay and deep-sea fishing, see South Padre Island and Port Isabel.

ANNUAL EVENTS

February

CHARRO DAYS
Various locations around Brownsville
542-4245
Four-day weekend in middle or end of month
Admission for some activities
W variable

A *grito*, the Mexican cowboys' yell of exuberance, usually opens Charro Days at the Gateway International Bridge. *Charro* used to refer only to landowning Mexican horsemen whose formal attire was the traditional costume of black or striped pants covered with fancy chaps, a bolero jacket with ornamental embroidery, and a sombrero covered with silver or gold filigree. The charro traditions have been adopted by a number of charro associations on both sides of the border, and it is the spirit of the charro and the working Mexican cowboy that inspired this fiesta. Held annually since 1938, festivities usually start on Thursday and run through Sunday afternoon. These include several parades, mariachi music, Mexican folk dancing and regular dances, a jalapeño-eating and other contests, a children's fiesta, a *charreada* (Mexican rodeo), and other sports competitions and events.

September

FIESTA INTERNATIONAL
Various locations around Matamoros and Brownsville
542-4341
Three-day weekend in mid month
Admission to some activities
W variable

This is a two-nation celebration of Mexican Independence Day (September 16th) as well as of the cotton harvest (it used to be called the Cotton Carnival). Parades, receptions, fireworks, and other activities are held on both sides of the border as the citizens of the sister cities entertain each other.

HOTELS & MOTELS

Rates for a double:
   $: under $30
   $$: $35–$45
   $$$: $46–$60
   $$$$: over $60

BEST WESTERN FORT BROWN HOTEL
1900 E. Elizabeth, three blocks east of Gateway International Bridge
546-2201 or in Texas 1-800-582-3333, outside Texas 1-800-541-3333
$$$–$$$$
W
   Palm trees swaying in the breeze and the quiet waters of a lagoon, called a *resaca* here, give the impression of a tropical oasis in the midst of a bustling city. Among the 278 units are four rooms with private patios, each sheltering a whirlpool about the size of a double bed ($$$$). The Coffee Shop features a noon buffet Monday through Friday. The Resaca Club offers evening dining and entertainment (see Clubs & Bars) as well as a champagne brunch on Sundays. One of the two outdoor pools has a Jacuzzi and is for adults only. The Riverview Municipal Golf Course is adjacent. Lighted tennis courts. Short walk to downtown and the bridge to Matamoros.

EL PRESIDENTE HOTEL
Matamoros
249 Avenida Alvaro Obregón at Constitución
39440
$$–$$$
W
   If you'd like to stay on the Mexican side of the Rio Grande, this is a good choice if it's open. Call the hotel, or the Brownsville Chamber of Commerce first, because this hotel has been closed before by strikes. When open it offers 150 large rooms, a colorful garden, a pool, restaurant, nightclub, and nearby shopping.

FLAMINGO MOTEL
1741 Central (U.S. 77-83), half a block north of Boca Chica
546-2478
$
W
   Ten of the 29 rooms in this moderately priced motel have kitchenettes, and 13 others have refrigerators. The rooms are small, but have all the amenities. Heated swimming pool. Several restaurants are within walking distance.

HOLIDAY INN
**1945 N. Expressway (U.S. 77-83), just south of FM Rd. 802,
approximately four miles north of downtown
546-4591 or 1-800-465-4329
$$$
W+ one room**
In addition to the 159 typical Holiday Inn rooms and suites, this two-story motel has a small exercise room with sauna and Jacuzzi overlooking the pool. The restaurant offerings include a buffet for both lunch and dinner as well as a pleasant view of the nearby river. Lounge with live entertainment. Sunrise Mall two blocks north.

LA QUINTA
**55 Sam Perl Rd. (southern extension of 12th St.), four blocks
southwest of Gateway International Bridge
546-0381 or 1-800-531-5900
$$
W+ two rooms**
The renovation of the 143 units in this motel included new door locks that open with a plastic card key instead of a regular metal key. Pool. Lounge. Located between the old and new bridges to Matamoros and near Amigoland Mall. The Denny's Restaurant next door is open 24 hours.

RAMADA INN
**715 N. Frontage Rd. (U.S. 77-83), approximately three and a half
miles north of downtown
541-2201 or 1-800-272-6232
$
W+ 10 rooms**
Recent remodeling included an expansion of the restaurant, which features all-you-can-eat buffets for all three meals every day. There are 120 rooms in this two-story motel. Each upstairs room has a small balcony overlooking the heated pool. The small but cozy lounge offers live entertainment every night but Sunday.

RANCHO VIEJO RESORT
**U.S. 77-83 at Ranch Viejo Dr., approximately nine miles north of
downtown
350-4000 or in Texas 1-800-292-7263, outside Texas 1-800-531-7400
$$$$
W**
"Turn off at the golf ball." That's the directions they give for finding this resort if you're traveling on U.S. 77-83. The golf ball is hard to miss since it's a water tower painted to look like one. It also marks one of the two 18-hole golf courses on the resort's 1,400 acres. To round out the sports picture there is also a putting green and driving range, eight tennis courts (four lighted), jogging track, bicycle rentals, and a large pool with waterfall and swim-up bar. Accommodations range from

hotel-type rooms and suites to two- and three-bedroom villas. The original hacienda building, on a peninsula in the *resaca*, was converted into a supper club that is open Tuesday through Saturday and for Sunday brunch. You can also make reservations for cocktails on the resort's barge, *Delta Dawn*, which cruises the gently curving three miles of the Resaca del Rancho Viejo between the clubhouse and the supper club. The Ranchero Clubhouse restaurant is open for all meals every day, and there is a poolside snack bar. Other resort facilities include a boutique and men's shop, beauty salon, and barbershop.

RODEWAY INN
845 N. Expressway at Old Alice Rd.
546-5501 or 1-800-228-2000
$
W

This moderately priced motel has 121 units in three two-story buildings. Amenities include a pool, a restaurant open for all meals daily, and a lounge offering live entertainment.

SHERATON PLAZA ROYALE
3777 N. Expressway, approximately six miles north of downtown
350-9191 or 1-800-325-3535
$$$
W+ four rooms

The indoor-outdoor pool lets you swim right into the dining area here. The Spanish motif of the exterior is carried over into the Galleria restaurant and the Tavern lounge, which are almost extensions of the lobby. The restaurant features a popular luncheon buffet six days a week and a buffet brunch on Sunday. The 142 rooms in this two-story motel include two suites with private whirlpools.

VALLEY INN AND COUNTRY CLUB
Central Blvd. (U.S. 77) at FM Rd. 802
546-5331
$$$-$$$$
W

This resort complex sits at the north edge of town, across from Sunrise Mall and just below the Brownsville Information Center. In addition to an 18-hole golf course and a nine-hole executive course, it has an Olympic-size swimming pool at the main clubhouse, a heated pool at the club's Conference Center, and 14—count 'em, that's 14—other smaller pools located around the club's 350 acres. There are also eight tennis courts (four lighted), a restaurant (closed Monday), and a lounge. Accommodations range from large efficiency apartments to three-bedroom villas located on the golf course. About 100 of the 500 units are available through the rental pool.

OTHER ACCOMMODATIONS

VISTA VERDE RESORT TOWNHOMES
2100 W. San Marcelo, off FM Rd. 802 behind Sunrise Mall
544-6461
$$$–$$$$
W

Renting one of these one- to three-bedroom townhouses automatically includes full use of the adjacent Brownsville Country Club's facilities. That means an 18-hole golf course, gym, pool, sauna, three tennis courts, and other recreational facilities, plus a restaurant and lounge. There are approximately 110 townhouse units available for rent. All are comfortably furnished and have two-car garages, central atriums, and maid service.

RESTAURANTS

Dinner for Two

THE DRIVE INN
Matamoros
6th and Hidalgo, approximately one mile southwest of Gateway International Bridge
33022
Open seven days for lunch and dinner
$$; Cr.
W

Don't let the name fool you—you can't drive in. In fact, parking is across the street, and inside, the crystal chandeliers, red plush seats, the aviary with peacocks, macaws, and other tropical birds, and the extensive menu will quickly dispel any lingering thoughts of fast food. Choices range through *chateaubriand*, lobster, frog legs, shrimp, steaks, and, of course, Mexican dishes, with the top price under $12. This should leave you enough money to top off the meal with one of the house's special flaming desserts. The spacious restaurant has a bar and large lounge, strolling musicians, and dinner dancing. From the waiters' dark suits and bow ties to the soft lighting, the atmosphere is definitely continental. But the family that has owned this restaurant for close to 70 years has never forgotten its origin, as evidenced by the plate of jalapeño peppers and hot sauce routinely served with every dinner.

GARCIA'S
Matamoros
82 Avenida Alvaro Obregón and Puerta, one block south of Gateway
International Bridge
31566
Open seven days for lunch and dinner
$$; Cr.

This comfortable, upstairs restaurant offers a view of the bridge, strolling musicians, and a menu that features A and B dinners, which let you order a little of this and a little of that and put them together at one price. Turkey, frog legs, shrimp, quail, steaks, lobster, and *cabrito* are all available. There are even some Mexican dishes buried in the menu. The kitchen is not always up to the menu, but the atmosphere covers the infrequent lapses. One of the nice things about Garcia's is it's just a short stroll over the bridge from downtown Brownsville. Gift shop downstairs (see Shopping).

Mexican

LAVIO'S
2474 Boca Chica, approximately half a mile east of U.S. 77-83
546-4636
Open seven days for lunch and dinner
$–$$; Cr.
W

Survival of a Mexican restaurant on the American side of the Rio Grande is chancy at best, but Lavio's makes it by being a little different from what you usually can get across the border or at most other places in town. Most dishes are HOT, but they'll make them milder if you ask. In any case, servings are bountiful and inexpensive. Curio shop and dress shop inside restaurant entrance. Bar.

LOS PORTALES
Matamoros
Sexta and Della Garza
23338
Open seven days for lunch and dinner
$–$$; AE, MC, V
W

The parking lot, itself a rarity in downtown Matamoros, is decorated with old wagon wheels, and this rustic decor is carried over to the restaurant's interior. Specialties include large portions of *cabrito*, shish kabob, and ribs, as well as the more popular Mexican dishes. There is a patio, but unfortunately, all it overlooks is the parking lot. Bar.

CLUBS & BARS

RESACA CLUB
Fort Brown Motor Hotel
1900 E. Elizabeth
546-2201
Open seven days
No cover, but minimum during floor shows; Cr.
W

The Las Vegas–style floor shows—vaudeville with a flash—seem to fit in well with the plush red velvet decor accented by brass and a stained glass ceiling. Usually two shows are presented a night, at 10 and midnight, Monday through Saturday. The talent is mostly from the Valley, but they also have traveling comics, singers, dancers, and musicians. The dress rules aren't strict, but the club attracts a dress-up crowd. The kitchen serves dinner at least up to floor show time. Dancing every night.

OFFBEAT

WHITMAN'S ARMY STORE, PAWN SHOP, AND GUN MUSEUM
629 E. 11th, between Washington and Adams
542-2541
W

The slogan of this store is "if you haven't seen Whitman's, you haven't seen Brownsville." This may or may not be true, but if you're looking for something a little bit different in a shopping experience, this could be it. The "gun museum" in the name refers to an extensive, but dusty, gun collection displayed high on the walls over the merchandise. Other decorations include a skeleton and a knight in tarnished armor. For sale are new guns, knives, low-priced jewelry, pawned items, and furniture that includes some antiques. Its reputation for the bizarre has dimmed some since the death of the founder, Mr. Whitman, but it's still worth a drop-in if you're wandering around downtown.